Finding Aids to the Microfilmed Manuscript Collection of the Genealogical Society of Utah

BIBLIOGRAPHIC GUIDE TO THE GUATEMALAN COLLECTION

NUMBER 7

FINDING AIDS
TO THE MICROFILMED MANUSCRIPT COLLECTION
OF THE GENEALOGICAL SOCIETY OF UTAH

ROGER M. HAIGH, EDITOR

BIBLIOGRAPHIC GUIDE
TO THE GUATEMALAN COLLECTION

BY

SHIRLEY A. WEATHERS

WITH

PATRICIA HART MOLEN, JACKIE PERRY, AND TOM GRAMAN

UNIVERSITY OF UTAH PRESS
SALT LAKE CITY
1981

Prepared with the assistance of
The Center for Historical Population Studies
University of Utah
Dean May, Director

The series Finding Aids to the Microfilmed Manuscript Collection of the Genealogical Society of Utah is funded in part by grants from the National Endowment for the Humanities and the University of Utah.

Anne Mette Haigh, Associate Editor

Number 1.   Preliminary Survey of the Mexican Collection, 1978.

             Supplement to the Preliminary Survey of the Mexican Collection, 1979.

Number 2.   Preliminary Survey of the German Collection, 1979.

Number 3.   Descriptive Inventory of the English Collection, 1979.

Number 4.   Descriptive Inventory of the New York Collection, 1980.

Number 5.   Preliminary Survey of the French Collection, 1980.

Number 6.   Research Inventory of the Mexican Collection of Colonial Parish Registers, 1980.

Copyright 1981 by the University of Utah Press
Published and distributed by the University of Utah Press,
Salt Lake City, Utah 84112
International Standard Book Number 0-87480-198-2
Printed in the United States of America

CONTENTS

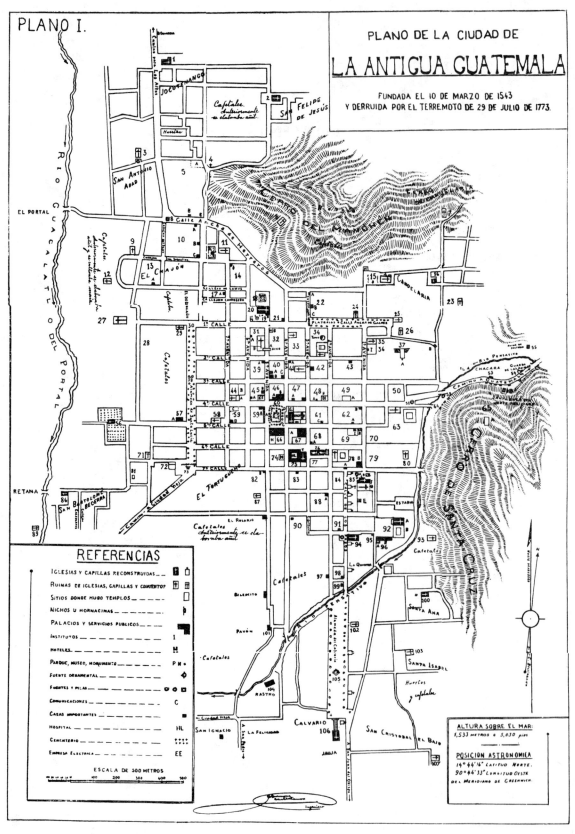

Maps of Antigua Guatemala as it was before the earthquake of 1773. A sizable portion of the documentation included in the Archivo General de Centroamérica originated here during the period Antigua Guatemala served as the capital city

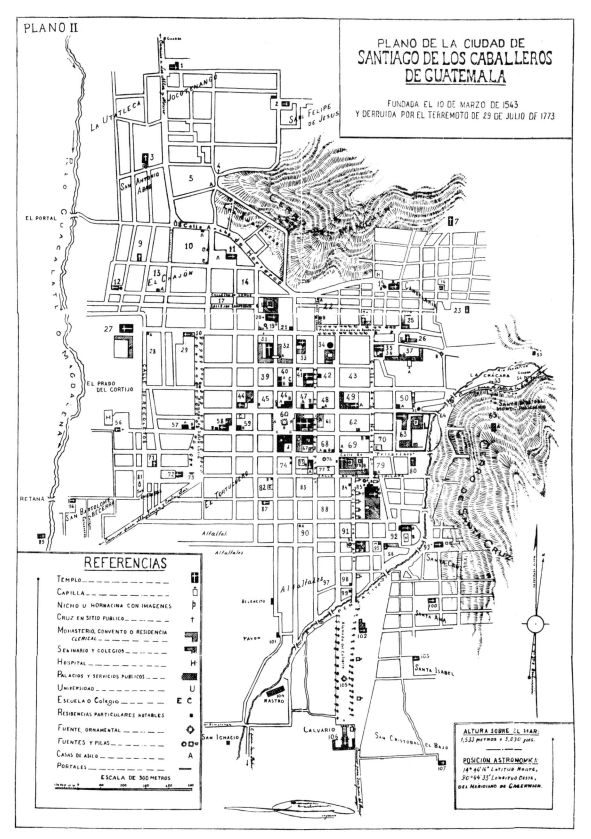

(see explanation in note 3 of the Introduction). From J. Joaquín Pardo, Pedro Zamora Castellanos, and Luis Luján Muñoz, Guía de Antigua Guatemala, 2nd edition (Guatemala: Editorial "José de Pinada Iberra," 1968).

ACKNOWLEDGMENTS

I would like to express my gratitude to a number of people who helped make possible the preparation of this Guide. At the Genealogical Society of Utah, Ray Wright, Jim Streeter, Lyman Platt, and Steve Fox provided valuable information and assistance. On a day-to-day basis, special thanks go to Laurie Jensen and Winona Welch, as well as the staff of the Latin American section. Numerous other employees at the Society, too many to name, also deserve thanks for their time and help.

At the University of Utah, I wish to thank the staff at the Center for Historical Populations Studies. Without the financial backing of the University Institutional Funds Committee, the project would not have been done--my profound thanks to that body. I would also like to thank Penny Tadman of the history department for helping with various administrative matters; Jim McMurrin for his advice on the visual layout of material; and Helen Swapp for transcribing list information.

Copy editing and typing of this volume were perhaps more complicated and time-consuming than for any of the previous ones due to the variety in document types and geographical locations. I am indebted to Anne Mette Haigh for her advice and work as copy editor. Cheryl Willey deserves thanks for the careful typing of material that can often be tedious, yet challenging.

Mention last of Roger Haigh reflects in no way on his valuable contributions to this project. His experience, help, and support from the initial stages to the completion of this Guide were indispensable. I am deeply grateful for his involvement in the project, as well as for his friendship.

S.A.W.

PREFACE

The largest collection of filmed manuscripts in the world, more than a million 100-foot rolls, is used only sparingly by the world's academic community and other genealogical researchers. This problem is a result of misinformation or lack of information about the Genealogical Society of Utah's collection. It is precisely this situation that the series <u>Finding Aids to the Microfilmed Manuscript Collection of the Genealogical Society of Utah</u> is designed to correct.

The scope of the collection is truly international. The declared intention of the Society is "to gather records on everyone who has ever lived." As astonishing as this statement may appear, this is the Society's goal. At the present time significant collections of microfilmed manuscripts exist for the United States, Europe, Latin America, and the Far East.

The bulk of this awesome collection is comprised of civil and parish registers of births, marriages, deaths, and whatever other kinds of information records of this type may contain. However, the remaining rolls of film alone constitute the largest collection of non-parish or non-civil register in the world! Included here is an amazing variety of types of materials--letters, maps, factory records, guild records, immigration material, to name a few. Whereas the parish and civil registers are usually adequately cataloged, these other kinds of records are not. The primary aim of the <u>Finding Aids</u> is to acquaint scholars with the nature and location of these historical manuscripts.

Three types of aids will be offered through the series: preliminary surveys, descriptive inventories, and bibliographic guides.

The <u>preliminary survey</u> is planned to give the researcher rather precise information about the holdings of parish and civil registers in large national collections. Designed as much to indicate regions within a national area where records are missing as those for which there are extensive holdings, the survey attempts to insure that those coming to use the collection are not disappointed, and that the library can have requested rolls available for the researcher upon arrival. The surveys also provide a general idea of the types of other materials that, for a variety of reasons, are a part of the Society's holdings in a given national area. Finally, the surveys identify sections for which existing cataloging is reliable and those for which it is not.

The descriptive inventory is a more precise bibliographic instrument. Aimed at collections less than 50 percent complete (as estimated by the Society), the inventories classify and record manuscripts and indicate film footage. The material is cross-referenced to give an interested researcher quite an accurate picture of holdings of particular types of records, holdings in given time periods, and holdings of various types of records within given geographic regions.

The bibliographic guide is the most detailed of the aids. It is designed to focus on smaller collections of previously uncataloged material. The bibliographic guide requires the reading of each roll of film in the collection and a precise description of its contents. The rolls are then cross-referenced by manuscript type, time span, region, etc. Bibliographic guides are planned only for collections the Society regards as complete.

The Finding Aids series represents the response of the University of Utah to needs expressed by the international community of scholars. This process began in 1976, when the University Institutional Funds Committee generously granted funds to the Department of History to bring in a team of social scientists to evaluate the scholarly potential of the collection and to make recommendations to facilitate its use. Jerome Clubb, Samuel Hays, and Jackson Turner Main represented researchers with an interest in holdings for the United States; and Louise Tilly, Lewis Hanke, and Richard Wall, the latter representing the Cambridge Population Studies program, investigated the potential of the international holdings. Their recommendations varied, but they were in complete agreement on two points: (1) The collection has fantastic potential for many types of scholarly research; and (2) a series of finding aids is urgently needed to make the collection more accessible to and more efficiently usable by scholars and other researchers.

As this book goes to press, preliminary surveys of the Mexican, German, and French holdings have been published. Descriptive inventories of the English collection, the New York collection, and the collection of Mexican colonial parish registers are also available. This Guide and the Mexican, German, and English aids were completed with funds allocated by the University of Utah. The French Survey and the New York Inventory were supported by a grant from the National Endowment for the Humanities and administered through the Center for Historical Population Studies, Dean May, Director. Financial support for Professor Robinson's Inventory of Mexican colonial parish registers emanated from Syracuse University's Dellplain Program in Latin American Geography.

These aids will be kept current through supplements issued as needed listing all pertinent newly cataloged material. Supplements will be made available at minimal cost to purchasers of the books; and the first, the Supplement to the Preliminary Survey of the Mexican Collection, is ready for distribution.

This is the first bibliographic guide of the series. Guides are particularly difficult to produce because of the high cost per roll of film and the necessity of reading and cataloging every item on a particular roll. Whereas the cost of preparation of a guide is high, it is my conviction as editor that the presentation to researchers of material in such an exact manner will certainly justify the expenditure.

Two more aids are in preparation: a bibliographic guide to the Michoacán material and an inventory of the Society's pre-1600 holdings. When these are completed the series will be reevaluated. If the response of the scholarly community is favorable, another publication program will be outlined, and if funding can be obtained the series will be continued.

The authors and the publisher want these finding aids to be as effective tools as possible. With this in mind, we earnestly solicit suggestions for improving their usefulness, as well as manuscripts that will fit the series' format.

Roger M. Haigh

INTRODUCTION

This bibliographic guide describes the holdings of the Genealogical Society of Utah as filmed at the Archivo General de Centroamérica (AGCA) in Guatemala City. Those familiar with this archive recognize it as a valuable repository of impressive amounts of civil, governmental, and judicial documentation of the Reino de Guatemala, as well as of some major document groups for the nineteenth and early twentieth centuries. We hope that the academic community is at least somewhat aware of the enormity and richness of the microfilm library of the Society and of the goal of this Finding Aid Series to publicize and facilitate its use. This volume is the result of a year-long project, funded by University of Utah Institutional Funds. The project involved reading the majority of the Society's AGCA collection, which consists of documents recorded on over 3,600 rolls of microfilm.

Priorities of the Society precluded the filming of the entire archive; nevertheless, a great number of different document types are represented in this collection, suggesting a variety of research possibilities heretofore available only to scholars willing and able to travel to the AGCA. Several portions of the film collection appear to represent most, if not all, documents of those types in the archive, i.e., Bienes de Difuntos, Información Matrimonial, Información Personal, Poblaciones y Tributos, Protocolos, and Tierras. Scholars interested in utilizing these document types may be able to exhaust the AGCA's resources at the Society's library in Salt Lake City, or through its branch library system, leaving Guatemalan research time for materials not available in the United States.[1]

---

[1] The Society branch library system extends throughout the United States, allowing nationwide access to microfilms. The procedure is somewhat more time-consuming and precludes the possibility of making use of the expertise of library and Center of Historical Population Studies employees. Those interested in more information about the system are encouraged to contact the Genealogical Society of Utah, 50 East North Temple, Salt Lake City, Utah 84111.

Other portions, often tending to be interspersed with various document types, are so limited in number and deal with such scattered years and locations that their inclusion in the microfilming program appears to have been an error, albeit a welcome one.[2]

Before describing individual document types found in the collection, some general comments regarding the lists are appropriate.

> a. Geographical locations: Within document type group-
> ings, material is organized by current-day political juris-
> dictions, specifying locations where the documentation was
> executed. Listings of documents originating in the capital
> city, whether during the Colonial, Confederation or
> National periods, appear first under each major document
> classification.[3] Listings of documents originating else-
> where in current-day Guatemala follow in alphabetical
> order. Location headings proceed from departamento, to
> municipio, to site of the document's origin. When known,
> the rank of the latter (whether ciudad, pueblo, villa,
> etc.) is provided (see Abbreviations). Detail varies
> somewhat depending on the gazetteer or map used to identify

---

[2]Scholars should be aware that the Central American collection at the Society goes far beyond films from this archive. A description of the entire holdings as of 1978 is contained in Shirley A. Weathers, "Holdings of the Genealogical Society of Utah--Central America," in R. L. Woodward, ed., "Research Guide to Central America and the Caribbean": Projected publication date, 1981.

[3]For the reader's information, changes of the capital city location are as follows:

1572-1542	Located at the site of current-day Ciudad Vieja, cabecera municipal in Sacatepéquez.
1542-1776	Located at the site of current-day Antigua Guatemala, cabecera municipal in Sacatepéquez.
by 1776-present	Located in the departamento of Guatemala, is now generally known as the Ciudad de Guatemala and is also the cabecera municipal of that departamento.

individual population centers.

Problems with geographical precision remain as names of populated areas have changed and political boundaries have been redrawn. Some towns for which records are extant have ceased to exist. Document damage and illegible handwriting add to the problem. No document type illustrates these difficulties more emphatically than Poblaciones y Tributos. Listings here, as with other document types, are organized in the guide by site of document origin--populations were enumerated and their tributo recorded wherever a population is evident. Gazetteers and maps allowed reference to the majority of these locations by current-day jurisdictions. Records for town names not appearing in either of those types of sources are listed separately and arranged alphabetically by town name. If the documents themselves specify the provincial jurisdiction of the town at the time, this information is provided in the Comments section, as are other pertinent data. In order to avoid misrepresentation of the territories involved, a section of statistical summary data for provinces is listed by jurisdictions appearing on the documents.

b. Years covered: Time period covered by the documents is noted for each entry. Where a time span is indicated, documents covering most, if not all, of those years are included, unless otherwise noted in the Comments.

c. Roll number entries: To facilitate locating specific document groups on any one roll of film, a system was created based on the existing divisions of the rolls and formed by the insertion of a heading frame prepared by the

camera operator to announce a new set of documents,
volume, legajo, etc.

On occasion, the existing card catalog at the Society
(which will be superseded by information in this volume
in the upcoming computerized cataloging system) states
that the camera operator's first heading frame of a
particular six-digit roll number specifies, for example,
Bienes de Difuntos, while the second heading frame specifies
Información Personal by adding "1st Item" and "2nd Item",
respectively, after the appropriate roll number. Such
existing divisions on rolls are consistently noted herein
as xxx,xxx/y, the first six digits referring to the roll
number and the "y" referring to the "Item" number. Generally speaking, camera operators filmed whole runs of
documents without seeing the need to insert a new heading
frame. There is, however, a significant number of rolls
on which a new heading frame precedes each complete (or
extant) group of documents. For example, Tutela case
follows Tutela case with heading frames preceding each
one. In both cases, the xxx,xxx/y system is used. For
rolls containing a number of different document types
and/or interspersed locations, ODT/OL (other document
types/other locations) has been placed in the Comments
to alert researchers to the disorganization, as well as
to allow film ordering to be prioritized. Rolls with such
mixed content may include only a few groups of documents
of each type and/or location noted. Therefore, it is often
more productive to identify, order, and read whole rolls of
desired material before rolls with mixed content are con-
fronted. This is particularly advisable since 99 percent
of the AGCA films are still negatives. Printing positive

copies makes waiting time from order to receipt even longer than the usual three to five days required in the reading of the negatives.[4] For roll numbers where the condition is ODT/OL, entries appear under their appropriate headings in the lists.

Rolls of Poblaciones y Tributos are frequently rife with different and often geographically distant locations, from the tiniest pueblo to entire provinces. Different forms of population- and/or tribute-reporting formats and years add to the disorder. This necessitated the addition of a numbering system to that already described, i.e., xxx,xxx/y/z where "z" indicates the relative location (our addition) within the camera operator's "Item" ("y") on roll number xxx,xxx. The researcher will undoubtedly find the task of locating specific entries on a 100-foot roll of film tedious, but the numbering does become a valuable contribution in view of the paucity of location entries in the Society's existing catalog.

d. Comments section: This is intended to aid the researcher in a variety of ways. The readability of the film, legajo number when known, roll numbers of continued material when roll numbers are not consecutive, ODT/OL notations, and geographical information are the most common entries. Gazetteers and maps used are listed in the bibliography.

---

[4]The Society allowed negative films to be read for this project due to our need to study the entire collection, heretofore little used. As researchers request films from the AGCA, positives will be produced. (Many films held by the library are immediately available in the positive form.)

The following comments on document types are based on the reading of the films and consist, at least, of reference to the kinds of information provided within each type. Sources reported by the Society are noted at the end of each applicable description.

Geographic organization of the various document types under major subject headings is designed to facilitate location of entries and reflects the organizational scheme existing in the AGCA. Entries for various sub-types of manuscripts are located within major headings such as Documentos Jurídicos and Gubernamentales as appropriate. Subject headings such as Bienes de Difuntos, Información Matrimonial, Información Personal, Poblaciones y Tributos, Protocolos, and Tierras are set apart because of the size of these portions of the collection and as camera operator procedures indicate that filming followed the organization of records in Guatemala. Small collections of ambiguous material not clearly fitting under the major headings have been placed under Documentos Misceláneos.

Bienes de Difuntos

Bienes de Difuntos refer to records of probate cases and fill over 360 rolls of microfilm. Most cases include a will (see Testamentos in Documentos Misceláneos), a list of interested parties present at the reading of the will, an inventory of the goods of the deceased, and records of limosnas and/or capellanías. An outline of burial costs and of property liquidated for payment of debts may appear. Documentation also reflects any extraordinary circumstances regarding the estate, a common example being the absence of a will. Given the cost of legal procedures, what is found among these records refers to individuals constituting a minority of Central Americans during the years covered. Nevertheless, these films present a valuable source of information on landholding, slavery, and commercial activities, to name but a few.

Source: Juzgado General de Bienes de Difuntos

Documentos Gubernamentales

Considering the size of the AGCA collection on microfilm at the Society, a relatively small amount of film reflects governmental activities. Aside from Poblaciones y Tributos, which is treated separately, most of the materials were miscataloged as Bienes de Difuntos. The following descriptions are provided to aid in the understanding of the documentation, although contents are too varied and scattered to allow more than a generalization.

Archivo de la Independencia, a unique collection within the AGCA, is listed separately. Most of the materials are minutes of the Cabildo Ordinario, Ayuntamiento, and Junta Provisional del Gobierno sessions, depending on the time between 1808 and 1822. Others originated in the Audiencia. Beginning in 1808, researchers can follow the official actions of the Cabildo Ordinario as it dealt primarily with matters of local interest, i.e., education, public works, commerce, revenues and expenditures, land, public safety, etc. This format continues with Avisos, Circulares, Correspondencia, Oficios del Gobierno, Reales Cédulas y Decretos, etc. interspersed among the minutes as they relate to the issues under discussion. Business as usual began to suffer from interruptions in the session of August 16, 1808, when news of the abdication of Carlos IV was recorded. The resultant flurry of documents, including Gazeta extracts from Spain and elsewhere, correspondence, and memos reflect first confusion, then outrage, and finally resolve in reaction to the crisis. Rolls in the 741,000's indicate a degree of local disagreement regarding the appropriate response. As news of the actions of other Spanish colonies arrived, the Cabildo busied itself with discussions of the local implications. After the Constitution of 1812, the records trace the activities of the new Ayuntamiento. The last section of film is devoted to the minutes of the Junta Provisional del Gobierno de Guatemala, 1818-1821, a body serving the last Captain General of Central America prior to Independence.

Circulares apparently were sent by government officials (most commonly the Jefe Político) to inform officials on lower levels and laymen (particularly finqueros) of items of local interest. Subject matter ranges from education to names and descriptions of wanted criminals--documentation is miscellaneous in content.

Correspondencia included in this section of the collection is primarily between local officials. Much of it reflects the efforts of the Jefe Político to advise and coordinate actions in outlying areas under his jurisdiction. Other examples are scattered and miscellaneous (see also Correspondencia in Poblaciones y Tributos).

Elecciones refer to documentation which pertains specifically to election practices. On most rolls of film where they appear, numerous consecutive frames contain instructions on upcoming elections, including legal means of running polls, selection of judges, transmittal of ballots, etc.

Indice del Antiguo Archivo del Supremo Gobierno, contained on two rolls of film, indexes a portion of the documents included in the collection from the AGCA. However, attempts to correlate the organization of the index and the documents led to the conclusion that these two rolls are of limited value to researchers.

Libros de Cuentas generally record the administrative activities of the various departments within the Real Hacienda. The context often indicates the treasury records solicited either for periodic or special audits. In some cases wrong-doing was alleged. Other cases record investigations of local businesses, industries, or haciendas, providing accounting records as part of the procedure. As with other types of governmental records, these do not appear to constitute a complete collection; rather, they are found interspersed on rolls containing information of genealogical significance (usually Información Personal or Bienes de Difuntos).

Memorias/Sesiones Municipales outline local governmental activities. Whether appearing in the form of Memorias (summary reports) or Sesiones (minutes of the municipal body), local affairs regarding public works, agriculture, public safety, communication, justice, resources, finances, etc. are represented. It should be noted that Memorias include some information of types found elsewhere in the archive. Particularly for the purposes of genealogical work, some entries from the existing card catalog are retained (see Listas de Difunciones and Revistas de Comisario in Documentos Misceláneos).

Oficios del Gobierno are orders originating with the Crown's governing officials prescribing both general policies and solutions to specific problems. Many of the case reports begin with a title page indicating the issue at hand. This type of documentation is mixed in subject matter and in terms of information provided.

Pasaportes contained in the collection were issued in the capital city by the Jefe del Estado. The documentation suggests at least that the policy regarding the movement of people, even from one province to another, was strictly supervised. The standard format begins with the petition stating name, desired destination and duration of stay, and often a fairly detailed description of reasons for travel and planned activities. The occupation of the petitioner is usually obvious or may even be stated. Many cases continue with a record of witnesses testifying to the good character of the petitioner, the Auto granting the passport, and often a copy of that document. Extenuating circumstances and previous violation of passport limitations resulted in extensive discussions, correspondence, and litigation. The most outstanding example of this phenomenon can be found on rolls cross-referenced under the Revolución de 1828 when passports were issued to alleged dissidents.

Source: Ministro General de Gobernación

Reales Cédulas/Decretos are occasionally found on AGCA rolls. They appear sporadically; however, some seem to have been kept together by particularly organized record keepers and/or archivists. The King's orders cover a wide range of issues and often include detailed explanations. They are listed in the guide under the location in Central America in which they were recorded and from which they were dispatched.

Revolución de 1828 is the designation for a group of documents found on two rolls of Pasaportes. Indeed, the records were collected as part of the passport issuance procedure. To justify the issuance of passports to persons suspected of participating in the revolution, the recording officials provide a detailed account of the uprising, often including letters and testimonies of accusors and defendants.

Visitas record surveillance of government officials by agents of the Crown. It suggests royal concern with colonial rule by providing a local forum for comments and complaints regarding officials.

Documentos Juridicos

This section confines itself to scattered documentation of civil and criminal cases, as well as of Divorcios and Vecinos y Vecindades. The relatively small size of this collection should not discourage scholars from using the valuable and varied documents it contains.

Causas Civiles document those civil cases heard by the Audiencia that can not be categorized under more specific document designations. Such papers are interspersed throughout other document types on a number of rolls.

Source: Real Audiencia

Causas Criminales are also found on rolls of various major document types. Some refer to the activities of arraignment courts, providing name, age, sex, caste, place of origin, occupation, offense, and sentence of each defendant. Longer criminal proceedings, more detailed and varied in content than arraignment court records, make up the remainder of the collection. See also Despojos in Tierras.

Source: Real Sala del Crimen

Divorcios describe the litigation and include names of both parties involved in the proceeding. Often explicit testimony brought before the judge appears. Names of the parents of the wife are included. Decisions appear along with justifications by the involved justices. Some cases include a description of the religious procedure executed, and some show property inventories.

Source: Juzgado Matrimonial

Vecinos y Vecindad cases, whether handled on the provincial level or decided in the main seat of government, concern themselves with local issues. The majority relate to individuals either desirous of establishing residency (in the strict legal sense--the word radicarse seems to lack an equivalent in English), or being charged with some form of inappropriate behavior which threatened to result in exile from an area. Other cases reflect the existence of local interests ranging from the need for increased police protection to a collective desire to change zoning ordinances. No precise descriptive format is possible as the information provided varies greatly depending on the issue and exigencies of each case.

Información Matrimonial

The AGCA microfilms provide a variety of information on late nineteenth and early twentieth century marriages. Of all the document types contained in the collection, these provide the most detailed descriptions of what might be assumed to be average Central American males and females, at least those who pursued the legal sanction of the marriage ceremony once civil authorities were empowered to perform it.[5]

Source: Registro Civil

Actas Matrimoniales provide the names, dates, and places of registered marriages.

Autos de Disenso give insight into the results of the Aviso gone awry (see Expedientes Matrimoniales, below). Couples whose posted marriage banns were challenged could confront serious bureaucratic difficulties. Although not

---

[5]David J. Robinson, Research Inventory of the Mexican Collection of Colonial Parish Registers, Number VI of Finding Aids to the Microfilmed Manuscript Collection of the Genealogical Society of Utah, Roger M. Haigh, ed., Salt Lake City: University of Utah Press, 1980, provides an instructive discussion of the limitations of marriage-related materials as well as their usefulness as research sources.

numerous, these records differ markedly from the standardization of Expedientes Matrimoniales, and provide an opportunity to view the workings of the legal and social systems which constitute the context of these cases.

Causas Matrimoniales document extraordinary marriage petitions. Circumstances requiring special handling vary, the most common being marriages between castes, of widows unable to produce the appropriate death certificate for husbands, and of couples unable to acquire parental consent where required by law.

Expedientes Matrimoniales record individual marriage transactions from application to ceremony. These originated in the various cabeceras municipales throughout the Reino de Guatemala from 1880-1938. Although cases appearing sporadically on rolls containing other document types make any exact roll count impossible, more than 1,800 rolls reflect the civil marriage procedures and show a relatively standardized type of material. The petitions or applications for marriages include the names, ages, occupations, places of birth, places of residence, names of parents, grandparents, and witnesses of each couple. Age verification--usually certification by the Encargante del Registro Civil or baptizing cura (this consists of literal copies of birth certificates or baptismal partidas respectively)--is also shown. Notarized testimonies of witnesses permitted the couples to post banns. If the case was affirmed, an authorization of impending marriage appears, as well as a copy of the marriage certificate which includes the names of witnesses and padrinos. Also found in many cases are certificates of vaccination.

Matrimonios Suspensos appear to be Expedientes Matrimoniales halted for either no apparent reason, or because of inappropriate or unavailable witnesses, failure to produce necessary documentation, or the existence of some other impediment.

Información Personal

This category of documents records compliance with social mores and legal processes unique to Latin culture. Whether the petitioner sought a desired honor, position, or right, the various types of procedures reflect the values of the society through the fulfillment of established legal requirements. The general heading, Información Personal, has been divided into more specific document designations based on the procedures as named by recording officials. It is then described in terms of the information contained in the document type. Certain of these types tend to consist of several phases of documentation, some of which may appear separately as types in their own right. An example is Méritos y Servicios, so called because of the highest goal of the procedure, although proof of Calidad and Legitimidad were required procedures and therefore are included in the documentation.

Source: Fiscalía and Real Audiencia

Absueltos result from an individual's attempt to establish the fact that he was absolved of a crime. This document type seems to lack any association with any other, although it is conceivable that the procedure could have been initiated by a person desirous of marrying, or gaining a governmental position, etc.

Calidades are documents which result in the establishment of nobility of lineage on the part of the applicant. Included are Legitimidades, genealogical descriptions (often in the form of family trees). Examples of this document type appear separately as well as in conjunction with other types such as Comisiones. An alternate name for this procedure is Limpieza de Sangre; however, if the goal in any of these cases were to prove an absence of Jewish or Moorish heritage, the means is subtle--the genealogical account may state that a certain ancestor was "español" and a "natural" or "vecino" of a town in Spain.

Comisiones resulted from successful attempts by individuals to gain military, civil, or ecclesiastical positions. Generally, both blood line and past services rendered are described, as are the duties and rights of the position.

Hidalguías, in the initial phases, appear identical to Méritos y Servicios; however, here the services refer to those of the supplicant's conquistador ancestors. The stated result is generally the right to the title of "Don" in the traditional sense; however, at times there is an indication that the procedure was a step toward achieving a larger goal.

Legitimidades required proof of marriage of ancestors further removed than one generation. Generally, the supplicant's birth certificate is shown. This document type may be found separately with only the explicit goal of proving legitimacy, or it may be part of a longer procedure such as Calidades, Méritos y Servicios, etc.

Mercedes y Nombramientos begin with a decoration of some type (usually military in nature) for a lavishly described deed. The nombramiento follows as the reward entitling the recipient to an official post. These documents resemble Méritos y Servicios in the initial phase; however, the specificity of purpose for the procedure seems to set the two types apart.

Méritos y Servicios provide detailed descriptions of the individuals in question, albeit with no apparent purpose other than to establish the descriptions on record. The procedure can be divided into two sections, (a) Méritos include Calidad, Legitimidad, and at least a brief genealogical account, and (b) Servicios amount to a listing of posts held, deeds done, and services rendered. This document type is sometimes found as part of a marriage case among the nobility, or as a Pensión, Comisión, Hidalguía, etc.

Pensiones reflect efforts by families of deceased or disabled military men or civil servants to obtain remuneration. Past services and statements of financial need are emphasized.

Probanzas de Mayorazgo involve documents to gain title to inherited land. The procedure required proof of majority (often a copy of the birth certificate appears); in some cases, the heir attempts to prove himself equal to the responsibility he is undertaking. A description of the lands in question is often included.

Probanzas de Pobreza establish the supplicant as destitute, usually due to the death of a breadwinner. It would seem obvious that aid of some sort is sought through the procedure; however, rarely is there any mention of either this or of any prospective source of aid. Perhaps these probanzas have become separated from corresponding Pensiones.

Títulos de Encomienda are documents granting a specific type of Pensión. Usually the number of Indios vacos is specified.

Poblaciones y Tributos

Enumeration of the population as necessary for the computation and collection of tribute provides researchers with detailed census records as early as the sixteenth century.

Censos originate in the twentieth century and do not mention tribute or taxation. Otherwise, the censos provide information similar to that provided by Padrones Generales with some expansion of data to include comments on literacy, physical or "moral" handicap (presumably illegitimacy), religion, and commercial use of a residence, as well as standard information traditionally gathered for population enumeration.

Correspondencia contains information pertaining specifically to populations and/or tribute. Besides providing specific statistical data which supplement the other document types, the correspondence often describes census-taking procedures, as well as the means of collecting tribute.

Padrón entries represent all documentation providing statistical information referring to populations other than the regularized Padrón General. Usually, data are limited to totals by sex, marital status, and perhaps caste. Where names of individuals are noted, they are listed without reference to the individuals' positions within the community.

Padrón General, a name drawn from the documents, refers to the periodic, stylized censuses taken throughout Central America to allow officials to assign and predict tribute collection for each population center. These documents provide information similar to current-day censuses. Name, age, marital status, race or caste, and tribute payment status of individuals are noted by household within each enumeration district (usually by town and surrounding population centers). Frequently, the occupation of the head of household is given.

Tributos represent the remaining documentation type in this section --that referring directly to tribute. The majority of records so designated reveal the means by which towns discharged the requirement of tribute, whether in specie or in kind, allowing insight into the value of payment by town, as well as agricultural activities of the area. Records dated 1877 or later are likely to indicate payment of tribute by labor on public works. This is undoubtedly part of the internal improvements program instigated during the Positivist period of the latter nineteenth century.

Protocolos

Filling 887 rolls of microfilm in the AGCA collection, protocolos record the official activities of notary publics from 1541-1898. Over 99 percent of the rolls in this portion of the collection contain documentation originating in the capital city.

Roll-by-roll reading of this group was not possible; however, fifty randomly selected rolls were examined to determine the accuracy of the existing card catalog entries. In that sample, the dates proved to be 80 percent accurate (with only one roll more significantly in error than one year). The assumption that, unless otherwise noted, the location of the notary process was the capital city proved to be 100 percent correct. On all rolls read, the name of the notary provided in the card catalog corresponded to that on the documents. Based on the accuracy rates, the card catalog entries were reorganized and repro- duced. The new organization presents Protocolos emphasizing the name of the notary in the Comments section.

On ninety rolls of microfilm at the Society library are Indices de Protocolos which correspond to Protocolos collected by notary publics throughout Guatemala between 1877 and 1921. According to information provided by Lyman Platt, the Society's specialist on the AGCA and many other Latin American archives, the actual Protocolos are housed not at the AGCA, but at the Archivo Nacional de Protocolos, also in Guatemala City. These records have not been filmed by the Society; therefore, roll-by-roll reading of this portion of the collection seemed unnecessary. However, the Indices can be useful to researchers who plan eventually to travel to Guatemala, especially those who intend to utilize notarial records by dates. Although handwritten, they are in relatively good condition, easily readable, and appear to have been prepared carefully. The format is standardized. Organized by notary and year, each entry provides the location, date, names of clients and witnesses, folio number, and a brief reference to the object of the notarized transaction. This section of the guide presents a direct reproduction of the existing card catalog.

Tierras

A sizable collection of land records dating from the sixteenth to the nineteenth century offers researchers information on a variety of transactions. While the Genealogical Society has cataloged the applicable rolls of film under the general heading of Tierras, examination revealed twenty-eight separate document types as designated by the record generating officials--document types varied enough in terms of both name and information contained to list each. Again, some of the document types appear separately or as part of other transactions. The designation assigned is that of the recording officials.

Source: Secretaria de Hacienda y Crédito Público

Alcabalas refer to paragraph-long register entries acknowledging payment of alcabalas (transfer tax) on specific pieces of property. Grouped by town or village, the registers provide the name of the taxpayer and a description of his property.

Autos de Amparo were executed when a party other than the owner paid rent or tribute on land. The names of the land owner, his benefactor, and a description of the land are included.

Autos de Avivamiento amount to requests for the right to live on and/or make use of land that was either tierra realenga or owned by the municipality. Names of supplicants and a description of the land are provided. An alternative name for this type of transaction also appears as Solicitudes de Sitios.

Autos de Denuncia are declarations of land for tax purposes. La Administración de Rentas recorded the means by which the owner came into possession of the land, his proof of title (if not a copy of the title itself), estimated monthly income from the land, and the amount of taxes to be paid. An alternate designation is Declaraciones.

Autos de Posesión result in satisfactory proof of ownership; however, they differ from Títulos in rigidity of proof presented. In Autos de Posesión, a legally registered title to the land described was sometimes lacking, but the owner was allowed to retain the land by virtue of proof of acquisition through a grant or inheritance in the distant past, length of time of possession constituting assumption of ownership. A less formal procedure than Presentaciones de Títulos, contents of the individual transactions noted in Autos de Posesión tend to be more varied.

Autos de Residencia constitute proof that the supplicant occupied a certain piece of land. These documents appear separately on the microfilms; however, they seem to be a stage in larger transactions such as Títulos Supletorios. The supplicant's residency claim is often backed by testimony of witnesses.

Confirmaciones de Títulos, alternately known as Comprobaciones de Títulos, Reafirmaciones de Títulos, and Títulos de Confirmaciones, result in proof of ownership. The owner established legal title, unlike Presentaciones de Títulos; however, the high degree of detail as to the means of acquisition differentiates this group from Títulos. That confirmation was a response to a specific challenge to title is only implied.

Despojos relate criminal actions brought as a result of charges of improper and/or destructive use of land or water. These cases are varied in content and detail depending on the exigencies.

Diligencias de Renovación refer to procedures required for the renewal of a deed with all accompanying rights. Those procedures included the testimonies of witnesses, some means of public notice, and a description of the means of acquisition of the land. Maps appear in some cases.

Entregas de Títulos involve transfer of titles. Events leading to the transfer may or may not be outlined in individual cases. Complete cases provide a description of the land, its location, and an estimate of either its monetary worth or the monthly income it produced.

Hipotecas provide as standard information a description of land being mortgaged, its location, and estimated monthly income produced. In addition, a variety of transactions related to the land title may be included; title search is an example.

Libros Ejidales consist of short certifications of completion of transactions by recipients of grants of ejidal lands. The locations of the land are outlined, as well as the fees extracted by municipalities for the certification.

Medidas reflect land surveys executed for various reasons. Often the release of tierra realenga to private ownership precipitated the action, although other cases indicate Títulos Supletorios, Reclamas, Ventas, or planned construction of public buildings as the cause. Still others seem to have originated with an order for routine, periodic surveys. Maps are sometimes included.

Pajas de Agua either refer to actions required to gain rights to water or to registers of holders of those rights.

Presentaciones de Títulos specify the names of both the party requesting the presentation and the property owner. Besides proof of legal title, the owner usually produced witnesses verifying his use of the land over a period of years and the circumstances leading to ownership, i.e., inheritance, purchase, etc.

Reales Concesiones resulted from services rendered to the Crown, usually by a member of the armed forces or the noble class. Expedientes of this type generally originated with the King and provide detailed descriptions of the deeds leading to the concession.

Reclamas originated over disputes between two parties over title to the same piece of land. Allegations of the means of acquisition by both parties are recorded; often witnesses' testimony bolsters both sides of the dispute. Researchers should not necessarily expect to discover the final disposition of these cases.

Remates record land auctions, outline the circumstances necessitating the action, describe the land, and provide the price and name of the buyer. Often the Entrega de Título is included.

Redenciones de Tierra resemble Confirmaciones de Títulos in format; however, the action resulted specifically from the loss of possession of land at some earlier time.

Títulos, probably the most numerous land record type, are land titles. These documents provide the name of the owner, the location and description of the land, and usually the monetary value. Testimonios de Títulos is an alternate name.

Títulos Concedidos, also called Títulos Otorgados, notified supplicants of the successful completion of cases of Títulos Supletorios. Through these documents, the town clerk reported that title had been granted. In some instances, the Título Supletorio procedure appears.

Títulos Registrados refer to titles to land held by virtue of Reales Concesiones. Otherwise these records are identical to Títulos.

Títulos Supletorios resulted from a request for title to land already in undisputed possession of the supplicant. Besides a description of the land and of the means of acquisition, the recording official certified that the correct procedure had been executed. This consisted of witnesses' testimony and the posting of Avisos and/or pregones until printing presses made possible the use of newspaper ads. Copies of the public notices generally appear. Estimated monthly income from the property is often specified, as well as some information about the supplicant such as age, sex, place of origin, and legitimacy status. In cases where the supplicant was of the aristocracy, more detail is presented.

Ventas record land sales. Generally the bill of sale appears--if that document fails to describe the land, a description appears separately. Some applicable Entregas de Títulos are included or can be found separately elsewhere in the collection

Vistas are documents in response to various land-related issues such as taxation and petitions for home improvement permits. Seemingly, these cases required a statement to the effect that a certain party was in charge of the property.

Documentos Miscelaneos

Avisos, besides appearing as one of the final stages in Expedientes Matrimoniales, as well as in some forms of Tierras, are found interspersed among other document types. These, however, are miscellaneous public notices (handbills) announcing livestock for sale, auctions, festivals, etc.

Bautismos, recording the Sacrament as executed by a priest, are rare in this archive of almost exclusively secular documents (the volume of entries in this guide is due to "Items" consisting of only one or two cases each). As noted, some cases of Expedientes Matrimoniales include copies of baptismal certificates; some partidas, however, appear separately. This document type is very well represented at the Society library, due to filming of Registros Parroquiales outside of the AGCA.

Cuentas Desudotes record procedures followed in returning dowries in cases of divorce or death of wives under special circumstances. An inventory of goods included appears along with valuations. Usually a discussion of events leading to the action is part of the documentation.

Exhumaciones as contained in the collection apply to the Cementarios General, Antiguo, and Nuevo in Guatemala City and date from 1895 to 1920. The procedure was required to allow expansion of the Hospital General; or it resulted from requests filed by relatives of the deceased for a variety of reasons. A copy of the death certificate, issued by the Depositorio del Registro Civil, the bill of sale for the original burial plot, and applicable correspondence between the applicant and officials of the Administración del Servicio Funebre are usually shown. Of interest are several cases which include descriptions of special burial and exhumation procedures due to death by various diseases.

Source: Administración del Servicio Funebre, Dirección del Hospital General
          y sus Dependéncias

Guías appear almost exclusively interspersed with Poblaciones y
Tributos. These documents are short-term business permits issued to venders,
allowing them to sell within a particular town for a particular length of time.
The fee paid for this privilege is shown.

Inventarios de Agricultura provide detailed information on land use
and crop production. Usually, they appear in groups in conjunction with the
corresponding governmental order. Occasionally, information relating to hacienda
residents can be found.

Listas de Difunciones are usually intermingled with miscellaneous
document types. Information on age, sex, and cause of death is often supple-
mented by notations regarding quarantine and symptoms. Researchers interested in
civil registers which include partidas of Difunciones are directed to the
Society's Guatemala collection microfilmed at various Archivos del Registro Civil
throughout Central America.

Matrículas de Armas consist of rifle and machine-gun registrations.
The names and occupations of the owners, makes, calibres, and registration fees
are listed.

Mausoleos amount to local governmental records of the process
whereby burial plots and/or mausoleum niches were obtained--generally following
the procedure through the final record of sale. The name of supplicant and
location of the plot or niche are standard information here; however, roll
#744,583/2 contains records of the purchase of 20 varas in the Cementario Nuevo
by the Sociedad de Beneficencia Española as well as negotiations for the construction of a pantheon on the site.

Nacimientos are partidas listing births registered at the civil
level. They follow a strict format which includes the location of the registry;
date; name of witness appearing to register the birth; date, time and place of
birth; name of child; names of parents and their race; and name of madrina and
her place of residence. The madrina also attested to her acceptance of attendant

obligations. In cases of illegitimacy, there is a statement that the mother is a soltera. The bulk of this type of documentation is contained in Society holdings filmed at Registros Civiles throughout Central America.

Revistas de Comisario enumerate military personnel, stating ranks and wages. One list also gives the citizenship of the soldiers.

Source: Mayor de Plaza

Testamentos, found as standard documentation included in Bienes de Difuntos, also appear separately in the collection. Wills vary in content depending on the wealth of the maker as well as his particular family and situation; however, standard information includes names of survivors and witnesses, bequests, and often an outline of debts and debtors.

Tutelas, although cataloged by the Society as guardianship papers, are described more accurately as settlements of custody problems. Names of wards and guardians plus verifications of the identities of the guardians are standard information. Often, a copy of the parents' death certificates or a description of circumstances surrounding their deaths appears as part of the documentation, either of which may provide information on diseases or suggest local social conditions.

Source: Registro Civil

ABBREVIATIONS

Locations

aldea	a
barrio	bar
cabecera	cab
capital	cap
caserío	cas
ciudad	cd
departamental	dl
estado	e
municipal	ml
nacional	nl
pueblo	p
villa	v

Dates

Enero	Enn
Marzo	Mr
Abril	Ab
Junio	Jn
Julio	Jl
Septiembre	Se
Octubre	Oc
Diciembre	Dc

Comments

Diccionario Geográfico de Guatemala	DGG
Indicated town name did not appear in available gazetteers	Gaz/no
Indicated town name is common--appears various times in gazetteers	Gaz/var
Index to Map of Hispanic America	IMAH
Indicated documents are interspersed with documents of other types and/or for other locations	ODT/OL

BIBLIOGRAPHY

The following sources were consulted for information on current-day
jurisdictions of the various geographical locations.

Gazetteers:

"Costa Rican Gazetteer," prepared by the Genealogical Society of Utah, n.d.

Diccionario Geográfico de El Salvador, Vols. 1-4, San Salvador: Ministerio
de Obras Públicas, Instituto Geográfico Nacional, 1970.

Diccionario Geográfico de Guatemala, Tomos 1-2, Guatemala: Dirección
General de Cartografía, 1961, referred to as DGG.

Division Municipal de las Entidades Federativas, México, D.F.: n.p., 1963.

"Documentos acerca de la cooperación de Guatemala en la independencia de
Centro América," Boletín del Archivo General del Gobierno, Vol. IV, No. 2,
Enero de 1939, 169-176.

"El Salvador Gazetteer" prepared by the Genealogical Society of Utah, n.d.

"Honduras Gazetteer" prepared by the Genealogical Society of Utah, n.d.

Index to Map of Hispanic America. American Geographic Society, Washington,
D.C.: U.S. Printing Office, 1945.

Juarros, Domingo, A Statistical and Commercial History of the Kingdom of
Guatemala in Spanish America. Containing Important Particulars Relative to Its
Productions, Manufactures, Customs, etc., etc., with an Account of Its Conquest
by the Spanish and a Narrative of Events Down to the Present Time: From
Original Records in the Archives; Actual Observations; and Other Authentic
Sources. Translated by J. Baily, Lieutenant R.M. New York: AMS Press, Inc.,
1971 (reprint from first edition London: J. F. Dove, 1823).

"Mexico Gazetteer" prepared by the Genealogical Society of Utah, n.d.

"Nicaragua Gazetteer" prepared by the Genealogical Society of Utah, n.d.

Atlases and Maps:

Arbingast, Stanley A., Clark C. Gill, Robert K. Holz, Robert H. Ryan,
William L. Hezlep. Atlas of Central America. Austin: The University of Texas
at Austin, Bureau of Business Research, 1979.

Garcia de Miranda, Enrique and Zaida Falcón de Gyves, Nuevo Atlas Porrúa de
la República Mexicana, México, D.F.: Editorial Porrúa, S. A., 1972.

Geographical Branch, Military Intelligence Division, (6-2), General Staff,
U.S.A., 1935-1947, 2nd edition.

Rand McNally Standard Map of Mexico. Chicago: Rand McNally & Company, 1927.

BIENES DE DIFUNTOS

Location/ Document Type	Years	Roll No.	Comments
		GUATEMALA nación	
Capital			
	1543,1610, 1620, 1642-1659, 1708-1735	744,868	Disordered Document damage Legajo 2339
	1557, 1562-1577	746,581	Legajo 4808
	1574	744,876/1	Legajo 2453
	1577-1602	746,582/2	Disordered Document damage Legajo 4810
	1580-1583	746,582/1	Legajo 4809
	1587	746,583/1	Legajo 4812
	1590,1594	746,583/2	Document damage Legajo 4814
	1593	744,566/1	ODT/OL Legajo 122
	1593-1599	746,585	Legajo 4818
	1593-1609, 1626	746,874/1	Disordered Legajo 4834
	1594,1596	746,584/1	Legajo 4816
	1596-1608	746,874/3	Legajo 4836
	1597, 1612-1613	746,879/2	Legajo 4845
	1598,1677	751,731/6	Legajo 5772

Location/ Document Type	Years	Roll No.	Comments
	1598-1599	746,584/2	Legajo 4817
	1599	746,586/1	Legajo 4819
	1599-1600	746,586/3	Legajo 4821
	1600-1601	746,586/2	Legajo 4820
	1602	746,586/4	Legajo 4322
	1602-1603	746,587/1	Legajo 4823
	1603	746,587/2	Legajo 4824
	1603-1604	746,587/3	Disordered Legajo 4825
	1604	746,588/1-2	Legajos 4827-4828
	1604	751,732/10	Legajo 6071
	1605	746,589/1	Legajo 4829
	1605	747,177/1	Legajo 4913
	1605-1606	746,590/1	Legajo 4832
	1605-1606, 1635	747,168/1	Legajo 4895
	1606	745,811/6	Legajo 4833
	1606	746,589/2-3	Legajos 4830-4831
	1606-1607	746,874/2	Legajo 4835
	1606-1636	751,732/2	Legajo 5925
	1607	746,590/2	Legajo 4833
	1607,1610, 1613, 1616-1617, 1622-1623, 1625-1626, 1635-1637	746,876	Legajo 4839
	1607-1621	751,731/7	Legajo 5903
	1608	751,732/11	Written in Indian language Legajo 6074
	1610	741,886/7	Legajo 5925
	1610-1611	746,875	Document damage Legajo 4838

Location/ Document Type	Years	Roll No.	Comments
	1610-1613, 1620,1625	746,877	Legajo 4840
	1610-1616	746,880/2	Legajo 4849
	1611,1616, 1618	746,885/1	Document damage Legajo 4860
	1611-1612, 1617, 1625-1626	746,878/3	Legajo 4843
	1611-1613	746,878/1	Legajo 4841
	1612	745,811/18	Legajo 4845
	1612	746,879/1	Legajo 4844
	1612-1613	746,879/3	Legajo 4847
	1612-1651	744,957/1	Disordered ODT/OL Legajo 235
	1612-1714	751,732/12	Written partially in Indian language Legajo 6083
	1613	746,880/1	Legajo 4848
	1613	751,731/4	Legajo 5532
	1613,1615	746,883/1	Disordered Legajo 4856
	1613-1616	746,881/1	Legajo 4850
	1613-1618	746,881/2	Legajo 4851
	1614	746,882/3	Legajo 4855
	1614, 1616-1617, 1619	746,884/1	Disordered Legajo 4858
	1615-1616	746,883/2	Legajo 4857
	1616	746,570/9	Legajo 2731
	1616	746,884/2	Document damage Legajo 4859
	1616-1624, 1629-1632 1637-1642, 1668, 1675-1676	746,886/2	Disordered Legajo 4865

Location/ Document Type	Years	Roll No.	Comments
	1617,1619	746,885/2	Legajo 4861
	1617, 1657-1660	747,260/3	Document damage Legajo 4926
	1618, 1624-1626, 1639-1640	747,161	Document damage Legajo 4880
	1618-1619	746,882/2	Legajo 4853
	1618-1619, 1631	746,886/3	Disordered Legajo 4866
	1618-1625	746,893/3	Disordered Legajo 4876
	1619-1620	746,887	Legajo 4867
	1620, 1623-1624	746,888	Legajo 4868
	1620-1623	746,889	Continued on 746,890 Legajo 4868
	1620-1623	746,891/1	Disordered Legajo 4869
	1620-1623, 1634-1652, 1661-1674	744,876/2	Legajo 2658
	1621	745,811/7	Legajo 4870
	1621, 1623-1624	746,893/1	Legajo 4875
	1621-1622	746,891/4	Disordered Legajo 4872
	1621-1626	746,891/2	Disordered Legajo 4870
	1622	746,891/3	Legajo 4871
	1622-1623	746,886/1	
	1622-1624	746,892/2	Disordered Legajo 4873
	1623	746,892/1	
	1623	746,892/3	Legajo 4873
	1623-1625	746,890	Continued from 746,889 Legajo 4868
	1623-1632	747,165/1	Legajo 4888

Location/ Document Type	Years	Roll No.	Comments
	1624-1628, 1630, 1632-1633, 1636, 1640-1641, 1647	747,170	Disordered Document damage Legajo 4900
	1625	741,886/8	Legajo 5925
	1625	746,893/2	Legajo 4876
	1625	746,894/1	Legajo 4877
	1625-1626	746,895/1	
	1625-1627	747,162/1	Legajo 4881
	1626	741,886/9	Legajo 5925
	1626	746,578/8	Legajo 4107
	1626-1627	746,894/2	Disordered Legajo 4878
	1626-1627	746,895/2	Legajo 4879
	1626-1721	747,284/3	Disordered Legajo 5000
	1627,1629, 1633, 1638-1639	747,162/2	Legajo 4882
	1627,1635, 1638	747,169/1	Legajo 4898
	1627-1629	745,811/19	Legajo 4884
	1628	747,163/1	Legajo 4883
	1628,1630	747,163/2	Legajo 4884
	1629	741,750/2	Legajo 278
	1629	747,163/3	Legajo 4885
	1629-1630	746,885/3	Legajo 4864
	1629-1644	747,164/1	Legajo 4886
	1630	746,579/1	Legajo 4109
	1630	747,164/2	Legajo 4887
	1630, 1634-1639	747,168/2	Disordered Legajo 4897

Location/ Document Type	Years	Roll No.	Comments
	1631-1632	747,165/2	Legajo 4889
	1631-1635, 1637	747,166/2	Legajo 4892
	1632-1633, 1635-1637, 1639-1640	747,166/1	Disordered Legajo 4891
	1632-1633, 1635-1640	747,165/3	Legajo 4890
	1633	747,153/1	Legajo 1123
	1633-1634, 1663-1667, 1674-1675	747,167/1	Legajo 4893
	1634	747,167/2	Legajo 4894
	1635	741,886/10	Legajo 5925
	1635	745,812/3	Legajo 5925
	1635	746,579/2	Legajo 4110
	1636	747,153/2	Legajo 1125
	1636	751,731/1	Legajo 5321
	1637-1638	744,779/2	Illegible Legajo 1126
	1639	745,811/8	Legajo 4898
	1639-1642, 1651-1653	747,169/2	Legajo 4899
	1640	741,886/11	Legajo 5926
	1640-1641	751,732/5	Legajo 5925
	1640-1642	747,171/1	Legajo 4902
	1640-1643	747,172/1	Legajo 4904
	1640-1657	747,178/2	Disordered Legajo 4918
	1641?	746,579/3	Document damage Legajo 4113
	1641-1643, 1647	747,171/2	Disordered Legajo 4902
	1642	744,779/3	Legajo 1559

Location/ Document Type	Years	Roll No.	Comments
	1643-1644, 1650	747,172/2	Legajo 4905
	1644	745,811/9	Legajo 4906
	1644	745,811/12	Legajo 5926
	1644-1646, 1648,1650	747,173/1	Legajo 4906
	1644-1652	747,176/2	Legajo 4912
	1645,1655	744,867/14	Legajo 2023
	1645-1647	747,173/2	Legajo 4907
	1646-1648	747,174	Legajo 4908
	1646-1648	747,175/2	Legajo 4910
	1646-1649, 1656	747,179/2	Legajo 4920
	1646-1654	747,175/1	Legajo 4909
	1648	741,886/5	Legajo 5765
	1649	744,867/1	Legajo 1560
	1649-1650, 1657,1659	747,260/2	Disordered Legajo 4927
	1649-1651	747,176/1	Disordered Legajo 4911
	1649-1651	747,177/2	Disordered Legajo 4915
	1649-1652	747,178/1	Legajo 4917
	1649-1705	751,732/4	Legajo 5926
	1651	747,177/3	Legajo 4916
	1651-1652	745,812/1	Legajo 4915
	1653-1655	747,179/1	Legajo 4919
	1654	746,578/3	Legajo 3012
	1656	747,179/3	Legajo 4921
	1657	747,257/2	Legajo 4923
	1657	747,258	Legajo 4924
	1657-1675	747,257/1	Legajo 4922

Location/ Document Type	Years	Roll No.	Comments
	1658	741,886/1	Legajo 4926
	1658	744,867/2	Legajo 1562
	1658	745,076/17	Legajo 1562
	1658-1659	747,259	Document damage Legajo 4925
	1658-1660	747,260/1	Document damage Legajo 4926
	1659	745,811/13	Legajo 5926
	1659,1661	747,261/2	Legajo 4930
	1659-1661	747,261/1	Disordered Legajo 4929
	1659-1663	747,261/3	Disordered Legajo 4931
	1660	745,811/10	ODT/OL Legajo 4927
	1662-1667	747,262/2	Legajo 4937
	1663-1667	747,261/4	Legajo 4934
	1664-1665	747,262/1	Legajo 4936
	1665	741,886/13	Legajo 5926
	1665-1667	747,263/1	Legajo 4938
	1665-1668	744,761/2	Legajo 4939
	1665-1766	751,732/3	Intermittent years Legajo 5926
	1667	747,263/2	Legajo 4939
	1668	747,265/1-2	Legajos 4941-4942
	1668-1670	747,264	Disordered Legajo 4940
	1668-1674	747,265/3	Disordered Legajo 4943
	1670	747,266/1	Legajo 4944
	1672-1678	747,266/4	Disordered Legajo 4947
	1673	747,266/2	ODT/OL Document damage Legajo 4945

Location/ Document Type	Years	Roll No.	Comments
	1674	747,266/3	ODT/OL Legajo 4946
	1674-1701	744,877	Legajo 2659
	1675	744,867/15	Legajo 2298
	1675	744,867/17	Legajo 2318
	1675	746,579/4	Legajo 4119
	1675	747,267/1	Legajo 4948
	1675-1689	744,869	Legajo 2340
	1676, 1679-1680	741,863/1	Disordered ODT/OL Legajo 246
	1676-1678	747,267/2-3	Legajos 4949-4950
	1677	744,867/3	Legajo 1565
	1677	745,076/18	Legajo 1565
	1677	746,878/2	Legajo 4842
	1677-1680	747,267/4	Legajo 4951
	1677-1680	747,268/1	Legajo 4952
	1679-1681	747,268/2-3	Legajos 4953-4954
	1679-1684	747,269/2	Disordered Legajo 4957
	1680-1681	747,268/4	Legajo 4955
	1680-1685	747,269/1	Legajo 4956
	1681	744,867/4	Legajo 1566
	1682-1683	747,270/1	Legajo 4959
	1684-1686	747,270/2	Legajo 4960
	1685-1686	747,270/3	Legajo 4961
	1685-1686	747,271/1	Legajo 4962
	1685-1694	747,271/2	Legajo 4963
	1686-1687	747,271/3-4	Legajos 4964-4965
	1686-1693	747,272/2	Legajo 4968
	1687-1689	747,272/3	Legajo 4969

Location/ Document Type	Years	Roll No.	Comments
	1687–1692	747,273/3	Legajo 4972
	1688	747,272/1	Legajo 4967
	1689–1693	747,273/1	Legajo 4970
	1689–1695	747,274	Legajo 4973
	1690–1692	747,273/2	Legajo 4971
	1690–1706	744,870	Legajo 2341
	1691	746,579/5	Legajo 4125
	1693–1694	747,275/1	Legajo 4974
	1693–1695	751,731/5	Legajo 5533
	1695	747,275/2	Legajo 4975
	1696	747,275/3	ODT/OL Legajo 4976
	1698?	745,811/17	Illegible Legajo 1570
	1698–1706	747,276/1	Legajo 4978
	1699	741,886/12	Legajo 5926
	1699	747,276/2–3	Legajos 4979–4980
	1700	744,867/6	Legajo 1571
	1700	751,732/7	Legajo 5983
	1701	744,867/7	Legajo 1572
	1702,1763	744,875/3	Legajo 2363
	1703	744,867/8	Legajo 1573
	1703	746,571/5	ODT/OL Legajo 2890
	1703	747,277	Legajo 4982
	1703–1706	746,751/6	Legajo 2891
	1703–1818	744,878/1	ODT/OL Legajo 2660
	1705	741,886/14	Legajo 5926
	1705–1799	746,571/2	Legajo 2881
	1706–1707	747,279/2	Legajo 4987

Location/ Document Type	Years	Roll No.	Comments
	1707	744,867/9	Legajo 1576
	1707-1711	747,280/2	Disordered Legajo 4989
	1707-1737	747,280/1	Disordered Legajo 4988
	1708-1709	747,279/1	Legajo 4986
	1709	746,579/6	Legajo 4137
	1710	751,732/9	Legajo 6039
	1710-1711	747,281/1	Legajo 4990
	1711-1717	747,283/2	Legajo 4995
	1712	745,076/19	Legajo 1579
	1712	747,281/2	Legajo 4991
	1712-1715	747,281/3	Legajo 4992
	1713	744,867/10	Legajo 1580
	1713	746,579/7	Document damage Legajo 4140
	1713-1714	747,282/1	Legajo 4993
	1713-1719	744,871	Legajo 2342
	1715	747,283/1	
	1715,1725	744,867/16	Legajo 2300
	1715-1730	747,282/2	Disordered Legajo 4994
	1716-1719	747,283/3	Document damage Legajo 4996
	1717-1719	747,284/1	ODT/OL Legajo 4998
	1717-1720	747,283/4	Legajo 4997
	1719	744,867/11	Legajo 1583
	1720	747,284/2	Legajo 4999
	1720-1728	744,872	Legajo 2343
	1722	747,284/4	ODT/OL Legajo 5001
	1722	747,284/5	Legajo 5002

Location/ Document Type	Years	Roll No.	Comments
	1723–1731	747,287/1	Document damage Legajo 5014
	1724	747,285/1	Legajo 5006
	1725	747,285/2-4	Legajos 5007–5009
	1725–1743, 1758	751,732/1	Legajo 5904
	1726	744,867/12	Legajo 1585
	1726–1727	747,286/1	Legajo 5010
	1727	747,286	Legajo 5012
	1727–1729	744,878/2	Legajo 2661
	1728–1729	747,286/3	Legajo 5013
	1728–1746	744,873	Legajo 2344
	1730	741,886/2	Legajo 5015
	1730–1733	747,288/1	Legajo 5017
	1730–1734	747,287/2	Legajo 5015
	1731–1733	744,878/3	Legajo 2662
	1731–1737	747,288/2	Legajo 5018
	1732–1735	747,289/1	Legajo 5019
	1732–1743	747,289/2	Legajo 5020
	1733–1734	747,289/3	Legajo 5021
	1733–1738	747,291/1	Legajo 5027
	1734	741,886/15	Legajo 5926
	1734	747,290/1	Legajo 5023
	1735–1736	747,290/2	Legajo 5024
	1736	741,865/1	ODT/OL Legajo 257
	1736–1737	747,290/3	Legajo 5025
	1736–1739	747,291/2	Legajo 5028
	1736–1749	744,879/1	ODT/OL Legajo 2663
	1737–1752	744,765/1-2	Legajos 5,7

Location/ Document Type	Years	Roll No.	Comments
	1738	741,886/3	Legajo 5027
	1738-1743	744,562/2	ODT/OL Legajo 4066
	1739-1740	746,580/1	Legajo 4165
	1739	747,291/3	Document damage Legajo 5029
	1740-1741	748,135/1	Legajo 5031
	1740-1743	744,879/2	Legajo 2664
	1742-1747	748,135/2	Legajo 5033
	1743	746,580/2	Legajo 4167
	1743	748,135/3-4	Legajos 5034-5035
	1744	744,875/4	Legajo 2374
	1745	744,875/1	Legajo 2361
	1745	748,135/5	Legajo 5036
	1745-1761	748,135/6	Legajo 5037
	1746-1750	744,880/1	Disordered Legajo 2665
	1746-1786	744,874	Legajo 2345
	1747	748,136/1	Legajo 5038
	1748-1749	748,136/3	Legajo 5041
	1748-1760	748,136/2	Legajo 5039
	1749	748,137/1	Legajo 5043
	1749-1754	748,137/2	Legajo 5044
	1749-1756	744,880/2	Legajo 2666
	1749-1757	748,136/4	Legajo 5042
	1750-1751	748,138/1	Legajo 5047
	1750-1756	748,137/3	Document damage Legajo 5045
	1750-1761	748,137/4	Legajo 5046
	1751	746,578/7	Legajo 4067
	1751	748,138/2	Legajo 5049

Location/ Document Type	Years	Roll No.	Comments
	1752	746,561/1	Legajo 2667
	1752	748,138/3-4	Legajos 5050-5051
	1752	748,139/1	Document damage Legajo 5053
	1753-1755	748,139/2	Document damage Legajo 5054
	1753-1764	751,573/1	Legajo 5084
	1754	748,139/3	ODT/OL Legajo 5055
	1755-1756	748,141/1	Legajo 5057
	1755-1772	748,140	Document damage Legajo 5056
	1755-1756	746,561/2	Legajo 2668
	1756-1760	746,561/3	Legajo 2669
	1757	746,576/1	ODT/OL Legajo 2930
	1757	748,141/2	Legajo 5058
	1758	748,141/3	Legajo 5059
	1758	751,565/1	Legajo 5061
	1758-1759	751,565/2	Disordered Legajo 5062
	1758-1766	748,142	Legajo 5060
	1758-1775	751,774/1	Legajo 5115
	1759	741,872/1	ODT/OL Legajo 265
	1759	741,886/16	Legajo 5926
	1759-1761	751,565/3	Legajo 5063
	1760	751,566/1-2	Legajos 5064-5065
	1760	751,567/1	Legajo 5066
	1760-1765	751,567/2	Disordered Legajo 5067
	1761	751,568/1-2	Legajos 5068-5069
	1762	751,569/1-4	Legajos 5070, 5072-5074

Location/ Document Type	Years	Roll No.	Comments
	1762	751,570/2	ODT/OL Legajo 5076
	1762	751,750/1,3	Legajos 5075, 5077
	1763	746,562/1	Legajo 2670
	1763	751,571/2	Legajo 5079
	1763	751,573/2	Legajo 5085
	1763-1766	751,571/3	Disordered Legajo 5080
	1764	751,572/1,3	Legajos 5081, 5083
	1764,1794	751,572/2	Legajo 5082
	1764-1765	751,574/2	Legajo 5090
	1764-1766	751,573/4	ODT/OL Legajo 5088
	1764-1766	751,576/1	Legajo 5096
	1764-1773	751,780/1	Legajo 5136
	1765	741,886/17	Legajo 5926
	1765	746,580/3	Legajo 4198
	1765	751,574/3	Legajo 5091
	1765	751,575/1	ODT/OL Legajo 5092
	1765	751,575/2	Legajo 5094
	1765-1766	746,562/2	Legajo 2671
	1765-1775	751,574/1	Disordered Legajo 5089
	1765-1781	751,586/3	Legajo 5193
	1766	741,872/1	ODT/OL Legajo 265
	1766	746,580/4	Legajo 4200
	1766	751,576/2	Legajo 5097
	1766	751,576/3	ODT/OL Legajo 5098
	1766-1767	751,576/4	Disordered Legajo 5099

Location/ Document Type	Years	Roll No.	Comments
	1766-1767	751,577/1	Legajo 5100
	1767	746,562/3	ODT/OL Legajo 2672
	1767	751,577/2	Legajo 5101
	1767-1768	746,562/4	ODT/OL Legajo 2673
	1767-1770	751,774/2	Legajo 5117
	1767-1772	751,775/1	Disordered Legajo 5121
	1767-1773	751,577/3	Legajo 5103
	1768	751,578/1-3	Legajos 5104, 5106, 5108
	1768,1772, 1782	746,563/9	Legajo 2683
	1768-1772	751,774/3	Legajo 5118
	1769	751,772/1	Legajo 5109
	1769-1770	746,563/1	Legajo 2674
	1769-1771	751,772/3	Legajo 5111
	1769-1775	751,772/2	Legajo 5110
	1769-1808	751,732/6	Legajo 5927
	1770	744,765/3	Legajo 8
	1770	746,563/2	Legajo 2675
	1770-1772	751,583/1	Legajo 5176
	1770-1772	751,773/2	Legajo 5113
	1770-1773	741,873/1	ODT/OL Legajo 266
	1770-1779	751,773/3-4	Legajos 5114, 5119
	1770-1780	746,860/4	ODT/OL Legajo 4683
	1770-1794	751,773/1	Legajo 5112
	1771	751,776/1-2	Legajos 5124-5125
	1771	751,776/3	ODT/OL Legajo 5126
	1771-1773	751,775/3	Legajo 5123

Location/ Document Type	Years	Roll No.	Comments
	1771-1776	751,579/4	ODT/OL Legajo 5157
	1772	746,563/3	Legajo 2676
	1772	745,812/2	Legajo 5135
	1772	751,778/1	Legajo 5130
	1772-1773	751,778/3	Legajo 5132
	1772-1773	751,779/3	Legajo 5135
	1772-1778	751,778/2	Legajo 5131
	1772-1779	751,777/1	Disordered Legajo 5127
	1772-1787	751,777/2	Disordered Legajo 5128
	1772-1792	751,599/3	Legajo 5250
	1772-1793	751,598/3	Legajo 5247
	1773	741,886/4	Legajo 5138
	1773, 1780-1814	751,587/3	Legajo 5198
	1773-1774	746,563/4	Legajo 2677
	1773-1775	751,780/3	Legajo 5138
	1773-1782	751,780/2	Legajo 5137
	1773-1779	751,779/1-2	Legajos 5133-5134
	1774	746,563/5	Legajo 2678
	1774	751,732/8	Legajo 6025
	1774	751,781/1	Legajo 5140
	1774	751,782/1	Legajo 5145
	1774-1776	751,782/2	Legajo 5146
	1774-1781	751,781/2	Legajo 5141
	1774-1783	751,781/3	Legajo 5142
	1775	746,563/6	Legajo 2679
	1775	751,732/13	Legajo 6096
	1775	751,783/1-2,6	Legajos 5147-5148, 5152

Location/ Document Type	Years	Roll No.	Comments
	1775-1777	751,783/3,5	Legajos 5149, 5151
	1775-1782	751,783/4	Legajo 5150
	1776	744,765/4	ODT/OL Legajo 9
	1776	751,579/1,5	Legajos 5154, 5158
	1776	751,579/2	ODT/OL Legajo 5155
	1776	751,579/3	ODT/OL Legajo 5156
	1776-1785	751,783/7	Legajo 5153
	1777	751,580/1-3	Legajos 5162-5164
	1777-1778	746,563/7	Document damage Legajo 2680
	1778	744,765/4	ODT/OL Legajo 9
	1778	744,875/2	Legajo 2362
	1778	751,581/1,3	Legajos 5166, 5170
	1778	751,582/1	ODT/OL Legajo 5171
	1778	751,582/2-3	Legajos 5172-5173
	1778-1779	751,583/2	Legajo 5177
	1778-1785	751,581/2	Legajo 5167
	1779	745,108/10	ODT/OL Legajo 2757
	1779	751,583/3-4	Legajos 5178, 5180
	1779	751,583/5	ODT/OL Legajo 5181
	1780	744,765/4	ODT/OL Legajo 9
	1780	751,584/2	Legajo 5183
	1780-1781	746,563/8	Legajo 2682
	1780-1782	751,731/3	Legajo 5440
	1780-1786	751,585/1-3	Legajos 5186-5188
	1780-1786	751,588/1	Legajo 5199

Location/ Document Type	Years	Roll No.	Comments
	1780-1787	751,587/2	Legajo 5197
	1780-1788	751,594/2	Legajo 5229
	1780-1793	751,584/3	Legajo 5185
	1781	751,586/1	Legajo 5190
	1781-1783	741,886/6	Legajo 5190
	1781-1784	751,586/2	Legajo 5191
	1781-1789	751,586/4	Legajo 5194
	1781-1790	751,586/5	Legajo 5195
	1782	741,770/1	ODT/OL Legajo 334
	1782	745,811/4	ODT/OL Legajo 2678
	1782-1783	746,564/1	ODT/OL Legajo 2684
	1782-1785	751,588/2	Legajo 5201
	1782-1793	751,600/2	Disordered Legajo 5253
	1782-1814	751,587/1	Legajo 5196
	1783	751,589/2-4	Legajos 5203-5205
	1783	751,591/2	Legajo 5211
	1783-1785	751,589/1	Legajo 5202
	1783-1809	751,590/1	Legajo 5207
	1784	751,591/1	Legajo 5210
	1784-1793	751,591/7	Intermittent years Legajo 5218
	1785	751,591/6	ODT/OL Legajo 5217
	1785	751,591/2	Document damage Legajo 5214
	1785	751,591/4-5	Legajos 5215-5216
	1785-1789	746,564/2	Disordered Legajo 2685
	1785-1811	751,597/3	Legajo 5243

Location/ Document Type	Years	Roll No.	Comments
	1786	746,564/3	Legajo 2686
	1786	751,592/2	Legajo 5220
	1786, 1791-1792, 1806-1807	746,565/1	ODT/OL Legajo 2690
	1786-1791	751,597/1	Legajo 5239
	1786-1793	751,592/1	Document damage Legajo 5219
	1786-1794	751,592/3	Legajo 5221
	1787-1789	751,594/1	Legajo 5226
	1787-1794	751,593/3	Legajo 5224
	1787-1799	751,593/1	Legajo 5222
	1787-1807	751,593/2	Legajo 5223
	1788	751,594/4	Legajo 5232
	1788-1789	746,577/4	ODT/OL Legajo 2936
	1788-1789	751,594/3	Legajo 5231
	1788-1791	746,565/3	Legajo 2692
	1789	744,778	ODT/OL Legajo 217
	1789	746,564/4	Legajo 2688
	1789	751,596/2	Legajo 5237
	1789-1790	746,564/5	Legajo 2689
	1789-1791	751,595/1	Legajo 5233
	1789-1797	751,596/3	Legajo 5238
	1789-1807	751,595/2	Legajo 5235
	1789-1811	751,596/1	Legajo 5236
	1790	751,599/2	ODT/OL Legajo 5249
	1791	751,598/1-2	Legajos 5245-5246
	1792	751,599/1,4	Legajos 5248, 5251
	1793	746,566/1	Legajo 2693

Location/ Document Type	Years	Roll No.	Comments
	1793	746,577/5	Legajo 2938
	1793	751,600/1	Legajo 5252
	1793,1802	744,867/13	Legajo 1977
	1793-1800	751,597/2	Legajo 5242
	1794	746,565/2	Legajo 2691
	1794	746,566/3	ODT/OL Legajo 2696
	1794	746,570/10	Legajo 2863
	1794	751,600/3-5	Legajos 5255-5257
	1794-1795	746,566/2	Legajo 2695
	1794-1795	751,601/1	Legajo 5258
	1794-1796	744,552/1	ODT/OL Legajo 278
	1795	746,577/6	Legajo 2939
	1795	751,601/2-3	Legajos 5259-5260
	1795-1799	751,725/1	Disordered Legajo 5272
	1796	746,566/5	ODT/OL Legajo 2698
	1796	746,571/4	Legajo 2888
	1796	751,601/4	Legajo 5261
	1796-1803	746,567/2/2	Document damage Legajo 2700
	1797	751,602/1-2	Legajos 5265, 5267
	1797	751,731/2	Legajo 5329
	1797, 1799-1800	746,568/4	Disordered Legajo 2705
	1797-1798	746,568/1	Legajo 2702
	1797-1799	751,602/3	ODT/OL Legajo 5268
	1798	744,768	ODT/OL Legajo 18
	1798	746,568/2	Legajo 2703

Location/ Document Type	Years	Roll No.	Comments
	1798	751,602/4	Legajo 5269
	1798	751,603/1-2	Legajos 5270-5271
	1799	746,567/2	
	1799	746,578/1	Legajo 2943
	1799	751,725/2	Document damage Legajo 5273
	1799-1800	746,575/2	Legajo 2918
	1799-1818	751,730/3	Legajo 5299
	1800	746,580/5	Legajo 4370
	1800	751,726/1	Legajo 5276
	1800,1804	746,569/4	Document damage Legajo 2715
	1800-1801	746,568/5	Legajo 2707
	1800-1819	751,725/3	Legajo 5275
	1801	751,726/2-3	Legajos 5277-5278
	1802	744,761/3	Legajo 5281
	1802	744,770	ODT/OL Legajo 22
	1802	746,568/6-8	Legajos 2708-2710
	1802	746,571/3	Legajo 2882
	1802	751,726/4	Legajo 5280
	1802-1804	751,726/5	Legajo 5281
	1802-1805	744,779/1	Legajo 218
	1803	746,569/1-2	Legajos 2712-2713
	1803	751,726/6	Legajo 5282
	1803-1808	751,726/7	Legajo 5283
	1804	746,569/3	ODT/OL Legajo 2714
	1804	746,569/5-6	Legajos 2716-2717
	1804-1806	751,727/3	Legajo 5286
	1804-1810	751,727/2	Legajo 5285

Location/ Document Type	Years	Roll No.	Comments
	1804–1816	751,727/1	Legajo 5284
	1805	746,569/7–8	Legajos 2718–2719
	1805	746,575/4	ODT/OL Legajo 2922
	1805–1806	741,776/2	ODT/OL Legajo 357
	1805–1806	751,728/1	Legajo 5287
	1805–1808	751,728/2	Legajo 5288
	1805–1817	751,728/3	Legajo 5289
	1806	746,569/9	Legajo 2720
	1806–1808	751,729/1	Legajo 5290
	1806–1809	751,729/3	Legajo 5293
	1806–1811	751,729/2	Legajo 5292
	1807	746,570/1,3	Legajos 2722, 2724
	1807	746,571/1	Legajo 2868
	1807	746,580/6	Legajo 4430
	1807	751,729/4	Legajo 5296
	1807–1808	746,570/2	Legajo 2723
	1808	746,570/4–5	Legajos 2725, 2727
	1808	751,730/2	Legajo 5298
	1808,1812, 1813	746,569/3	ODT/OL Legajo 2714
	1808–1809	751,730/1	Legajo 5297
	1809	745,076/14	Legajo 1072
	1809	746,570/6	Legajo 2728
	1809	751,730/4–5	Legajos 5300–5301
	1810	746,570/7–8	Legajos 2729–2730
	1810	751,730/7	Legajo 5303
	1810–1812	751,730/6	Document damage Legajo 5302
	1894	741,776/1	ODT/OL Legajo 356

Location/ Document Type	Years	Roll No.	Comments
Alta Verapaz 　Cobán 　　<u>Cobán</u> (c/cd)			
	1765	751,575/1	ODT/OL Legajo 5092
Chimaltenango 　Chimaltenango 　　<u>Chimaltenango</u> (c/cd)			
	1771	751,776/3	ODT/OL Legajo 5126
	1792	746,565/1	ODT/OL Legajo 2690
	1799	745,418/1	ODT/OL
	1799	746,568/3	Legajo 2704
Chiquimula 　Chiquimula 　　<u>Chiquimula</u> (c/cd)			
	1754	748,139/3	ODT/OL Legajo 5055
	1762-1764	751,573/3	Legajo 5086
	1764-1766	751,573/4	ODT/OL Legajo 5088
	1769	751,571/1	Legajo 5078
	1776	751,579/2	ODT/OL Legajo 5155
	1779	751,583/5	ODT/OL Legajo 5181
	1784-1785	746,564/1	ODT/OL Legajo 2684
	1795-1796	746,566/5	ODT/OL Legajo 2698
	1796-1800	746,567/1	Legajo 2699
	1797-1799	751,602/3	ODT/OL Legajo 5268
	1798	744,776/2	Legajo 177
	1808	744,776/3	Legajo 180

Location/ Document Type	Years	Roll No.	Comments
Jocotán Jocotán (c/v)			
	1754	748,139/3	ODT/OL Legajo 5055

El Quiché
  Chichicastenango
    Chichicastenango (c/v)			

	1827,1835	715,141/1	

Escuintla
  Escuintla
    Escuintla (c/cd)			

	1653–1663	744,957/2	Disordered ODT/OL Legajo 244
	1653–1668	741,589	ODT/OL Legajo 244
	1679	741,863/1	Disordered ODT/OL Legajo 246
	1765–1766	741,871/1	ODT/OL Legajo 264
	1766	741,872/1	ODT/OL Legajo 265
	1793	744,961/3	ODT/OL Legajo 278
	1802	744,961/4	ODT/OL Legajo 280
	1808	744,776/1	Legajo 174

Guatemala
  Mixco
    Mixco (c/p)			

	1673	747,266/2	ODT/OL Legajo 4945
	1736	744,879/1	ODT/OL Legajo 2663
San Juan Sacatepéquez San Juan Sacatepéquez (c/v)			
	1780	746,576/2	Legajo 2931
	1782–1783	746,577/1	Legajo 2932

Location/ Document Type	Years	Roll No.	Comments
	1784	746,577/2	ODT/OL Legajo 2933
	1789	746,577/4	ODT/OL Legajo 2936

Huehuetenango
  Huehuetenango
    Huehuetenango (c/cd)			

	1674	747,266/3	ODT/OL Legajo 4946
	1686,1695, 1701	746,571/5	ODT/OL Legajo 2890
	1689	741,864/1	ODT/OL Legajo 249
	1717	747,284/1	ODT/OL Legajo 4998
	1735-1738	746,572/3	Document damage Legajo 2894
	1744	746,572/4	Legajo 2895
	1759	746,573/1	Legajo 2896
	1762	751,570/2	ODT/OL Legajo 5076
	1776	746,573/3	ODT/OL Legajo 2900
	1776	751,579/3	ODT/OL Legajo 5156
	1780-1781	746,573/4	ODT/OL Legajo 2900
	1781	746,573/5	Legajo 2902
	1782	746,573/6	Legajo 2903
	1792-1796	746,574/5	Legajo 2909
	1793-1797	746,575/1	Legajo 2915
	1796	746,578/5	Legajo 3026

Location/ Document Type	Years	Roll No.	Comments

Jalapa
  Jalapa
    Jalapa (c/cd)			

	1630	744,577/1	ODT/OL Legajo 237

Jutiapa
  Zapotitlán
    Zapotitlán (c/p)			

	1771-1772	751,775/2	Legajo 5122

Quezaltenango
  Quezaltenango
    Quezaltenango (c/cd)			

	1696	747,275/3	ODT/OL Legajo 4976

Sacatepéquez
  Antigua Guatemala
    Antigua Guatemala (c/cd)			

	1788-1789	746,577/3	Legajo 2935
	1789	746,577/4	ODT/OL Legajo 2936
	1796-1797	751,601/5	Legajo 5264
	1799	746,577/7	Legajo 2942
	1802	746,578/2	Legajo 2949
Ciudad Vieja Ciudad Vieja (c/p)			
	1772	746,576/1	ODT/OL Legajo 2930
Jocotenango Jocotenango (c/p)			
	1762	751,570/2	ODT/OL Legajo 5076

Location/ Document Type	Years	Roll No.	Comments
San Miguel Dueñas San Miguel Dueñas (c/p)			
	1761-1767	746,562/4	ODT/OL Legajo 2672

San Marcos
  San Antonio Sacatepéquez
    San Antonio Sacatepéquez (c/p)			

	1614	746,882/1	Legajo 4852

Santa Rosa
  Guazacapán
    Guazacapán (c/v)			

	1794	744,774/1	Legajo 129

Sololá
  Sololá
    Sololá (c/cd)			

	1612-1651	744,957/1	Disordered ODT/OL Legajo 235

Suchitepéquez
  Mazatenango
    Mazatenango (c/cd)			

	1802	744,961/4	ODT/OL Legajo 280
Patulul Patulul (c/p)			
	1915	738,331	ODT/OL
San Antonio Suchitepéquez San Antonio Suchitepéquez (c/v)			
	1592	744,566/1	ODT/OL Legajo 12?
	1717	747,284/1	ODT/OL Legajo 4998
	1722	747,284/4	ODT/OL Legajo 5001

Location/ Document Type	Years	Roll No.	Comments
Totonicapán Momostenango Momostenango (c/v)			
	1703	747,278/1	Legajo 4983
San Cristóbal Totonicapán San Cristóbal Totonicapán (c/v)			
	1773–1776	746,573/3	ODT/OL Legajo 2900
	1784	746,577/2	ODT/OL Legajo 2933
	1802	746,575/3	Legajo 2921
Totonicapán Totonicapán (c/cd)			
	1706–1715	746,572/1	Legajo 2892
	1722–1729	746,572/2	Document damage Legajo 2893
	1744	746,578/4	ODT/OL Legajo 3025
	1755–1764	746,573/2	Document damage Legajo 2897
	1779–1783	746,578/4	ODT/OL Legajo 3025
	1786	746,574/1	Legajo 2905
	1788–1789	746,574/2	Legajo 2906
	1791–1792	746,574/4	Legajo 2908
	1791–1798	746,574/3	Legajo 2907
	1796	746,574/6-7	Legajos 2912–2913
	1799	746,578/6	Legajo 3027
	1805	746,575/4	ODT/OL Legajo 2922
	1806–1807	746,575/5	Legajo 2923

Location/ Document Type	Years	Roll No.	Comments

Zacapa
  Zacapa
    Zacapa (c/cd)			

	1728	745,811/16	Legajo 5926
	1778	751,582/1	ODT/OL Legajo 5171
	1779	751,583/5	ODT/OL Legajo 5181
	1780	751,584/1	Legajo 5182

EL SALVADOR
nación

Location/ Document Type	Years	Roll No.	Comments

Chalatenango
  Chalatenango
    Chalatenango (c/cd)			

	1766	751,576/3	ODT/OL Legajo 5098

San Miguel
  San Miguel
    San Miguel (c/cd)			

	1776	741,750/4	Document damage Legajo 492

San Salvador
  San Salvador
    San Salvador (cap nl)			

	1611, 1617-1619	741,885/1	Legajo 4842
	1617-1618	741,885/2	Legajo 4862
	1620	741,885/3	Legajo 4867
	1622	741,885/4	Legajo 4871
	1632-1637	741,871	ODT/OL Legajo 1557
	1640-1642	741,885/5	Legajo 4899
	1643-1644	741,885/6	Legajo 4905

Location/ Document Type	Years	Roll No.	Comments
	1776	741,874/2-3	Legajos 4739-4740
	1790	751,599/2	ODT/OL Legajo 5249

Sonsonate
  Sonsonate
    Sonsonate (c/cd)			

	1776	741,874/1	Legajo 4737

HONDURAS
nación

Location/ Document Type	Years	Roll No.	Comments
Colón Trujillo (cap dl)			
	1627	741,750/1	Legajo 277
	1815	741,744/1	ODT/OL Legajo 98
	1815-1817	741,777/2	Legajo 363
Comayagua Comayagua (cap dl)			
	1572-1574, 1602	741,745/1	Legajo 258
	1588-1590	741,745/2	Disordered ODT/OL Legajo 259
	1600	741,745/3	Legajo 260
	1601	741,745/4	ODT/OL Legajo 261
	1605-1606	741,746/1	Legajo 262
	1606-1608	741,746/2	Legajo 263
	1609-1616	741,747/1	Legajo 264
	1611	741,747/2	Legajo 265
	1611-1621	741,747/3	Legajo 266
	1612	741,748/1	Legajo 267
	1615	741,748/2	Legajo 269

Location/ Document Type	Years	Roll No.	Comments
	1620	741,748/3	Legajo 272
	1621-1622	741,748/4	Legajo 273
	1625	741,749/1	ODT/OL Legajo 275
	1626	741,749/2-3	Legajos 275-276
	1628-1642	741,754/2	Document damage Legajo 286
	1630	741,750/3	Illegible Legajo 279
	1630-1636	741,753	Legajo 284
	1631-1632	741,751/1	Legajo 280
	1633	741,751/2	Legajo 281
	1633-1635	741,752/1	Legajo 282
	1635-1636	741,752/2	Legajo 283
	1635-1642	741,754/1	Legajo 285
	1641	741,755/1	Legajo 287
	1642-1647	741,755/2	Legajo 288
	1648	741,756/1	Legajo 289
	1649-1651	741,756/2	Legajo 290
	1652-1653	741,756/3	Legajo 291
	1656-1664	741,756/4	Legajo 292
	1663-1665	741,757/1	Legajo 293
	1664-1671	741,757/2	Legajo 294
	1667-1677	741,757/3	Legajo 295
	1679-1680	741,757/4	Legajo 296
	1680	741,758/1	Legajo 297
	1680-1684	741,758/2	Legajo 298
	1680-1688	741,758/3	Legajo 299
	1683-1687	741,759/1	Legajo 300
	1686	741,864/1	ODT/OL Legajo 249

Location/ Document Type	Years	Roll No.	Comments
	1689	741,759/2	Legajo 301
	1697-1698	741,760/2	Legajo 305
	1698-1699	741,760/1	Legajo 304
	1702	741,759/3	Legajo 303
	1708-1712	741,760/3	Legajo 306
	1721-1723	741,761/2	Legajo 308
	1733	741,774/2	Legajo 351
	1735	741,761/3	Legajo 309
	1738-1741	741,762/1	Legajo 310
	1750	741,762/2	Legajo 312
	1753	741,762/3	Legajo 313
	1754	741,763/1	Legajo 314
	1756-1758	741,763/2	Legajo 316
	1761	741,764/1	Legajo 317
	1762	741,764/2	Legajo 317
	1764-1765	741,764/3	Legajo 319
	1765-1767	741,765/1	Legajo 320
	1767	741,765/2	Legajo 321
	1767	746,562/3	ODT/OL Legajo 2672
	1769	741,765/3	Legajo 322
	1774	741,765/5	Legajo 324
	1774-1775	741,766/2	Legajo 326
	1774-1793	741,766/1	Legajo 325
	1775	741,767/1	Legajo 327
	1776	741,767/2	Legajo 328
	1778	741,768/1	Legajo 330
	1778-1779	741,768/2-3	Legajo 331
	1779-1783	741,769/1	Disordered Legajo 332

Location/ Document Type	Years	Roll No.	Comments
	1780-1791	741,772/1-2	Legajo 342
	1781	741,769/2	Legajo 333
	1783	741,770/2	Legajo 336
	1785	741,770/3	Legajo 337
	1785	751,591/6	ODT/OL
	1786-1787	741,770/4	Legajo 338
	1787	741,771/1	Legajo 339
	1787-1789	741,771/2	Legajo 340
	1789	741,771/3	Legajo 341
	1791	741,772/3	Legajo 343
	1791-1792	741,772/4	Legajo 344
	1792,1794	741,773/1	Legajo 346
	1792-1793	741,772/5	Legajo 345
	1794	741,761/1	Legajo 307
	1794	741,773/2	Legajo 347
	1795	741,773/3	Legajo 348
	1796-1797	741,773/4	Legajo 349
	1797	741,774/1	Legajo 350
	1800-1801	741,774/3	Legajo 352
	1801-1802	741,775/1	Legajo 353
	1803	741,775/2	Legajo 354
	1803-1804	741,775/3	Legajo 355
	1805-1806	741,776/2	ODT/OL Legajo 357
	1806	744,397/5	Legajo 367
	1807	744,397/6	Poor exposure Legajo 397
	1809-1810	741,776/3	Legajo 359
	1810-1815	741,776/4	Legajo 360
	1814	741,777/1	Legajo 362

Location/ Document Type	Years	Roll No.	Comments
	1815	744,397/3	Legajo 365
	1815-1818	744,397/2	Legajo 364
	1817	744,397/1	Legajo 364
	1819	744,397/4	Legajo 366
	1894	741,776/1	ODT/OL Legajo 356

Cortes
  Omoa (c mpl)

	1771-1776	751,579/4	ODT/OL Legajo 5157
	1780-1783, 1787-1792	741,742	Legajo 96
	1790	751,599/2	ODT/OL Legajo 5249
	1796-1805	741,744/1	ODT/OL Legajo 98
	1797-1800	741,743	Legajo 97

Teguicigalpa
  Teguciagalpa (cap dl)

	1795	746,566/4	ODT/OL Legajo 2697

MEXICO
nación

Campeche
  Campeche
    Campeche (cap del e)

	1640	741,587/2	ODT/OL Legajo 241

Chiapas
  Acapetagua
    Soconusco

	1612-1651	744,957/1	Disordered ODT/OL Legajo 235

Location/ Document Type	Years	Roll No.	Comments
	1634-1647	741,588/1	ODT/OL Legajo 242
	1653-1663	744,957/2	Disordered ODT/OL Legajo 244
	1653-1668	741,589	ODT/OL Legajo 244
	1671	744,958/1	Legajo 245
	1678-1689	774,315	Legajos 245-249
	1681	744,961/2	Legajo 1566
	1686-1687, 1692-1693	744,958/2	Document damage Legajo 249
	1694-1695	744,959/1	Legajo 259
	1714,1716	744,958/3	Legajo 252
	1760, 1766-1772	744,959/2	Legajo 262
	1770-1773	744,960/1	Legajo 266
	1772-1774	744,544/2	ODT/OL Legajo 267
	1772-1778	744,545/1	ODT/OL Legajo 269
	1773	744,960/2	Legajo 268
	1780	744,960/3	Legajo 269
	1782-1785	744,960/5	Legajo 271
	1784	744,960/4	Legajo 270
	1790	744,960/6	Legajo 274
	1802-1805	744,960/7	Legajo 281
	1807	744,961/1	Legajo 283

Chiapas
  San Cristóbal las Casas
    San Cristóbal las Casas

	Years	Roll No.	Comments
	1554	744,567	Legajo 247
	1578-1597	741,588/1	Document damage ODT/OL Legajo 242

Location/ Document Type	Years	Roll No.	Comments
	1588	744,566/1	ODT/OL Legajo 122
	1596	744,566/1	ODT/OL Legajo 122
	1603-1604	744,570	Legajo 222
	1610-1619	744,562/3	ODT/OL Legajo 4679
	1606	744,571	Legajo 223
	1606-1607	744,572/1	Disordered Legajo 224
	1607	744,572/2	Legajo 225
	1607	744,573	Document damage Illegible Legajo 226
	1615-1617	744,574	Document damage Illegible Legajo 232
	1625,1694	741,580/2	ODT/OL Legajo 35
	1633-1635	741,585	Legajo 238
	1634	744,764/1	ODT/OL Legajo 1
	1634,1644, 1647	741,588/1	ODT/OL Legajo 243
	1635-1636	741,586/2	Legajo 239
	1636	741,586/1	Legajo 239
	1637	741,863/1	Disordered ODT/OL Legajo 246
	1637,1640	741,587/4	Legajo 242
	1638-1647	741,587/1	Document damage Legajo 241
	1639	741,587/2	ODT/OL Legajo 241
	1639	741,587/3	Legajo 242
	1639-1640	741,587/4	Legajo 242

Location/ Document Type	Years	Roll No.	Comments
	1649-1651	741,588/2	Document damage Legajo 243
	1653-1654	741,581/1	Disordered Legajo 126
	1661-1679	741,862	Intermittent years Legajo 245
	1665	741,580/1	ODT/OL Legajo 22
	1685-1689	741,864/1	ODT/OL Legajo 249
	1688	744,562/1	Legajo 341
	1706-1711	744,764/2	ODT/OL Legajo 3
	1715,1730, 1780-1795	741,581/2	Legajo 134
	1715, 1771-1773	744,544	Intermittent years Legajo 267
	1730-1743	744,562/2	ODT/OL Legajo 4066
	1737-1743	741,865/1	ODT/OL Legajo 257
	1738-1750	741,867	Disordered Legajo 260
	1743-1745	741,866	Legajo 258
	1744,1762, 1772	741,580/1	ODT/OL Legajo 22
	1747-1748	741,582/2	Legajo 137
	1748-1749	741,582/1	Document damage ODT/OL Legajo 137
	1753-1760	741,582/3	ODT/OL Legajo 142
	1756-1759	741,868	Legajo 261
	1760-1768	741,869	Disordered Legajo 262
	1762-1763, 1771-1773, 1783	744,546/3	Document damage ODT/OL Legajo 270

Location/ Document Type	Years	Roll No.	Comments
	1764-1765	741,870	Legajo 263
	1765-1766	741,871/1	ODT/OL Legajo 264
	1766	741,872/1	ODT/OL Legajo 265
	1769-1772	741,873/1	ODT/OL Legajo 266
	1770	741,579/1	ODT/OL
	1776	744,544/2	ODT/OL Legajo 267
	1778	744,545/1	ODT/OL Legajo 269
	1780	744,546/3	ODT/OL Legajo 270
	1781-1782	744,545/1	Incomplete ODT/OL Legajo 269
	1783-1789	744,546/1	Legajo 271
	1785	744,546/2	ODT/OL Legajo 271
	1786	744,546/2	ODT/OL Legajo 271
	1786-1792	744,546/2	ODT/OL Legajo 271
	1787, 1807-1808	744,563	Legajo 5295
	1787-1796	744,545/1	ODT/OL Legajo 269
	1789	744,547/1	Legajo 273
	1789	744,547/2	ODT/OL Legajo 273
	1790-1793	744,548/1-2	Legajo 274
	1790-1795	744,549	ODT/OL Legajo 275
	1791	744,550	ODT/OL Legajo 276

Location/ Document Type	Years	Roll No.	Comments
	1791–1793	744,551/1-2	Legajo 277
	1791–1794	744,550/2	Legajo 276
	1793	744,961/3	ODT/OL Legajo 278
	1793–1798	744,552/2	ODT/OL Legajo 279
	1796	741,583/3	ODT/OL Legajo 154
	1798–1800	744,552/3	ODT/OL Legajo 279
	1800	741,583/3	ODT/OL Legajo 154
	1802	744,961/4	ODT/OL Legajo 280
	1802–1803	744,553	Legajo 280
	1806	744,554	Legajo 282
	1807	744,555	Legajo 283
	1808	744,557	Legajo 285
	1808–1809	744,556	Legajo 284
	1809	741,584/1	ODT/OL Legajo 164
	1809	741,584/2	ODT/OL Legajo 164
	1810	744,558/1	ODT/OL Legajo 286
	1810–1811	744,558/1	ODT/OL Legajo 286
	1813,1815	744,560/1	Legajo 288
	1813–1815	744,560/2	Legajo 288
	1818–1819	744,561/1	ODT/OL Legajo 289
	1819–1821	744,561/1	ODT/OL Legajo 289
	1821	744,563/2	Document damage Legajo 5321

Location/ Document Type	Years	Roll No.	Comments
Tapachula Tapachula			
	1802	744,961/4	ODT/OL Legajo 280
Tuxtla Tuxtla Gutiérrez (cap del e)			
	1793-1798	744,552/2	ODT/OL Legajo 279
	1798-1800	744,552/3	ODT/OL Legajo 279
	1804, 1811-1813	744,559	Legajo 287

México
  Distrito Federal
    Ciudad de México (cap nl)			

	1600	744,761/1	Document damage Legajo 4820

Oaxaca
  Oaxaca de Juárez
    Oaxaca de Juárez (cap del e)			

	1689-1693	741,864/1	ODT/OL Legajo 249
	1770	744,545/1	ODT/OL Legajo 269

NICARAGUA
nación

Location/ Document Type	Years	Roll No.	Comments
Granada Granada (cap dl)			
	1628	741,750/2	Legajo 277

León
  León
    León (cap dl)			

	1603	745,311/11	Illegible Legajo 5925

Location/ Document Type	Years	Roll No.	Comments
	1625	741,749/1	ODT/OL Legajo 275
	1641	745,811/20	Legajo 4903
	1704	747,278/2	Legajo 4984
	1713	745,811/1	Poor focus Legajo 1580
	1714	745,811/2	Legajo 1581
	1717	745,811/3	Poor focus Legajo 1582
	1749	745,811/5	Legajo 4652
	1758	745,816/1	ODT/OL Legajo 152
	1769-1782	745,811/4	ODT/OL Legajo 2678
	1800-1803	745,817/2	ODT/OL Legajo 159
	1810-1815	741,744/1	ODT/OL Legajo 98

Matagalpa
   Matagalpa (cap dl)

	Years	Roll No.	Comments
	1640	745,811/21	Legajo 4899
	1660	745,811/10	ODT/OL Legajo 4927
	1705	745,811/14	Legajo 5926
	1718	745,811/15	Legajo 5926

PERU
nación

Lima (cap nl)

	Years	Roll No.	Comments
	1615	744,762/4	Legajo 4857
	1622	744,762/5	Legajo 4871
	1714-1716	744,762/6	Document damage Legajo 4996
	1767	744,762/3	Legajo 2345

Location/ Document Type	Years	Roll No.	Comments
			Current jurisdictions are unknown or unavailable for the following entries
Anteguera			Documents place in Oaxaca, México
	1612-1651	744,957/1	Disordered ODT/OL Legajo 235
	1767	741,872/1	ODT/OL Legajo 265
Jicalapa			
	1722	747,284/4	ODT/OL Legajo 5001
Sacatepéquez			Documents fail to specify whether San Juan, San Lucas, San Pedro, or Santiago Sacatepéquez
	1794	746,566/3	ODT/OL Legajo 2696
Villa Nueva			Documents place in Chiapas, México
	1773	741,583/2	Legajo 144

Documentos Gubernamentales

Location/ Document Type	Years	Roll No.	Comments

GUATEMALA
nación

Capital

Archivo de la Independencia

	Years	Roll No.	Comments
	1808	744,835/1	
	1808	744,837	
	1808-1811	741,854	
	1808-1811	741,855	
	1808-1812	741,856	
	1808-1812	741,857	
	1808-1813	744,838	
	1808-1817	741,859	
	1808-1820	717,356	
	1809	741,858	
	1809	744,835/2	
	1809-1814	744,839	
	1810	744,835/3	
	1811-1814, 1820	741,861	
	1811-1822	744,840	
	1812	744,836/1-2	
	1813	741,860	
	1813	744,836/3	
	1820-1821?	744,834	Unreadable due to processing
	1821-1822	744,847	

Location/ Document Type	Years	Roll No.	Comments
	1821-1823	744,849/1-2	
	1822	744,848	
Correspondencia			
	1763	744,398/4	ODT/OL Legajo 88
	1776-1805	744,765/4	ODT/OL Legajo 9
	1813-1820	741,861	ODT/OL
	1815	741,893	ODT/OL Legajo 1811
	1826-1828	745,107/2	ODT/OL Legajo 1977
	1827	745,420/9	Legajo 2515
	1831	745,421/1	ODT/OL Legajo 2556
Elecciones			
	1802	744,779/1	ODT/OL Legajo 218
Indice del Antiguo Archivo del Supremo Gobierno			
	1607-1823	744,844	Legajo 2420
	1636-1833	744,845	Legajo 2422
Inventario e Indice del Archivo Municipal de Guatemala			
	1573-1878	744,846	Legajo 2424
Libros de Cuentas			
	1688-1691	746,828/2/6	
	1787	746,827/1/12	Document damage
	1798	744,401/1	ODT/OL Legajo 382

Location/ Document Type	Years	Roll No.	Comments
	1801-1803	745,419/11	ODT/OL Legajo 1334
	1802-1803	745,419/10	ODT/OL Legajo 1334
	1815	741,893	ODT/OL Legajo 1811
	1826-1828	745,107/2	ODT/OL Legajo 1977
Oficios del Gobierno			
	1515	746,755/34	Legajo 1515
	1610	746,755/21	Legajo 212
	1658	744,867/5	Legajo 1568
	1676	746,756/32	Legajo 4583
	1687	746,755/25	Legajo 800
	1691	746,755/14	Legajo 25
	1699	746,755/6	Legajo 23
	1701	741,738	Indexed ODT/OL Legajo 1572
	1732-1734	744,562/2	ODT/OL Legajo 4066
	1760	746,755/3	Legajo 7
	1766	746,755/20	Legajo 109
	1768-1801	744,778	ODT/OL Legajo 217
	1776	746,755/32	Legajo 1297
	1778-1796	744,772	Legajo 35
	1780-1785	744,766/1	Legajo 10
	1786-1798	744,774/2	Legajo 149
	1792	746,755/17	Legajo 25
	1792	763,388/7/28	
	1792-1800	744,775	Legajo 154

Location/ Document Type	Years	Roll No.	Comments
	1794	744,766/2	Legajo 16
	1796-1797	744,767	Legajo 17
	1798	744,768	ODT/OL Legajo 18
	1798-1805	744,773	Legajo 43
	1799	745,076/7	Legajo 157
	1800	746,756/9	ODT/OL Legajo 1943
	1800-1801	744,769	ODT/OL Legajo 21
	1801-1802	744,770	ODT/OL Legajo 22
	1801-1803	745,419/11	ODT/OL Legajo 1334
	1802-1805	744,779/1	ODT/OL Legajo 218
	1803	745,419/10	ODT/OL Legajo 1334
	1805	744,779/1	ODT/OL Legajo 218
	1813	745,421/17	ODT/OL Legajo 6116
	1815	746,851	ODT/OL Legajo 2620
	1820-1821	744,771	Legajo 32
	1821-1825	748,130/3/1	
	1831	745,421/1	ODT/OL Legajo 2556
	1832	744,860/3	ODT/OL Legajo 2561
Pasaportes			
	1579, 1691-1759, 1785-1811	745,421/15	Intermittent years Disordered Legajo 5366
	1693-1694	745,421/14	Legajo 4563

Location/ Document Type	Years	Roll No.	Comments
	1744	744,562/2	ODT/OL Legajo 4066
	1744	745,114/1	Legajo 6
	1744	745,421/10	Legajo 4066
	1761	745,114/2	Legajo 7
	1772	745,421/11	Legajo 4069
	1772-1778	745,419/17	Legajo 2209
	1782	745,421/3	Legajo 2859
	1785	745,114/3	Legajo 10
	1785	745,114/11	ODT/OL Legajo 35
	1791	745,419/1	Legajo 272
	1792	745,421/12	Legajo 4070
	1793	745,114/4	Legajo 14
	1794	745,114/5	Legajo 16
	1794	745,421/6	Legajo 3068
	1796	745,114/6	Legajo 17
	1796	745,419/19	Legajo 2377
	1798	744,768	ODT/OL Legajo 18
	1798	745,114/12	Legajo 36
	1800?	745,421/2	Document damage Legajo 2605
	1801	744,769	ODT/OL Legajo 21
	1803	745,419/10	ODT/OL Legajo 1334
	1803	745,419/16	Legajo 1977
	1806	745,114	Legajo 24
	1807	745,114/8	Legajo 25
	1810	745,421/4	Document damage Legajo 2867

Location/ Document Type	Years	Roll No.	Comments
	1812	745,421/13	Legajo 4072
	1813	745,421/17	ODT/OL Legajo 6116
	1817	745,419/12	Legajo 1345
	1818	745,114/9	Legajo 29
	1818	745,114/13	Legajo 38
	1819	745,419/13-14	Legajos 1347, 1748
	1819-1820	745,421/5	Legajo 2870
	1820	745,419/18	Legajo 2210
	1824	745,419/2	Legajo 1146
	1824-1829	745,419/3	Document damage Legajo 1148
	1827, 1829-1846	745,421/9	Legajo 3644
	1828-1829	745,420/1-4	ODT/OL Legajos 2434-2436
	1829-1830	745,418/3	ODT/OL Legajo 159
	1830	745,419/4-5	Legajos 1149-1150
	1830	745,420/6	Legajo 2513
	1831	745,420/8	Legajo 2516
	1831	745,421/1	ODT/OL Legajo 2556
	1832	745,419/6	Legajo 1151
	1832	745,421/7	Legajo 3599
	1832-1873	745,419/15	Intermittent years Legajo 1757
	1833,1838	745,421/8	Legajo 3600
	1833-1834	745,419/7	Legajo 1152
	1835	745,419/8	Poor focus Legajo 1153
	1836	745,419/9	Legajo 1154
	1839	745,420/5	Legajo 2437

Location/ Document Type	Years	Roll No.	Comments
Real Cédulas/Decretos			
	1653	746,755/29	Legajo 1050
	1675	746,756/30	Legajo 4583
	1684	746,756/36	Legajo 4585
	1784–1785	745,114/11	ODT/OL Legajo 35
	1802–1805	744,779/1	ODT/OL Legajo 218
	1811–1820	741,861	ODT/OL
	1815	741,893	ODT/OL Legajo 1811
Revolución de 1828			
	1828–1829	745,420/1-4	ODT/OL Legajos 2434–2436
	1828–1830	745,418/3	ODT/OL Legajo 159

Alta Verapaz
  San Cristóbal Verapaz
    San Cristóbal Verapaz (c/v)

Oficios del Gobierno			
	1796–1805	744,771/1	Legajo 182
	1804	744,777/2	Legajo 187

Chimaltenango
  Chimaltenango
    Chimaltenango (c/cd)

Correspondencia			
	1794–1799	745,418/1	ODT/OL Legajos 164–166
	1797–1799	745,418/2	ODT/OL Legajos 164–166

Location/ Document Type	Years	Roll No.	Comments
Oficios del Gobierno			
	1794-1799	745,418/1	ODT/OL
	1797-1799	745,418/2	ODT/OL Legajos 164-166
Pasaportes			
	1803	745,418/2	ODT/OL Legajos 164-166

Chiquimula
  Chiquimula
    Chiquimula (c/cd)			

Pasaportes			
	1830	745,420/7	Legajo 2514
Visitas			
	1825	746,822/1/5	

Guatemala
  Guatemala
    Canalitos (a)			

Oficios del Gobierno			
	1884	744,589/11	Legajo 1430

Jutiapa
  Jérez
    Jérez (c/p)			

Circulares			Former name Chingo
	1887	737,249/6	Legajo 3
	1889	737,249/5	ODT/OL Legajo 3

Location/ Document Type	Years	Roll No.	Comments

Sacatepéquez
  San Juan Sacatepéquez
   San Juan Sacatepéquez (c/v)			

Oficios del Gobierno			
	1799	745,076/7	Legajo 157
San Lucas Sacatepéquez San Lucas Sacatepéquez (c/p)			
Memorias/Sesiones Municipales			
	1891,1902, 1910, 1918–1919	717,743/1	ODT/OL

San Marcos
  San Pedro Sacatepéquez
   San Pedro Sacatepéquez (c/cd)			

Circulares			
	1882	714,658/1	ODT/OL
Visitas			
	1882	714,658/1	ODT/OL

Sololá
  Sololá
   Sololá (c/cd)			

Correspondencia			
	1804	773,999/1	
	1915	738,331	ODT/OL

Suchitepéquez
  Chicacao
   Chicacao (c/p)			

Memorias/Sesiones Municipales			
	1900–1914	714,043	Indexed

Location/ Document Type	Years	Roll No.	Comments
	1914-1920	714,044	Indexed ODT/OL

Patulul
  Patulul (c/p)

Circulares

| | 1915 | 738,331 | ODT/OL |

Correspondencia

| | 1915-1916 | 738,331 | ODT/OL |

Elecciones

| | 1915-1916 | 738,331 | ODT/OL |

Memorias/Sesiones Municipales

	1900,1903	738,335/1	ODT/OL
	1905	738,334/1	ODT/OL
	1916	738,333/1	ODT/OL

Totonicapán
  Momostenango
    Momostenango (c/v)

Correspondencia

| | 1815 | 773,999/2 | |

EL SALVADOR
nación

Sonsonate
  Sonsonate
    Sonsonate (c/cd)

Libros de Cuentas

| | 1795 | 711,892/1/1 | |
| | 1795 | 741,892/1/2 | |

Location/ Document Type	Years	Roll No.	Comments

HONDURAS
nación

Colón
    Trujillo (cap dl)

Oficios del Gobierno

	1798	744,401	ODT/OL Legajo 382
	1815	746,755/5	ODT/OL Legajo 16

Comayagua
    Comayagua (cap dl)

Libros de Cuentas

	1798	744,401	ODT/OL Legajo 382
	1799-1801	744,398/2	Legajo 63
	1772-1787	744,402	Legajo 484

Oficios del Gobierno

	1774	744,398/6	ODT/OL Legajo 196

Visitas

	1748	744,758/3	Document damage ODT/OL Legajo 227

Location/ Document Type	Years	Roll No.	Comments

MEXICO
nación

Chiapas
  San Cristóbal las Casas
    San Cristóbal las Casas

Correspondencia

	Years	Roll No.	Comments
	1731-1734	741,579/1	ODT/OL
	1762-1769	741,579/1	ODT/OL
	1771-1785	741,579/1	ODT/OL
	1783-1789	744,546/3	ODT/OL Intermittent years Legajo 270
	1811-1821	741,579/2	

Memorias/Sesiones Municipales

	1766	741,871/1	ODT/OL Legajo 264

Oficios del Gobierno

	1712	741,579/1	ODT/OL

Visitas

	1568	741,588/1	ODT/OL Legajo 242

Documentos Jurídicos

Location/ Document Type	Years	Roll No.	Comments
	GUATEMALA nación		
Capital			
Causas Civiles			
	1579-1713	744,588/1	Indexed ODT/OL Legajo 443
	1673	746,860/1	ODT/OL Legajo 4681
	1735-1799	744,562/2	Intermittent years ODT/OL Legajo 4066
	1747	745,114/10	Incomplete Legajo 33
	1750	746,755/4	Legajo 7
	1778	744,765/4	ODT/OL Legajo 9
	1779	745,108/10	ODT/OL Legajo 2757
	1820	741,893	ODT/OL Legajo 1811
Causas Criminales			
	1572-1574	744,579/3	Illegible ODT/OL Legajo 354
	1779	745,108/10	ODT/OL Legajo 2757
	1797	741,583/3	ODT/OL Legajo 154
	1798	744,768	ODT/OL Legajo 18
	1801	746,863/1	ODT/OL Legajo 4694

Location/ Document Type	Years	Roll No.	Comments
Divorcios			
	1702,1779	745,075/11	Legajo 5343
	1756	745,075/8	ODT/OL Legajo 2924
	1777	745,075/13	Legajo 5888
	1806	745,075/6	Legajo 2884
	1818	745,075/5	Legajo 2810
	1836-1837	745,075/2	Legajo 1154
Vecinos y Vecindad			
	1579	747,154/19	Legajo 3068
	1587,1639	747,154/20	Legajo 4063
	1603	747,154/27	Legajo 4777
	1610	747,154/2	Document damage Legajo 1557
	1624	747,154/24	Legajo 4646
	1638	747,154/3	Document damage Legajo 1558
	1655	747,154/5	Legajo 1561
	1672	747,154/6	Legajo 1564
	1672	747,154/7	Document damage Legajo 1564
	1672	747,154/30	Legajo 5920
	1682	747,154/8	Legajo 1567
	1702	747,154/9	Document damage Legajo 2209
	1709	747,154/25	Legajo 4648
	1737	747,152/1	ODT/OL Legajo 5
	1742	747,154/17	Document damage Legajo 3016
	1743	747,154/23	Legajo 4066

Location/ Document Type	Years	Roll No.	Comments
	1762	747,154/28-29	Legajos 5508, 5765
	1805	747,154/13	Legajo 2867
	1818	747,154/31	Legajo 6118
	1833	747,154/16	Legajo 3600

Alta Verapaz
  San Cristóbal Verapaz
    San Cristóbal Verapaz (c/v)

Divorcios

	1795	745,075/4	Document damage Legajo 2759

Vecinos y Vecindad

	1799	747,152/3	Legajo 182

Chiquimula
  Concepción las Minas
    Ermita (a)

Divorcios

	1776	745,075/1	Legajo 1175

Chiquimula
  Chiquimula (c/cd)

Causas Civiles

	1743	747,142/1	ODT/OL Legajo 6016

Divorcios

	1888-1889	745,075/3	Legajo 1758

Vecinos y Vecindad

	1839	747,154/11	ODT/OL Legajo 2425
	1840	747,154/10	Legajo 2437

Location/ Document Type	Years	Roll No.	Comments

Escuintla
  Escuintla
    Escuintla (c/cd)			

Vecinos y Vecindad			
	1842	747,154/12	Legajo 2530

Guatemala
  Amatitlán
    Amatitlán (c/cd)			

Divorcios			
	1807	745,075/14	Legajo 5920
Mixco Mixco (c/p)			
Causas Civiles			
	1820	745,421/16	Legajo 5910

Huehuetenango
  Huehuetenango
    Huehuetenango (c/cd)			

Vecinos y Vecindad			
	1826	747,154/1	Legajo 1147

Jutiapa
    Jérez
      Jérez (c/p)			

Causas Civiles			
	1827-1879	737,249/1	Legajo 1
Causas Criminales			
	1889	737,249/5	ODT/OL Legajo 3
	1895-1903	737,249/4	Legajo 2
	1902	737,249/2	Legajo 1

Location/ Document Type	Years	Roll No.	Comments

Quezaltenango
  Quezaltenango
    Quezaltenango (c/cd)			

Causas Criminales			
	1766	744,546/2	ODT/OL Legajo 271

Sacatepéquez
  Ciudad Vieja
    Ciudad Vieja (c/p)			

Vecinos y Vecindad			
	1798	747,152/2	Legajo 154
San Lucas Sacatepéquez San Lucas Sacatepéquez (c/p)			
Causas Criminales			
	1873	717,742/1	

San Marcos
  San Antonio Sacatepéquez
    San Antonio Sacatepéquez (c/p)			

Divorcios			
	1702	745,075/10	Legajo 5337
Tejutla Tejutla (c/v)			
Causas Criminales			
	1891	716,910/1	ODT/OL

Sololá
  Sololá
    Sololá (c/cd)			

Causas Criminales			
	1767	745,075/12	Legajo 5509

Location/ Document Type	Years	Roll No.	Comments

Suchitepéquez
  Patulul
    Patulul (c/p)			

Causas Civiles			
	1899	738,335/1	ODT/OL
	1903	738,335/1	ODT/OL
	1912-1913	738,332/1	ODT/OL
	1916	738,331	ODT/OL
Causas Criminales			
	1903	738,335/1	ODT/OL
	1905	738,334/1	ODT/OL
	1915	738,331/1	ODT/OL
	1915	738,332/1	ODT/OL
	1916	738,331/1	ODT/OL
Vecinos y Vecindad			
	1768, 1773-1779	747,152/4	Legajo 201
	1905	738,334	ODT/OL

Totonicapán
  San Francisco el Alto
    San Francisco el Alto (c/p)			

Vecinos y Vecindad			
	1799	747,154/14	Legajo 2917
Totonicapán Totonicapán (c/cd)			
Causas Criminales			
	1779	746,578/4	ODT/OL Legajo 3025

Location/ Document Type	Years	Roll No.	Comments
Vecinos y Vecindad			
	1832	747,154/15	Legajo 3599

Zacapa
  Gualán
    Gualán (c/v)			

Vecinos y Vecindad			
	1839	747,154/11	ODT/OL Legajo 2425

EL SALVADOR
nación

Ahuachapán
  Apaneca
    Apaneca (c/v)			

Vecinos y Vecindad			
	1725-1727	747,154/22	Legajo 4065

HONDURAS
nación

Comayagua Comayagua (cap dl)			
Causas Civiles			
	1592	741,745/2	ODT/OL Legajo 259
	1749	744,758/3	ODT/OL Legajo 227
Causas Criminales			
	1787	744,864/4	ODT/OL Legajo 386

Location/ Document Type	Years	Roll No.	Comments
Divorcios			
	1798	744,864/2	Legajo 69
	1819	744,865/1-2	Legajos 386, 372

MEXICO
nación

Chiapas
  Acapetagua
    Soconusco

Causas Criminales			
	1594	744,566/1	ODT/OL Legajo 122

Comitán de Domínguez
  Comitán de Domínguez

Causas Civiles			
	1818	744,561/1	ODT/OL Legajo 289

San Cristóbal las Casas
  San Cristóbal las Casas

Causas Civiles			
	1711	744,764/2	ODT/OL Document damage Legajo 3
	1749-1750	741,582/1	ODT/OL Legajo 137
	1782	744,546/3	ODT/OL Legajo 270
	1791-1793	744,552/1	ODT/OL Legajo 278
Causas Criminales			
	1758-1770	741,583/1	ODT/OL Legajo 144

Location/ Document Type	Years	Roll No.	Comments
	1597	744,566/1	ODT/OL Legajo 122
	1609-1610	744,562/3	ODT/OL Legajo 4679
	1742	741,580/1	ODT/OL Legajo 22
	1782	741,584/3	ODT/OL Legajo 196
	1796	741,583/3	ODT/OL Legajo 154
	1797-1803	741,583/3	ODT/OL Legajo 154
	1809	741,584/2	ODT/OL Legajo 164
	1809-1810	741,584/1	ODT/OL Legajo 164
	1817	744,561/1	ODT/OL Legajo 289
	1821	744,561/1-2	ODT/OL Legajo 289

Vecinos y Vecindad

	1649	747,154/4	Document damage Legajo 1560

Tapachula
Tapachula

Causas Civiles

	1819	744,561/1	ODT/OL Legajo 289

Tuxtla
Tuxtla Gutiérrez (cap del e)

Causas Civiles

	1782	741,584/4	Legajo 196

Location/ Document Type	Years	Roll No.	Comments
Vecinos y Vecindad			
	1792	747,154/26	Legajo 4658

NICARAGUA
nación

Granada
    Granada (cap dl)

Divorcios			
	1807	745,075/8	ODT/OL Legajo 2924

León
    León
        León (cap dl)

Causas Civiles			
	1792-1800	745,816/1	ODT/OL Legajo 152
	1795	745,814/17	Legajo 148
	1797	745,814/18	ODT/OL Legajo 149
	1800	745,815/1	ODT/OL Legajo 151
	1802-1804, 1807	745,817/2	ODT/OL Legajo 159
Causas Criminales			
	1797	745,814/18	ODT/OL Legajo 149
	1800	745,815/1	ODT/OL Legajo 151
	1802	745,817/1/1	
	1802,1810	745,817/2	ODT/OL Legajo 159
	1802-1804	745,817/1	Legajo 158

Location/ Document Type	Years	Roll No.	Comments
Divorcios			
	1637-1638	745,073/1	Legajo 452
	1712-1796	745,073/2	Legajo 453
	1746	745,071/1	Legajo 75
	1783-1785, 1805-1808	745,071/3	Legajo 449
	1789-1791	745,071/4	Legajo 449
	1805	745,074	Legajo 454

<u>PERU</u>
nación

<u>Lima</u> (cap nl)

Causas Civiles

	1802	744,762/2	Legajo 5232

Current jurisdictions are unknown or
unavailable for the following entries

<u>Ojo de Agua</u>   Documents place in
                                                      Escuintla

Causas Criminales

	1817	747,829/3/1	

<u>San Juan</u>   Gaz/various

Vecinos y Vecindad

	1762	747,154/21	Legajo 4064

Location/ Document Type	Years	Roll No.	Comments
San Miguel			Documents place in Totonicapán
Divorcios			
	1776-1787	745,075/7	Legajo 2897

Información Matrimonial

Location/ Document Type	Years	Roll No.	Comments
	GUATEMALA nación		
Capital			
Actas Matrimoniales			
	1910-1912, 1916-1919	737,251/2	
	1910-1916	745,107/1	ODT/OL Legajo 1760
	1910-1919	737,251/2	
	1930-1931	737,251/3-4	
Autos de Disensos			
	1651-1807	745,113/6	Intermittent years ODT/OL Legajo 5927
	1707,1714	745,113/5	Legajo 5787
	1770, 1772,1795	745,113/4	Legajo 5772
	1773	745,113/8	Legajo 6096
	1780-1781	745,110/3	Legajo 2807
	1782	745,111/7	Legajo 4243
	1783	745,111/6	Legajo 4246
	1784	745,110/5	Legajo 2903
	1784	745,111/5	Legajo 4249
	1786-1790	745,110/4	Legajo 2884
	1787, 1800-1803, 1810-1812, 1819	745,113/2	Legajo 5342
	1788	745,110/6	Legajo 2906

Location/ Document Type	Years	Roll No.	Comments
	1790-1794	745,109/1	ODT/OL Legajo 2758
	1790-1794, 1797-1798	745,113/1	Legajo 5341
	1792	745,110/7	Legajo 2909
	1795-1811	745,112/2	ODT/OL
	1795	745,113/3	Legajo 5554
	1795-1800	745,109/2	Legajo 2759
	1797	745,110/8-9	Legajos 2913, 2915
	1797	745,111/3-4,14	Legajos 4340, 4336, 2941
	1798	745,110/10	Legajo 2916
	1799	745,110/11	Legajo 2917
	1799	745,111/16	Legajo 2918
	1800	745,111/13	Legajo 2945
	1800-1814	745,110/1	Legajo 2760
	1801	745,111/11-12	Legajo 2946
	1802	745,111/8	Legajo 2971
	1803	745,111/15	Legajo 2921
	1804	745,113/9	Legajo 6107
	1806	745,111/10	Legajo 2958
	1811	745,111/1	Legajo 4574
	1812	745,110/2	Legajo 2785
	1812	745,111/2,9	Legajos 4462, 2970
Causas Matrimoniales			
	1637	745,076/16	Legajo 1557
	1734	744,562/2	ODT/OL Legajo 4066
	1788	745,076/2	Legajo 12
	1792	745,076/1	Legajo 14

Location/ Document Type	Years	Roll No.	Comments
	1798	744,768	ODT/OL Legajo 18
	1798	745,076/3	Legajo 18
	1801	744,769	ODT/OL Legajo 21
	1804	745,076/15	Legajos 1484
	1804-1808	745,076/8	Legajo 177
	1805,1809	745,076/10	
	1808	744,763/4	Legajo 187
	1809	745,076/14	Legajo 1072
	1811	745,076/6	Legajo 38
	1811,1813	745,076/4	Legajo 28
	1818	745,076/5	Legajo 30
	1872	745,076/12	Legajo 860
	1886	745,076/13	Legajo 866
Expedientes Matrimoniales			
	1571	745,107/3	Legajo 2326
	1683	745,107/4	Legajo 2363
	1779	745,108/10	ODT/OL Legajo 2757
	1782	745,108/9	Incomplete Legajo 2588
	1785, 1787-1788	745,108/11	Illegible Legajo 2757
	1785-1788	745,108/10	Document damage ODT/OL Legajo 2757
	1790	745,107/5	Legajo 2495
	1794	745,107/6	Legajo 2509
	1795-1828	745,107/2	Disordered Legajo 1977
	1798	745,108/2	Incomplete Legajo 2523

Location/ Document Type	Years	Roll No.	Comments
	1822-1888	745,106/1	Intermittent years Disordered
	1830	745,108/5-7	Legajos 2553-2555
	1832	745,108/8	Incomplete Legajo 2560
	1836	745,107/7	Legajo 2521
	1837	745,108/1	Incomplete Legajo 2522
	1840	745,108/3-4	Incomplete Legajo 2544
	1881-1924	737,579	1923 indexed mid-roll Disordered
	1882(En-Jn)	756,547/1-2	Indexed
	1882(Jl-Dc)	756,548/1	Indexed
	1883(En-Jn)	756,548/2-3	Indexed
	1883(Jl-Dc)	756,549	Indexed
	1884(En-Jn)	756,550/1-2	Indexed
	1885(En-Jn)	756,551	Indexed
	1885(Jl-Dc)	756,556	Indexed
	1886	747,123/1	
	1886(En-Jn)	756,553	Indexed Incomplete
	1886(Jl-Dc)	756,554	Indexed
	1887	747,123/2	
	1887(En-Jn)	756,555	Indexed
	1887(Jl-Dc)	756,556/1-2	Indexed Volume 2
	1887-1892	745,106/2	
	1888	747,123/3	
	1888(En-Jn)	756,557/1-2	Indexed
	1888(Jl-Dc)	756,558	Indexed
	1889(En-Jn)	756,559/1-3	Indexed
	1889(Jl-Dc)	756,560	Indexed

Location/ Document Type	Years	Roll No.	Comments
	1889(Jl-Dc)	756,561	Indexed Volume 2
	1890(En-Jn)	756,562	Indexed
	1890(En-Jn	756,563	Indexed on 756,562
	1890(Jl-Dc)	756,564/1-2	Indexed
	1891(En-Jn)	756,565	Indexed
	1891(En-Jn)	756,566	Indexed on 756,565
	1891(Jl-Dc)	756,567	Indexed
	1891(Jl-Dc)	756,568	Indexed on 756,567
	1892(En-Jn)	756,569/1-2	Indexed
	1892(Jl-Dc)	756,570	Indexed
	1892(Jl-Dc)	756,571	Indexed on 756,570
	1893	745,107/1	ODT/OL Legajo 1760
	1893(En-Mr)	756,572/1-2	
	1893(Ab-Jn)	756,573	Legajo 27
	1893(Jl-Se)	756,574	Indexed Legajo 28
	1893(Oc-Dc)	756,575	Indexed Legajo 29
	1894(En-Mr)	756,576	Indexed Legajo 30
	1894(Ab-Jn)	756,577	Indexed Legajo 31
	1894(Jl-Se)	756,578	Indexed Legajo 32
	1894(Oc-Dc)	756,579	Indexed Legajo 33
	1895(En-Mr)	756,580	Indexed Legajo 34
	1895(Ab-Jn)	756,581	Indexed Legajo 35
	1895(Jl-Se)	756,582	Indexed Legajo 36

Location/ Document Type	Years	Roll No.	Comments
	1895(Oc-Dc)	756,583	Indexed Legajo 37
	1896	758,380	
	1896(En-Mr)	754,841	Indexed Legajo 38
	1896(Ab-Jn)	754,842	Indexed Legajo 39
	1896(Jl-Se)	754,843	Indexed Legajo 40
	1896(Oc-Dc)	754,844	Indexed Legajo 41
	1897(En-Mr)	754,845/1-2	Indexed Legajo 42
	1897(En-Mr)	754,846	Indexed on 754,845 Legajo 42
	1897(Ab-Jn)	754,847	Indexed Legajo 43
	1897(Jl-Se)	754,848	Indexed Legajo 44
	1897(Oc-Dc)	754,849	Indexed Legajo 45
	1898(En-Mr)	754,850	Indexed Legajo 46
	1898(Ab-Jn)	754,851	Indexed Legajo 47
	1898(Jl-Se)	754,852	Indexed Legajo 48
	1898(Oc-Dc)	754,853	Indexed Legajo 49
	1899(En-Mr)	754,854	Indexed Legajo 50
	1899(Ab-Jn)	754,855	Indexed Legajo 51
	1899(Jl-Se)	754,856	Indexed Legajo 52
	1899(Oc-Dc)	754,857	Indexed Legajo 53
	1900(En-Mr)	759,016/1-2	Indexed Legajo 54

Location/ Document Type	Years	Roll No.	Comments
	1900(Ab-Jn)	759,017	Indexed Legajo 55
	1900(Jl-Se)	759,018/1-2	Indexed Legajo 56
	1900(Oc-Dc)	759,019/1-2	Indexed Legajo 57
	1901(En-Mr)	759,020/1-2	Indexed Legajo 58
	1901(Ab-Jn)	759,021	Indexed Legajo 59
	1901(Jl-Se)	759,022	Indexed Legajo 60
	1901(Oc-Dc)	759,023	Indexed Legajo 61 Incomplete
	1902(En-Mr)	759,024	Indexed Incomplete Legajo 62
	1902(Ab-Jn)	759,025	Indexed Legajo 63
	1902(Jl-Se)	759,026	Indexed Legajo 64
	1902(Oc-Dc)	759,027	Indexed Legajo 65
	1903(Ja-Mr)	759,028	Indexed Legajo 66
	1903(Ab-Jn)	759,029/1-2	Indexed Legajo 67
	1903(Jl-Se)	759,030/1-2	Indexed Legajo 68
	1903(Oc-Dc)	759,031/1-2	Indexed Legajo 69
	1904(En-Mr)	759,032/1-2	Disordered Indexed Legajo 70
	1904(Ab-Jn)	759,033	Legajo 71
	1904(Jl-Se)	759,034	Indexed Legajo 72
	1904(Oc-Dc)	759,035/1-2	Indexed Legajo 73

Location/ Document Type	Years	Roll No.	Comments
	1905(En-Mr)	756,059	Indexed Legajo 74
	1905(Ab-Jn)	756,060	Indexed Legajo 75
	1905(Jl-Se)	756,036	Indexed Legajo 76
	1905(Oc-Dc)	756,037	Indexed Legajo 77
	1906(En-Mr)	756,038	Indexed Legajo 78
	1906(En-Mr)	756,039	Indexed on 756,038 Legajo 78
	1906(Ab-Jn)	756,040	Indexed Legajo 79
	1906(Jl-Se)	756,041	Indexed Legajo 80
	1906(Oc-Dc)	756,042	Indexed Legajo 81
	1907(En-Mr)	756,043	Indexed Legajo 82
	1907(Ab-Jn)	756,044	Indexed Legajo 83
	1907(Jl-Se)	756,045	Indexed Legajo 84
	1907(Oc-Dc)	756,046	Indexed Legajo 85
	1908(En-Mr)	754,872	Indexed Legajo 86
	1908(Ab-Jn)	754,873	Indexed Legajo 87
	1908(Jl-Se)	754,874	Indexed Legajo 88
	1908(Oc-Dc)	754,875	Indexed Legajo 89
	1909	754,876	Indexed Legajo 90
	1909(Ab-Jn)	754,877	Indexed Legajo 91

Location/ Document Type	Years	Roll No.	Comments
	1909(Jl-Se)	754,878	Incomplete Legajo 92
	1909(Oc-Dc)	754,879	Indexed Legajo 93
	1910(En-Mr)	754,880	Indexed Legajo 94
	1910(Ab-Jn)	754,881	Legajo 95
	1910(Ab-Jn)	754,882	Indexed on 754,881 Legajo 95
	1910(Jl-Se)	754,883	Indexed Legajo 96
	1910(Jl-Se)	754,817	Volume 96
	1910(Oc-De)	754,818	Indexed Volume 97
	1910(Oc-Dc)	754,840	Legajo 97
	1911(En-Mr)	754,819/1-2	Indexed Volume 94
	1911(Ab-Jn)	754,820/1-2	Indexed Volume 99
	1911(Jl-Se)	754,821	Indexed Volume 100
	1911(Oc-Dc)	754,822	Indexed Volume 101
	1911(Oc-Dc)	754,823	Volume 101
	1912(En-Mr)	754,824	Indexed Volume 102
	1912(En-Mr)	754,825	Volume 102
	1912(Ab-Jn)	754,326	Indexed Volume 103
	1912(Ab-Jn)	754,827	Volume 103
	1912(Jl-Se)	754,828	Indexed Volume 104
	1912(Jl-Se)	754,829	Volume 104
	1912(Oc-Dc)	754,830	Indexed Volume 105
	1912(Oc-Dc)	754,831	Volume 105

Location/ Document Type	Years	Roll No.	Comments
	1913(En-Mr)	754,832	Indexed Volume 106
	1913(Ab-Jn)	754,833	Indexed Volume 107
	1913(Ab-Jn)	754,834	Volume 107
	1913(Ab-Jn)	754,835	Volume 107
	1913(Jl-Se)	754,836	Indexed Volume 108
	1913(Jl-Se)	754,837	Volume 108
	1913(Oc-Dc)	754,838	Indexed Volume 109
	1913(Oc-Dc)	754,839	Volume 109
	1914(En-Mr)	756,002	Indexed Legajo 110
	1914(En-Mr)	756,003/1-2	Indexed on 756,002 Legajo 111
	1914(Ab-Jn)	756,004	Indexed Legajo 112
	1914(Ab-Jn)	756,005	Indexed Legajo 112
	1914(Jl-Se)	756,006/1-2	Indexed Legajo 113
	1914(Oc-Dc)	756,007	Indexed Legajo 114
	1914(Oc-Dc)	756,008	Indexed on 756,007 Legajo 114
	1915(En-Mr)	756,009	Indexed Legajo 115
	1915(En-Mr)	756,010	Indexed on 756,009 Legajo 115
	1915(Ab-Jn)	756,011	Indexed Legajo 116
	1915(Jl-Se)	756,012	Indexed Legajo 115
	1915(Jl-Se)	756,013	Indexed on 756,012 Legajo 117
	1915(Oc-Dc)	756,014	Indexed Legajo 118

Location/ Document Type	Years	Roll No.	Comments
	1916(En-Mr)	756,015	Indexed Legajo 119
	1916(Ab-Jn)	756,016/1-2	Indexed Legajo 120
	1916(Jl-Se)	756,017	Indexed Legajo 121
	1916(Oc-Dc)	756,018	Indexed Legajo 122
	1916(Oc-Dc)	756,019	Indexed Legajo 122
	1916(Oc-Dc)	756,020	Partially indexed Legajo 122
	1917(En-Mr)	756,021	Indexed Legajo 123
	1917(En-Mr)	759,001	Indexed Legajo 123
	1917(Ab-Jn)	759,002/1-2	Indexed Legajo 124
	1917(Jl-Se)	759,003/1-2	Indexed Legajo 125
	1917(Oc-Dc)	759,004/1-2	Indexed Legajo 126
	1917-1931	737,251/2	
	1918(En-Mr)	759,005/1-2	Indexed Legajo 127
	1918(Ab-Jn)	759,006/1-2	Indexed Legajo 128
	1918(Jl-Se)	759,007	Indexed Legajo 129
	1918(Oc-Dc)	759,008/1-2	Indexed Legajo 130
	1918-1956	737,251/3	
	1919(En-Mr)	759,009/1-2	Indexed Legajo 131
	1919(Ab-Jn)	759,010	Indexed Legajo 132
	1919(Jl-Se)	759,011	Indexed Legajo 133

Location/ Document Type	Years	Roll No.	Comments
	1919(Oc-Dc)	759,012	Indexed Legajo 134
	1920	773,998	
	1920(En-Mr)	759,013/1	Indexed Legajo 135
	1920(Ab-Jn)	759,013/2	Indexed Legajo 135
	1920(Jl-Se)	759,014	Indexed Legajo 137
	1920(Oc-Dc)	759,015/1-2	Indexed Legajo 138
	1921(En-Mr)	779,568	Poor exposure Indexed
	1921(Ab-Jn)	779,569	Indexed
	1921(Ab-Jn)	779,570	Indexed
	1921(Jl-Se)	779,571	Indexed
	1921(Jl-Se)	779,572	Indexed
	1921(Oc-Dc)	779,573	Indexed
	1921(Oc-Dc)	779,574	Indexed
	1922	779,166	
	1922(En-Mr)	779,575	Indexed
	1922(Ab-Jn)	779,577	Indexed
	1922(Ab-Jn)	779,578	Indexed on 779,577
	1922(Jl-Se)	779,579	Indexed
	1922(Jl-Se)	779,580	Indexed
	1922(Oc-Dc)	779,581	
	1922(Oc-Dc)	779,582	
	1923(En-Mr)	779,583	
	1923(En-Mr)	779,584	
	1923(Ab-Jn)	779,585	Indexed
	1923(Ab-Jn)	779,586	Indexed Incomplete

Location/ Document Type	Years	Roll No.	Comments
	1923(Ab-Jn)	773,233	Indexed Legajo 148
	1923(Jl-Se)	779,587	Indexed
	1923(Jl-Se)	779,588	Indexed
	1923(Oc-Dc)	779,589	Indexed
	1924(En-Mr)	779,590	Indexed
	1924(En-Mr)	779,591	Partially indexed
	1924(Ab-Jn)	776,305	Indexed
	1924(Ab-Jn)	779,592	Indexed
	1924(Ab-Jn)	779,593	Indexed
	1924(Jl-Se)	776,306	Indexed
	1924(Oc-Dc)	776,307	Indexed
	1924(Oc-Dc)	776,308	Indexed
	1925(En-Mr)	776,309	Indexed
	1925(En-Mr)	776,310	Indexed
	1925(Ab-Jn)	776,311	Indexed
	1925(Ab-Jn)	776,312	Indexed
	1925(Jl-Se)	776,313	Indexed
	1925(Jl-Se)	776,314	Indexed
	1925(Jl-Se)	778,721/1	
	1925(Oc-Dc)	778,721/2	Indexed
	1925(Oc-Dc)	778,722	Indexed
	1926	736,589	
	1926(En-Mr)	778,723	Indexed
	1926(En-Mr)	778,724	Indexed
	1926(Ab-Jn)	778,725	Indexed
	1926(Ab-Jn)	778,726	Indexed
	1930-1931	737,251/4-5	

Location/ Document Type	Years	Roll No.	Comments
Matrimonios Suspensos			
	1893-1895, 1902,1907, 1914-1915	745,107/1	ODT/OL Legajo 1760

Alta Verapaz
  Cahabón
    Cahabón (c/p)			

Actas Matrimoniales			
	1878-1879, 1882-1887	784,340/1	Document damage
	1907(Ja-Ap), 1909(Dc)-1918	784,340/2	Document damage
Cobán Cobán (c/cd)			
Expedientes Matrimoniales			
	1880	713,722	Disordered Indexed
	1880-1881	713,723	
	1881-1882	713,724	
	1883	713,725	
	1883	713,726	Document damage
	1884	713,727	Poor exposure
	1885	713,728	
	1886	713,729	
	1887-1888	713,730	
	1888	713,731	
	1889	713,732	
	1889	713,733	
	1889	713,734	
	1890	713,735	
	1890	713,736	

Location/ Document Type	Years	Roll No.	Comments
	1891	713,737	Document damage
	1891	713,738	
	1891	713,739	Document damage
	1892	713,740	
	1892	713,741	
	1893	713,742	
	1893	713,743	
	1893	713,744	
	1894	713,745	
	1894	713,746	
	1895	713,747	
	1895	713,748	
	1896	713,749	
	1896	713,750	
	1897	713,751	
	1897	713,752	
	1898	713,753	
	1899	713,754	
	1899	713,755	
	1900	713,756	
	1900	713,757	
	1900-1901	713,758	
	1901	713,759	
	1902	713,760	
	1902	713,761	
	1902	713,762	
	1903	713,763	
	1903	713,764	
	1904	714,634	

Location/ Document Type	Years	Roll No.	Comments
	1905	714,635	
	1906	714,636	
	1907	714,537/1	
	1908	714,637/2	
	1909	714,638	
	1910	714,639	
	1911	714,640	
	1912	714,641	
	1913	714,642	
	1913-1914, 1917-1918, 1924-1925	714,643	
	1915	714,644	
	1916-1917	714,645	
	1918	714,646/1	
	1919	714,646/2	
	1919-1920	714,647	
	1921-1922	776,065	
	1923-1924	776,066	
	1925-1926	776,067	

San Juan Chamelco
San Juan Chamelco (c/p)

Actas Matrimoniales

	Years	Roll No.	Comments
	1893-1896	786,296/1	Disordered
	1897-1902	786,296/2	

Expedientes Matrimoniales

	Years	Roll No.	Comments
	1902-1904	786,297/1	
	1908-1912	786,297/2	
	1912-1915	786,297/3	

Location/ Document Type	Years	Roll No.	Comments
	1916–1917	785,297/4	
	1917–1920	786,297/5	
	1921–1923	786,297/6	
	1924–1925	786,297/7	
	1925–1929	786,297/8	
	1929–1933	786,297/9	

Baja Verapaz
  El Chol
    El Chol (c/p)

Expedientes Matrimoniales

	Years	Roll No.	Comments
	1881	752,104/1	
	1882	752,104/2	
	1883	752,104/3	
	1885	752,104/4	
	1886	752,104/5	
	1887	752,104/6	
	1888	752,104/7	
	1889	752,104/8	
	1890	752,105/1-2	
	1891,1894	752,105/3	
	1892	752,105/4	
	1893	752,105/5	ODT/OL
	1894	752,106/1	
	1895	752,106/2-3	
	1896	752,106/4	
	1897	752,106/5	
	1898	752,106/6	
	1899	752,107/1	
	1900	752,107/2	

Location/ Document Type	Years	Roll No.	Comments
	1902	752,107/3	
	1903	752,107/4	
	1904	752,108/1	
	1905	752,108/2	
	1906	752,108/3	
	1908	752,108/4-5	
	1909	752,109/1	
	1910	752,109/2	
	1911	752,109/3	
	1912-1913	752,109/4-5	
	1914	752,110/1	
	1915	752,110/2	
	1916	752,110/3	
	1917	752,110/4	
	1918	752,110/5	
	1919	752,111/1	
	1920	752,111/2	Document damage
	1938	752,105/5	ODT/OL

Purulhá
  Purulhá (c/p)

Expedientes Matrimoniales

	Years	Roll No.	Comments
	1881-1889	751,921	
	1889-1890	751,922	
	1891-1896	751,923	Continued on 751,924 ODT/OL
	1892	751,926	
	1892	751,927	
	1896-1900	751,924	Continued from 751,923
	1901-1902	751,925	

Location/ Document Type	Years	Roll No.	Comments
	1902-1908, 1910,1915	751,926	
	1911-1920	751,927	
	1912	751,923/1	ODT/OL
	1921	779,665/1	
	1922	779,665/2	
	1923	779,665/3	
	1923	779,666/1	
	1924	779,666/2	
	1926	779,666/3	
	1927	779,666/4	
	1928	779,666/5	
	1929	779,666/6	Document damage

Rabinal
  Rabinal (c/cd)

Actas Matrimoniales

	Years	Roll No.	Comments
	1892	754,864/1	ODT/OL
	1910	756,521/2	ODT/OL
	1921	779,674/1	ODT/OL
	1923	779,678/2	ODT/OL

Expedientes Matrimoniales

	Years	Roll No.	Comments
	1880	752,112/1	
	1881	752,112/2	
	1882	752,113/1-2	
	1883	752,114	
	1884	752,115/1-2	
	1885	752,116	
	1886	752,117	
	1887	752,118	

Location/ Document Type	Years	Roll No.	Comments
	1888	752,119	
	1888	752,120	
	1888	758,013	
	1889	754,858	
	1889	754,859	
	1890	754,860	
	1891	754,861	Disordered
	1891	754,862	
	1892	754,863	Document damage
	1892	754,864	Document damage ODT/OL
	1893	754,865	
	1893	754,866	
	1894	754,867	
	1894	754,868	
	1895	754,869	
	1895	754,870	
	1896	754,871	
	1896	756,501	
	1896	756,502	
	1897	756,503	
	1897	756,504	
	1898	756,505	
	1898	756,506	
	1899	756,507	
	1900	756,508	
	1901	756,509	Document damage
	1902	756,510	
	1903	756,511	
	1903	756,512	

Location/ Document Type	Years	Roll No.	Comments
	1904	756,513	
	1904	756,514	
	1904-1905	756,515/1-2	
	1905,1908	756,519/1-2	
	1906	756,516	
	1907	756,517	
	1907,1919	756,518	
	1909	756,520/1-2	
	1910	756,521/1-2	ODT/OL
	1911	756,522	
	1911	756,523	
	1912	756,524	
	1913	756,525	
	1913	756,526	
	1915	756,527/1	
	1916	756,527/2	
	1917	756,528	
	1917	756,529	
	1918	756,530/1-2	
	1919	756,531/1-2	
	1920	756,532/1-2	
	1921	779,674/1	ODT/OL
	1921	779,675	
	1922	779,676	
	1922	779,677	
	1923	779,678/1-2	ODT/OL
	1924	779,679	Document damage
	1925	779,680	
	1926	779,681	

Location/ Document Type	Years	Roll No.	Comments
	1926–1928	779,398	
	1927	779,682/1-2	
	1929	779,399	
	1930	779,400	

Chimaltenango
  San Martín Jilotepeque
    <u>San Martín Jilotepeque</u> (c/v)

Actas Matrimoniales

	Years	Roll No.	Comments
	1911	717,357	ODT/OL
	1912	717,359	ODT/OL
	1913	717,361	ODT/OL
	1914	717,363	ODT/OL
	1915	717,365	ODT/OL
	1916	717,366	ODT/OL
	1919	717,372	ODT/OL
	1920	717,373	ODT/OL
	1925	776,333	ODT/OL
	1927	776,338	ODT/OL

Expedientes Matrimoniales

	Years	Roll No.	Comments
	1881–1882	715,146	
	1882–1885	715,147	
	1885–1886	715,148	
	1886–1887	715,149	
	1887–1888	715,150	
	1888	715,151	
	1888–1889	715,152	Document damage
	1890	715,153	
	1890–1891	715,154	

Location/ Document Type	Years	Roll No.	Comments
	1891	715,155	
	1891	715,156	
	1892	715,157	
	1892–1893	715,158	
	1893	715,159	
	1893	715,160	Disordered
	1894	715,161	
	1895	715,162	
	1896	715,163	
	1896	715,164	
	1897	715,165	
	1898	715,166	
	1899	715,167	
	1900–1901	715,791	
	1901	715,792	
	1902	715,793	
	1903	715,794	
	1904	715,795	
	1905	715,796	
	1906	715,797/1-2	
	1907	715,797/3	
	1908	715,798/1	
	1909	715,798/2	
	1910	715,799	
	1911	717,357	ODT/OL
	1911	717,358	
	1912	717,359	ODT/OL
	1912	717,360	
	1913	717,361	ODT/OL

Location/ Document Type	Years	Roll No.	Comments
	1914	717,363	ODT/OL
	1915	717,365	ODT/OL
	1916	717,366	ODT/OL
	1916	717,367	
	1916	717,368	
	1917	717,369	
	1917	717,370	
	1918	717,371	
	1919	717,372	ODT/OL
	1920	717,373	ODT/OL
	1920	717,374	
	1920	717,375	
	1921	776,326	
	1922	776,327	
	1922	776,328	
	1923	776,329	
	1923	776,330	
	1924	776,331	
	1924	776,332	
	1925	776,333	Document damage ODT/OL
	1925	776,334	
	1925	776,335	
	1926	776,336	
	1926	776,337	
	1927	776,338	ODT/OL
	1927-1928	778,460	
	1928	779,604	
	1929	778,461	

Location/ Document Type	Years	Roll No.	Comments
	1929	779,605	
	1930	778,462	
	1930	779,606	

Chiquimula
  Concepción las Minas
    <u>Concepción las Minas</u> (c/p)

Expedientes Matrimoniales

	Years	Roll No.	Comments
	1878-1879	753,549/1	1879 Indexed Document damage
	1880	753,549/2	
	1881	753,549/3	
	1882	753,549/4	
	1883	753,549/5	
	1884	753,549/6	
	1885	753,550/1	
	1886	753,550/2	
	1887	753,550/3	
	1888	753,550/4-5	
	1889	753,551/1	
	1890	753,551/2	
	1891	753,551/3	
	1892	753,551/4	
	1893	753,551/5-6	
	1894	753,552/1	
	1895	753,552/2	
	1896	753,552/3	
	1897	753,552/4	
	1898	753,553/1	
	1899	753,553/2	
	1900	753,553/3	

Location/ Document Type	Years	Roll No.	Comments
	1901	751,553/4-5	
	1902	753,554/1	
	1903	753,554/2	
	1904	753,554/3	
	1905	753,555/1-2	
	1906	753,555/3	
	1907	753,555/4	
	1908	753,556/1	
	1909	753,556/2	
	1910	753,556/3	
	1911	753,557/1-2	
	1912	753,557/3	
	1913	753,557/4	
	1914	753,557/5	
	1915	753,557/6	
	1916	753,558/1	
	1917	753,558/2	
	1918	753,558/3	
	1919	753,558/4	
	1920	753,558/5	
	1921-1922	779,727	
	1922-1925	779,728	
	1925-1928	779,729	
	1928-1930	779,730	

Chiquimula
   Chiquimula (c/cd)

Actas Matrimoniales

	1929-1930	779,733	

Location/ Document Type	Years	Roll No.	Comments
Causas Matrimoniales			
	1809	745,076/9	Legajo 178
Expedientes Matrimoniales			
	1911	762,300	ODT/OL
	1921-1925	779,731	
	1925-1929	779,732	
Esquipulas Esquipulas (c/v)			
Expedientes Matrimoniales			
	1881	752,166/1	
	1882	752,166/2	
	1883	752,116/3	
	1884	752,167/1	
	1885	752,167/2	
	1886	752,167/3	
	1887	752,167/4	
	1888	752,167/5	
	1889	754,759/1	
	1890	754,759/2	Document damage
	1891	754,760/1-2	
	1892	754,760/3	
	1893	754,761/1-2	
	1894	754,761/3	
	1895	754,762/1-2	
	1896	754,762/3	
	1897	754,762/4	
	1898	754,763/1-2	
	1899	754,763/3	

Location/ Document Type	Years	Roll No.	Comments
	1900	754,763/4	
	1901	754,764/1	
	1902	754,764/2-3	
	1903	754,765/1	
	1904	754,765/2-3	
	1905	754,766/1	Document damage
	1906	754,766/2	Document damage
	1907	754,766/3	Document damage
	1908	754,767/1	
	1909	754,767/2	Document damage
	1910	754,767/3-4	Document damage
	1910-1911	754,768/1	
	1912	754,768/2	
	1913	754,768/3-4	
	1914	754,769/1	
	1915	754,769/2	Document damage
	1916	754,769/3-4	Document damage
	1917	754,770/1	
	1918	754,770/2	
	1919	754,770/3	
	1920	754,770/4	Document damage
	1921	778,812/1	
	1923	778,812/2	
	1924	778,813/1	
	1925	778,813/2	
	1926	778,813/3	
	1926	778,814/1	
	1927	778,814/2	
	1929	778,814/3	

Location/ Document Type	Years	Roll No.	Comments
	1930	778,814/4	
	1930	778,815	

Ipala
  Ipala (c/p)

Expedientes Matrimoniales

	Years	Roll No.	Comments
	1880	754,771/1	
	1880-1886	751,928	
	1881	754,771/2	
	1882	754,771/3	
	1883	754,771/4	
	1884	754,771/5	Document damage
	1885	754,771/6	Document damage
	1886	754,772/1-2	Document damage
	1886-1889	751,929	
	1887	754,772/3	Document damage
	1888	754,773/1	Document damage
	1889	754,773/2	Document damage
	1889-1890	751,930	
	1890	754,773/3	Document damage
	1891	754,774/1	
	1891-1893	751,931	
	1892	754,774/2	
	1893	754,774/3-4	
	1893-1897	751,932	
	1894	754,775/1	
	1895	754,775/2	
	1896	754,775/3	
	1896-1899	756,025	
	1897	754,776/1	

Location/ Document Type	Years	Roll No.	Comments
	1898	754,776/2	
	1899	754,777/1	
	1899-1900	756,026	
	1900	754,777/2-3	
	1901	754,777/4	
	1901-1905	756,027	
	1902	754,777/5	
	1903	754,778/1	
	1904	754,778/2	
	1905	754,779/1-2	
	1905-1909	756,028	
	1906	754,779/3-4	
	1907	754,779/5	
	1908	754,779/6	
	1908-1910	756,029	Disordered
	1909	754,780/1-2	
	1910	754,780/3	
	1911	754,780/4	
	1911-1914	756,030	
	1912	754,781/1	
	1913	754,781/2	
	1913-1918	756,031	
	1914	754,781/3	
	1915	754,781/4	
	1916	754,781/5	
	1917	754,782/1	
	1917-1920	756,032	Disordered
	1918	754,782/2	
	1919	754,782/3	

Location/ Document Type	Years	Roll No.	Comments
	1920	754,783	
	1920	756,033	
	1921	779,667	
	1921-1922	779,668/1	
	1923,1929	779,668/2	
	1924-1927	779,669	
	1927-1930	779,670	
	1930	779,734	

Olopa
  Olopa (c/p)

Expedientes Matrimoniales

	1921	778,809/1	
	1922	778,809/2	
	1923	778,809/3	
	1924	778,810	Document damage
	1925	778,810/2	
	1926	778,810/3	
	1927	778,810/4	
	1928	778,810/1	
	1929	778,810/2	
	1930	778,810/3	

Quezaltepeque
  Azacualpa (a)

Expedientes Matrimoniales

	1882	748,057/1	
	1883	748,057/2	ODT/OL
	1884	748,057/3	
	1885	748,057/4	

Location/ Document Type	Years	Roll No.	Comments
	1886	748,057/5	ODT/OL
	1887	748,057/6	ODT/OL
	1888	748,057/7	
	1889	748,058/1	
	1890	748,058/2	
	1891	748,058/3	ODT/OL
	1894	748,059/2	Document damage
	1895	748,059/3	ODT/OL
	1896	748,059/4	ODT/OL
	1897	748,059/5	Document damage ODT/OL
	1904	748,061/1	
	1905	748,061/2	ODT/OL
	1906	748,061/3	
	1907	748,061/4	ODT/OL
	1908	748,061/5	
	1909	751,530/1	
	1910	751,530/2	
	1911	751,531/1	
	1912	751,531/2	
	1913	751,532/1	
	1914	751,532/2	
	1915	751,533/1	
	1916	751,533/2	
	1917	751,533/3	
	1918	751,534	
	1919	751,535/1-2	
	1920	751,536	
	1921	779,656	
	1922-1923	779,657	

Location/ Document Type	Years	Roll No.	Comments
	1923	779,658/1	
	1924	779,658/2	
	1925	779,658/3	
	1925	779,659/1	
	1926	779,659/2	
	1927	779,659/3	
	1928	779,660/1	
	1929	779,660/2	
	1930	779,660/3	

San Jacinto
San Jacinto (c/p)

Expedientes Matrimoniales

	Years	Roll No.	Comments
	1882	752,159/1	
	1886	752,159/2	
	1887	752,159/3	
	1889	752,159/4	
	1892	752,159/5	
	1893	752,159/6	
	1895	752,159/7	
	1896	752,159/8	
	1897	752,160/1	
	1898	752,160/2	
	1899	752,160/3	
	1901	752,160/4	
	1903	752,160/5	
	1904	752,160/6	
	1905	752,161/1	Document damage
	1906	752,161/2	
	1907	752,161/3	Document damage

Location/ Document Type	Years	Roll No.	Comments
	1908	752,161/4	Document damage
	1909	752,161/5	Document damage
	1910	752,162/1	
	1911	752,162/2	
	1912	752,162/3	
	1913	752,162/4	
	1914	752,163/1	
	1915	752,163/2	
	1916	752,164/1	
	1917	752,164/2	
	1918	752,164/3	
	1919	752,164/4	
	1920	752,165	
	1921-1923	779,724	
	1923-1925, 1927	779,725	
	1926-1927	779,726	Disordered ODT/OL
	1927-1930	779,726	Document damage ODT/OL

El Progreso
  El Progreso
    El Progreso (c/cd)

Expedientes Matrimoniales

	Years	Roll No.	
	1884	747,155/1,3	
	1885	747,155/2	
	1886	747,155/4	
	1887	747,155/5	
	1888	747,155/6	
	1889	747,156/1	
	1890	747,156/2	

Location/ Document Type	Years	Roll No.	Comments
	1891	747,156/3	
	1892	747,157/1-2	
	1893	747,157/3	
	1894	747,157/4	
	1895	747,158/1	
	1896	747,158/2-3	
	1897	747,158/4	
	1398	747,159/1	
	1899	747,159/2-3	
	1900	747,159/4	
	1901	747,160	
	1902	747,420/1	
	1903	747,420/2	
	1904	747,421	
	1905	748,143/1	
	1906	748,143/2	
	1908	748,145/1	
	1909	748,145/2	
	1910	748,146	
	1911	748,147	ODT/OL
	1912	748,148	
	1913	748,149	
	1914	748,150	
	1915	748,151/1-2	
	1916	748,151/3	
	1917	748,152/1	
	1918	748,152/2	
	1919	748,153	
	1920	748,154	

Location/ Document Type	Years	Roll No.	Comments
San Agustín Acasaguastlán San Agustín Acasaguastlán (c/p)			
Expedientes Matrimoniales			
	1921–1925	782,753	
	1925–1927	782,754	
San Antonio la Paz San Antonio la Paz (c/p)			
Expedientes Matrimoniales			
	1877–1880	756,543	Indexed
	1881(Ja–Jl)	756,544/1–2	Indexed
	1881(Ag–Dc)	756,545	Indexed
	1918–1919	756,546	
	1921–1924	782,755	
	1924–1928	782,756	Disordered
	1928–1930	782,757	
Sanarate Sanarate (c/p)			
Causas Matrimoniales			
	1809	745,076/9	Legajo 178
Expedientes Matrimoniales			
	1880	747,121/1	
	1881	747,121/2	
	1882	747,122/1	
	1884	747,122/2	
	1885	747,122	
	1889	747,124/1	
	1890	747,124/2	

Location/ Document Type	Years	Roll No.	Comments
	1891	747,124/3	
	1891	747,308	ODT/OL
	1892	747,124/4	
	1893	747,125/1	
	1894	747,125/2	
	1895	747,126/1	
	1895	747,313	ODT/OL
	1896	747,126/2	
	1897	747,126/3	
	1898	747,127	
	1899	747,128	
	1900	747,129/1	
	1901	747,129/2	
	1902	747,130/1	
	1903	747,130/2	
	1904	747,131/1	
	1905	747,131/2	
	1906	747,131/3	
	1907	747,131/4	
	1908	747,131/5	
	1909	747,132/1-2	Legajo 7
	1910	747,132/3	Legajo 7
	1911	762,300	ODT/OL
	1912	747,133/1	
	1913	747,133/2	
	1914	747,134/1	
	1915	747,134/2	
	1916	747,134/3	
	1917	747,135/1-2	

Location/ Document Type	Years	Roll No.	Comments
	1918	747,135/3	
	1919	747,136/1	Document damage
	1920	747,136/2	
	1921	779,465	
	1922	779,466	
	1923	779,467/1	
	1924	779,467/2	
	1925	779,468/1-2	
	1926	779,469	
	1927	782,750	
	1928	782,751	
	1929-1930	782,752	

El Quiché
  Cunén
    Cunén (c/p)

Expedientes Matrimoniales

	Years	Roll No.	
	1900-1920	715,196/1-2	
	1921	776,315/1	
	1922	776,315/2	
	1923	776,315/3	
	1924	776,315/4	
	1926	776,315/5	
	1927	776,316/1	
	1928	776,316/2	
	1929	776,316/3	
	1930	776,316/4	

Location/ Document Type	Years	Roll No.	Comments
Chiché			
Chiché (c/p)			
Expedientes Matrimoniales			
	1885,1888, 1893-1894, 1896-1899	714,159	
	1921	776,054/1	
	1922	776,054/2	
	1922	776,056/1	
	1923	776,054/3	
	1923	776,056/2	
	1924	776,054/4	
	1924	776,056/3	
	1925	776,054/5	
	1925	776,056/4	
	1926	776,055/1	
	1926	776,056/5	
	1927	776,055/2	
	1927	776,056/6	
	1928	776,055/3	
	1928	776,056/7	
	1929	776,055/4	
	1929	776,056/8	
	1930	776,055/5	
Chichicastenango			
Chichicastenango (c/v)			
Expedientes Matrimoniales			
	1880-1896	715,141/2	
	1892-1899	715,142	

Location/ Document Type	Years	Roll No.	Comments
	1899-1905	715,143	
	1905-1915	715,144	
	1915-1920	715,145	
	1921	776,317/1	
	1922	776,317/2	
	1923	776,317/3	
	1924	776,317/4	
	1925	776,318/1	
	1926	776,318/2	
	1927	776,318/3	
	1928	776,318/4	
	1929	776,318/5	
	1930	776,318/6	

Chinique
　Chinique (c/p)

Expedientes Matrimoniales

	Years	Roll No.	
	1879-1888	714,148	
	1888-1893	714,149	
	1893-1899	714,150	
	1900-1906	714,151	
	1907-1915	714,152	
	1916-1920	714,153	

El Quiché
　El Quiché (c/cd)

Expedientes Matrimoniales

	Years	Roll No.	
	1883, 1891-1894, 1899	714,145	

Location/ Document Type	Years	Roll No.	Comments
Joyabaj Joyabaj (c/v)			
Expedientes Matrimoniales			
	1880-1889	714,160	
	1889-1896	714,161	
	1897-1901	714,162	
	1900-1907	714,163	
	1908-1913	714,164	
	1913-1918	714,165	
	1918-1928	714,166	
	1921	776,070/1	
	1922	776,070/2	
	1923	776,070/3-4	
	1924	776,071/1	
	1925	776,071/2	
	1926	776,071/3	
	1927	773,997	
	1927	776,072/1-2	
	1929	776,072/3	
Nebaj Nebaj (c/p)			
Expedientes Matrimoniales			
	1881-1889	714,154	
	1890-1899	714,155	
	1900	714,156	

Location/ Document Type	Years	Roll No.	Comments
Patzite <u>Patzite</u> (c/p)			
Expedientes Matrimoniales			
	1908-1909	714,146/1-2	
	1922	776,052/1	
	1923	776,052/2	
	1925	776,052/3	
San Antonio Ilotenango <u>San Antonio Ilotenango</u> (c/p)			
Expedientes Matrimoniales			
	1900-1920	714,147	
	1921	776,053/1	
	1923	776,053/2	
	1925	776,053/3	
	1926	776,053/4	
	1928	776,053/5	
	1929	776,053/6	
	1930	776,053/7	
Zacualpa <u>Zacualpa</u> (c/p)			
Expedientes Matrimoniales			
	1883-1909	714,157	
	1909	714,158	Poor focus
	1920	776,057/1	
	1922	776,057/2	
	1923	776,057/3	
	1924	776,057/4	
	1925	776,057/5	

Location/ Document Type	Years	Roll No.	Comments
	1926	776,057/6	
	1927	776,058/1	
	1928	776,058/2	
	1929	776,058/3	
	1930	776,058/4	

Escuintla
  La Gomera
    <u>La Gomera</u> (c/v)

Expedientes Matrimoniales

	Years	Roll No.	Comments
	1912	752,158/3	
	1914	752,158/4	
	1917	752,158/5	
	1918	752,158/6	
	1919	752,158/7	
	1921	779,611/1	
	1925	779,611/2	
	1928	779,611/3	

Palín
  <u>Palín</u> (c/p)

Expedientes Matrimoniales

	Years	Roll No.	Comments
	1881–1890	751,912	Disordered
	1891–1892	751,913	
	1892–1895	751,914	
	1895–1897, 1899	751,915	
	1899–1900	751,916	
	1901–1913, 1918–1920	751,917	
	1920	751,918	
	1921–1922	779,741	

Location/ Document Type	Years	Roll No.	Comments
	1923-1926	779,742	
	1927-1930	779,743	Disordered

Santa Lucía Cotzumalguapa
  Santa Lucía Cotzumalguapa (c/p)

Expedientes Matrimoniales

	Years	Roll No.	Comments
	1881	752,144/1	
	1882	752,144/2	
	1883	752,145/1-2	
	1884	752,145/3	
	1885	752,146/1	
	1886	752,146/2	
	1887	752,147/1	
	1888	752,147/2-3	
	1889	752,148/1	
	1890	758,375/1-2	
	1891-1892	758,376	Disordered
	1892	758,377/1-2	
	1893	758,378/1	
	1894	758,378/2-3	
	1895	758,379	
	1897	758,381	
	1898	758,382/1	
	1899	758,382/2	
	1900	752,148/2	
	1901	752,149/1	
	1902	752,149/2	
	1903	752,149/3	
	1904	752,150/1	
	1905	752,150/2	

Location/ Document Type	Years	Roll No.	Comments
	1906	752,150/3-4	
	1907	752,151/1	
	1908	752,151/2	
	1909	752,151/3	
	1910	752,152/1-2	
	1911	752,152/3	
	1912	752,153/1-2	
	1913	752,153/3	
	1914	752,154/1-2	
	1915	752,154/3	
	1916	752,155/1-2	
	1917	752,155/3	
	1918	752,156/1	
	1919	752,156/2-3	
	1920	752,157	
	1921	779,744	
	1921-1924	779,745	
	1924-1926	779,746	
	1926-1929	779,747	
	1929-1930	779,748	

San Vicente Pacaya
San Vicente Pacya (c/p)

Expedientes Matrimoniales

	1881-1888	751,902	
	1888-1889	751,903	
	1890-1895	751,904	
	1895-1899	751,905	
	1900-1902	751,906	
	1902-1904	751,907	

Location/ Document Type	Years	Roll No.	Comments
	1905–1909	751,908	
	1910–1913	751,909	
	1914–1919	751,910	Disordered
	1918–1920	751,911	
	1921–1922	779,412	
	1922–1925	779,413	Disordered ODT/OL
	1925–1930	779,414	

Guatemala
  Chinautla
    Chinautla (c/p)

Expedientes Matrimoniales

	1905	774,312	

  Santa Catarina Pinula
    Santa Catarina Pinula (c/v)

Expedientes Matrimoniales

	1898	751,753/2	ODT/OL
	1901	751,756/1	ODT/OL

Huehuetenango
  Barrillas
    Barrillas (c/p)

Expedientes Matrimoniales

	1893	752,122/1-2	Legajo 25
	1893	752,123	Legajo 25
	1893	752,124	Legajo 25
	1894	752,125/1	
	1895	752,125/2	
	1896	752,125/3	
	1897	752,125/4	

Location/ Document Type	Years	Roll No.	Comments
	1898	752,125/5	
	1899	752,125/6	
	1900	752,125/7	
	1901	752,125/8	
	1902	752,125/9	
	1903	752,125/10	
	1904	752,125/11	
	1905	752,126/1	
	1906	752,126/2	
	1907	752,126/3	
	1908	752,126/4	
	1909	752,126/5	
	1911	752,126/6	
	1912	752,126/7	
	1913	752,126/8	
	1914	752,126/9	
	1916	752,126/10	
	1917	752,126/11	
	1918	752,126/12	
	1919	752,126/13	
	1920	752,126/14	
	1921	779,609/1	
	1922	779,609/2	
	1924	779,609/3	
	1925	779,609/4	
	1926	779,609/5	
	1928	779,610/1-2	
	1929	779,160/1	
	1930	779,160/2	

Location/ Document Type	Years	Roll No.	Comments
Colotenango Colotenango (c/p)			
Expedientes Matrimoniales			
	1882	752,133/1	
	1883	752,133/2	
	1886	752,133/3	
	1887	752,133/4	
	1888	752,134/1	
	1889	752,134/2	
	1890	752,135/1	
	1891	752,135/2	
	1892	752,135/3	
	1893	752,135/4	
	1894	752,135/5	
	1899	752,136/1	
	1900	752,136/2	
	1901	752,136/3	
	1902	752,136/4	
	1903	752,142/6	ODT/OL
	1904	752,136/5	
	1905	752,136/6	
	1906	752,137/1	
	1907	752,137/2	
	1908	752,138/1	
	1909	752,138/2	
	1910	752,138/3	
	1911	752,138/4	
	1912	752,138/5	
	1913	752,139/1	

Location/ Document Type	Years	Roll No.	Comments
	1915	752,139/2	
	1916	752,139/3	
	1917	752,139/4	
	1918	752,139/5	
	1919	752,139/6	

Chiantla
Chiantla (c/v)

Actas Matrimoniales

| | 1879-1880 | 751,944/1 | Incomplete
Legajo 17 |

Expedientes Matrimoniales

	1880	751,944/2	Legajo 17
	1880	752,140/2	
	1881	751,944/3	Legajo 17
	1882	751,944/4	Legajo 17
	1883	751,944/5	Legajo 17
	1883	752,140/5	ODT/OL
	1884	751,944/6	Legajo 17
	1885	751,944/7	Legajo 17
	1886	751,944/8	Legajo 17
	1887	751,945/1	Legajo 18
	1888	751,945/2	Legajo 18
	1889	751,946	Legajo 18
	1890	751,947/1	
	1891	751,947/2	
	1892	751,948/1	
	1893	751,948/2	
	1894	751,949/1	
	1895	751,949/2	

Location/ Document Type	Years	Roll No.	Comments
	1896	751,950/1	Legajo 19
	1897	751,950/2	Legajo 19
	1898	751,951/1	Legajo 19
	1899	751,951/2	Legajo 19
	1900	751,952	Legajo 19
	1901	751,953/1	Legajo 19
	1902	751,953/2	Legajo 19
	1902	751,954/2	
	1903	751,953/3	Legajo 19
	1903	751,954/3	
	1904	751,954/1	
	1906	751,955/1	
	1907	751,955/2	
	1908	751,956	
	1909	751,957/1	
	1910	751,957/2	
	1911	751,958	
	1912	751,959	
	1913	751,960	
	1914	751,961/1	
	1915	751,961/2	
	1916	751,962	
	1917	751,963	Legajo 24
	1918	751,964/1	Legajo 24
	1919	751,964/2	Legajo 24
	1920	752,121/1-2	Legajo 24
	1921	757,333	
	1922	757,334	
	1923	778,713	

Location/ Document Type	Years	Roll No.	Comments
	1924	778,714/1	
	1925	778,714/2	
	1926	778,715	
	1927	779,607/1	
	1928	779,607/2	
	1929	779,608/1	
	1930	779,608/2	

Huehuetenango
  Huehuetenango (c/cd)

Expedientes Matrimoniales

	Years	Roll No.	Comments
	1879	752,140/1	
	1880	752,140/2	ODT/OL
	1881	752,140/3	
	1882	752,140/4	
	1883	752,140/5	ODT/OL
	1884	752,140/6	
	1885	752,140/7	
	1886	752,140/8	
	1887	752,140/9	
	1888	752,140/10	
	1889	752,140/11	
	1890	752,141/1	
	1891	752,141/2	
	1892	752,141/3	
	1893	752,141/4	
	1894	752,141/5	
	1895	752,141/6	
	1896	752,141/7	

Location/ Document Type	Years	Roll No.	Comments
	1897	752,141/8	
	1898	752,142/1-2	
	1899	752,142/3	
	1900	752,142/4	
	1901	752,142/5	
	1903	752,142/6	ODT/OL
	1904	752,142/7	
	1905	752,142/8	
	1906	752,142/9	
	1907	752,142/10	
	1908	752,142/11	
	1909	752,142/12	
	1910	752,142/13	
	1912	752,142/14	
	1913	752,142/15	
	1914	752,143/1	
	1915	752,143/2	
	1916	752,143/3	
	1917	752,143/4	
	1918,1920	752,143/5	
	1918-1919	752,143/6	
	1920	752,143/7	
	1921	779,162/1	
	1922	779,162/2	
	1923	779,162/3	
	1924	779,162/4	
	1925	779,162/5	
	1926	779,162/6	
	1927	779,163/1	

Location/ Document Type	Years	Roll No.	Comments
	1928	779,163/2	
	1929	779,163/3	

Malacatancito
  Malacatancito (c/p)

Expedientes Matrimoniales

	Years	Roll No.	Comments
	1880-1888	717,199	
	1885	751,720/1	Legajo 48413
	1886	751,720/2	Document damage Legajo 48413
	1887	751,720/4	Document damage Legajo 48413
	1888	717,200	
	1888-1889	717,200	
	1889	751,721/1	Legajo 48415
	1890	751,720/3	Legajo 48413
	1890-1891	751,721/2	Legajo 48415
	1892	751,722/1	Document damage Legajo 48416
	1893	751,722/2-3	Document damage Legajo 48416
	1894	751,722/4	Legajo 48416
	1896	751,723/1	Legajo 48417
	1897	751,723/2	Legajo 48418

Nentón
  Nentón (c/p)

Expedientes Matrimoniales

	Years	Roll No.	Comments
	1914	751,943/1	Legajo 48454
	1916	751,943/2	Legajo 48454
	1917	751,943/3	Legajo 48454
	1918	751,943/4	Legajo 48454

Location/ Document Type	Years	Roll No.	Comments
	1920	751,943/5	Legajo 48454
	1921	779,161/1	
	1925	779,161/2	
	1927	779,161/3	
	1928	779,161/4	
	1929	779,161/5	
	1930	779,161/6	

San Mateo Ixtatán
  San Mateo Ixtatán (c/p)

Expedientes Matrimoniales

	Years	Roll No.	Comments
	1882–1916	717,197	Disordered
	1912–1917	717,198	
	1921–1927, 1929	779,601	

Santa Bárbara
  Santa Bárbara (c/p)

Expedientes Matrimoniales

	Years	Roll No.	Comments
	1882	717,678	Legajo 48456
	1887–1889	717,679/2	Legajo 48457
	1890	717,680	Poor focus Legajo 48458
	1890–1894	717,679/1	Legajo 48457
	1894	717,681	Legajo 48459
	1897	717,682	Legajo 48460
	1903–1908	717,683	Legajo 48461
	1908–1911	717,684	Legajo 48461
	1911–1913	717,685	Legajo 48463
	1913–1916	717,686	Legajo 48464
	1916–1921	717,687	Legajo 48465

Location/ Document Type	Years	Roll No.	Comments
Soloma 　Soloma (c/p)			
Expedientes Matrimoniales			
	1874–1882	717,688	Legajo 48595
	1883–1887	715,214/1	Legajo 48597
	1886–1888	715,214/2-3	Legajo 48598
	1888–1889	715,214/4	Legajo 48599
	1890–1893	717,899	Legajo 48600
	1893	734,021	Legajo 48601
	1893	751,709	
	1893	751,710	
	1894	751,711/1	
	1895	751,711/2	
	1896	751,711/3	
	1897–1898	751,711/4	
	1898	751,712/1	
	1899	751,712/2	
	1900–1901	751,712/3	
	1902	751,712/4	
	1903	751,713/1	Legajo 48606
	1904	751,713/2	
	1905–1906	751,713/3	
	1906	751,714/1	
	1907	751,714/2	
	1908	751,714/3	
	1909	751,714/4	
	1910	751,715/1	
	1911	751,715/2	

Location/ Document Type	Years	Roll No.	Comments
	1912	751,715/3	
	1913	751,716/1	
	1914	751,716/2	
	1915	751,716/3	
	1916	751,717/1	Document damage Legajo 48611
	1916	751,717/2	Poor focus Legajo 48612
	1917	751,718/1	Legajo 48612
	1918	751,718/2	Legajo 48613
	1919	751,718/3	Legajo 48613
	1920	751,719	Legajo 48614
	1921-1924	779,602	
	1928-1930	779,115	

Todos Santos Cuchamatán
San Martín (a)

Expedientes Matrimoniales

	Years	Roll No.	
	1882	752,127/1	
	1883	752,127/2	
	1885	752,127/3	
	1888	752,127/4	
	1889	752,127/5	
	1890	752,127/6	
	1893	752,127/7	
	1894	752,127/8	
	1895	752,128/1	
	1896	752,128/2	
	1897	752,128/3	
	1898	752,128/4	

Location/ Document Type	Years	Roll No.	Comments
	1899	752,128/5	
	1900	752,128/6	
	1902	752,128/7	
	1903	752,128/8	
	1907	752,128/9-10	
	1908,1910	752,128/10	
	1911	752,129/11	
	1912	752,128/12	
	1916	752,128/13	
	1917	752,128/14	
	1918	752,129/1	
	1919	752,129/2	
	1920	752,129/3	

Todos Santos Cuchumatán
  Todos Santos Cuchumatán (c/p)

Expedientes Matrimoniales

	Years	Roll No.	Comments
	1891	752,130/1	
	1891	752,130/2	No documents filmed
	1898	752,130/3	
	1901	752,130/4	
	1904	752,130/5	
	1905	752,130/6	
	1906	752,130/7	
	1907	752,130/8	
	1908	752,130/9	
	1909	752,131/1	
	1910	752,131/2	
	1911	752,131/3	
	1913	752,131/4	

Location/ Document Type	Years	Roll No.	Comments
	1914	752,131/5	
	1915	752,131/6	
	1916	752,131/7	
	1917	752,131/8	
	1918	752,132/1	
	1919	752,132/2	
	1920	752,132/3	

Izabal
  Livingston
    Livingston (c/p)

Expedientes Matrimoniales

	1880-1894	714,079	Indexed
	1894-1898	714,080	Indexed on 714,079
	1898-1912	714,081	Indexed on 714,079
	1912-1918	714,082	Indexed on 714,079
	1918-1920	714,083	Incomplete Indexed on 714,079

Morales
  Morales (c/p)

Expedientes Matrimoniales

	1920	776,068/1	
	1921	776,068/2	
	1922	776,068/3	
	1924	776,068/4	
	1925	776,068/5	
	1926	776,069/1-2	
	1928	776,069/3	
	1929	776,069/4	

Location/ Document Type	Years	Roll No.	Comments
Puerto Barrios Puerto Barrios (c/cd)			
Expedientes Matrimoniales			
	1921	776,059/1	
	1922	776,059/2	
	1923	776,059/3	
	1924	776,059/4	
	1925	776,059/5	
	1926	776,059/6	
	1927	776,059/7	
	1928	776,059/8	
	1929	776,059/9	
	1930	776,059/10	

Jalapa
  Jalpa
    Jalpa (c/cd)			

Expedientes Matrimoniales			
	1879	747,297/1	
	1880	747,297/2	
	1880-1897	747,319	Intermittent years Disordered
	1881	747,297/3	
	1882	747,298/1-2	
	1883	747,299/1-2	
	1884	747,300	
	1885	747,301/1-2	
	1886	747,301/1-2	
	1887	747,304	
	1888	747,305	

Location/ Document Type	Years	Roll No.	Comments
	1889	747,306	
	1890	747,307	
	1891	747,308	ODT/OL
	1892	747,309	
	1892	747,310	
	1893	747,311	
	1894	747,312	
	1895	747,313	ODT/OL
	1896	747,314	
	1897	747,315/1-2	
	1898	747,316	
	1899	747,317/1-2	
	1900	747,318/1-2	
	1902	747,320/1-2	
	1903	747,321	
	1904	747,322	
	1904	747,323	
	1905	747,324	
	1905	747,325	
	1906	747,326	
	1907	747,327	
	1907	751,225	
	1908	751,226	
	1908	751,227	
	1909	751,228	
	1910	751,229	
	1910	751,230	
	1911	751,231	
	1911	751,232	

Location/ Document Type	Years	Roll No.	Comments
	1912	751,233	
	1912	751,234	
	1913	751,235/1-2	
	1914	751,236	
	1914	751,604	
	1915	751,605	
	1915	751,606	
	1916	751,607/1-2	
	1917	751,608/1-2	
	1918	751,609/1	
	1919	751,609	
	1920	751,610	
	1921	779,124	
	1921	779,125	
	1921	779,175/1	
	1921-1930	779,395	
	1922	779,175/2	
	1922-1923	779,126	
	1922-1923	779,127	
	1922-1923	779,128	Document damage
	1923	779,175/3	
	1924	779,175/4	
	1924-1925	779,129	
	1924-1925	779,130	
	1925	779,175/5	
	1926	779,175/6	
	1926-1927	779,131	
	1926-1927	779,132	
	1927	779,194	

Location/ Document Type	Years	Roll No.	Comments
	1927	779,195	
	1927	779,196	
	1928	779,197	
	1928	779,198	
	1929	779,199	
	1929	779,200	
	1930	779,201	
	1930	779,202	
	1930	779,203	

Mataquescuintla
  Mataquescuintla (c/v)

Expedientes Matrimoniales

	Years	Roll No.	Comments
	1883	751,747/1	
	1887	751,747/2	
	1887-1888	751,747/3	
	1889	751,748	
	1892,1899	751,749	
	1893	751,750/1	
	1894	751,750/2	
	1895	751,751	
	1896	751,752	
	1897,1899	751,753/1	
	1898	751,753/2	ODT/OL
	1899	751,754	
	1900	751,755	
	1901	751,756/1	ODT/OL
	1902	751,756/2	
	1903	751,757	
	1904	751,758	

Location/ Document Type	Years	Roll No.	Comments
	1905	751,759/1	
	1906	751,759/2	
	1907	751,760	
	1908	751,761	
	1909	751,762	
	1910	751,763	
	1911	751,764	
	1912	751,765	
	1913-1914	751,766	
	1914	751,767	
	1915	751,768	
	1916	751,769	
	1917	751,770	
	1918	751,771/1	
	1919	751,771/2	
	1920	751,875	
	1921	779,190	
	1922	779,191	
	1923	779,192	
	1923	779,193/1	
	1924	779,193/2	
	1924	779,662/1	
	1925	779,662/2	

Monjas
Monjas (c/p)

Expedientes Matrimoniales

	Years	Roll No.	Comments
	1912	751,919	ODT/OL
	1919	751,920/1	
	1925-1928	779,396	

Location/ Document Type	Years	Roll No.	Comments
	1928-1930	779,397	

San Luís Jilotepeque
<u>San Luís Jilotepeque</u> (c/p)

Expedientes Matrimoniales

	Years	Roll No.	
	1921	779,177/1	
	1922	779,177/2	
	1922	779,178/1	
	1923	779,178/2	
	1923	779,179/1	
	1924	779,179/2	
	1924	779,180/1	
	1925	779,180/2	
	1926	779,180/3	
	1926	779,181/1	
	1927	779,181/2	
	1928	779,181/3	

San Manuel Chaparrón
<u>San Manuel Chaparrón</u> (c/p)

Expedientes Matrimoniales

	Years	Roll No.	
	1881	751,636/1	
	1883	751,636/2	
	1885-1887	751,636/3	
	1888-1889	751,636/4	
	1891	751,636/6	
	1892	751,636/7	
	1893	751,636/8	
	1895-1896	751,637/1	
	1896	751,637/2	

Location/ Document Type	Years	Roll No.	Comments
	1899	751,637/3	ODT/OL
	1900	751,637/4	ODT/OL
	1901	751,637/5	
	1902	751,638/1	
	1903	751,638/2	
	1904	751,638/3	
	1905	751,638/4	
	1906	751,638/5	
	1907	751,639/1	
	1908	751,639/2	
	1909	751,639/3	
	1910	751,639/4	
	1911	751,640/1	
	1912	751,640/2	
	1913	751,746/1	
	1914	751,746/2	
	1915	751,746/3	
	1916	751,746/4	
	1917	751,746/5	
	1918	751,746/6	
	1919	751,746/7	
	1927	779,176/1	
	1928	779,176/2	
	1929	779,176/3	
	1930	779,176/4	

Location/ Document Type	Years	Roll No.	Comments
San Pedro Pinula San Pedro Pinula (c/p)			
Expedientes Matrimoniales			
	1880	751,876/1	
	1881	751,876/2	
	1882	751,876/3	
	1883	751,876/4	
	1884	751,877/1	
	1885	751,877/2	
	1886	751,877/3	
	1887	751,878/1	
	1888	751,878/2	
	1889	751,879/1-2	
	1890	751,880	
	1891	751,881/1-2	
	1892	751,882/1-2	
	1893	751,883	
	1893	751,884	
	1894	751,885	
	1895	751,886	
	1896	751,887	
	1897	751,888/1-2	
	1898	751,889/1	
	1899	751,889/2	
	1900	751,890	
	1901	751,891	
	1902	751,892	
	1903	751,893	
	1904	751,894	

Location/ Document Type	Years	Roll No.	Comments
	1905	751,895/1	
	1906	751,895/2	
	1907	751,896	Document damage
	1908	751,897	
	1909	751,933/1-2	
	1910	751,934	
	1911	751,935	
	1911	751,936	
	1912	751,919	ODT/OL
	1912	751,937	
	1912	751,938	
	1913	751,939	
	1914	751,940	
	1915	751,941/1-2	
	1916	751,942	
	1917	753,546/1	
	1918	753,546/2	
	1919	753,547	
	1920	753,548	
	1920	773,998	
	1921	779,717	
	1922-1923	779,718	
	1923-1924	779,719	
	1924-1925	779,720	
	1925-1927	779,721	
	1927-1930	779,722	
	1930	779,723	

Location/ Document Type	Years	Roll No.	Comments

Jutiapa
  Agua Blanca
    <u>Agua Blanca</u> (c/p)

Expedientes Matrimoniales

	Years	Roll No.	
	1883,1885	751,790/1	
	1886	751,790/2	
	1887,1888	751,790/3	
	1889-1890	751,791/1	
	1891,1892	751,791/2	
	1893-1894	751,792/1-2	
	1895-1896	751,793/1	
	1897-1898	751,793/2-3	
	1899-1900	751,794/1	
	1901-1902	751,794/2-3	
	1903-1904	751,795	
	1905-1906	751,796	
	1907-1908	751,797	
	1909-1910	751,798	
	1911-1912	751,799	
	1913-1914	751,800	
	1915-1916	751,801	
	1918	751,802	
	1919-1920	751,803	
	1921	779,460/1	
	1921-1925	779,462/1-2	
	1922	779,460/2	
	1923	779,461/1-2	
	1924	779,461/3	
	1926	779,462/2	

Location/ Document Type	Years	Roll No.	Comments
	1927	779,463/1-2	
	1928	779,463/2	
	1929	779,464/1-2	
	1930	779,464/2	

Asunción Mita
  Asunción Mita (c/v)

Expedientes Matrimoniales

	Years	Roll No.	Comments
	1881	751,655/2	Document damage
	1881-1882	751,656	
	1883-1884	751,657	
	1885-1886	751,658	
	1887-1888	751,659	
	1388-1890	751,661	Disordered Document damage
	1889-1890	751,660	
	1891-1893	751,661	
	1893	751,663	
	1893-1894	751,664	
	1895	751,665	
	1896	751,666	
	1897	751,667	
	1899-1900	751,668	Disordered
	1900	751,669	
	1901-1902	751,670	
	1902-1903	751,671	
	1904	751,672	
	1904-1906	751,673	
	1906	751,674	
	1907-1908	751,675	

Location/ Document Type	Years	Roll No.	Comments
	1909–1910	751,676	
	1910	751,677	
	1911–1912	751,678	
	1911–1912	751,784	
	1913–1914, 1918	751,785	
	1915–1916	751,786	
	1917–1918	751,787	
	1918	751,788	
	1919–1920	751,789	
	1921	779,448/1	
	1922	779,448/2	
	1923	779,449/1	
	1924	779,449/2	
	1924	779,450/1	
	1925	779,450/2	
	1926	779,451/1	
	1927	779,451/2	
	1927	779,452/1	
	1928	779,452/2	
	1929–1930	779,453	
	1930	779,454	

Comapa
Comapa (c/p)

Expedientes Matrimoniales

	1881	751,557	
	1884	751,558	
	1887–1888	751,559	
	1888–1889	751,560	

Location/ Document Type	Years	Roll No.	Comments
	1889	751,655/1	
	1890-1891	751,561	
	1891-1892	751,562	
	1893-1894	751,563	
	1894-1895	751,564	
	1896-1898	751,641	
	1898	751,644/1	
	1899-1900	751,642/1-2	
	1901-1903	751,643/1-2	
	1904-1906	751,644/2	
	1906,1908	751,645	
	1909-1910	751,646	
	1910-1911	751,647	
	1911	751,648	
	1912-1913	751,649	
	1913-1914	751,650/1-2	
	1915-1917	751,651	
	1918-1919	751,652	
	1919-1920	751,653	
	1920	751,654	
	1921-1923	779,409	
	1923-1925	779,410	
	1925-1927	779,411	
	1927-1929	779,739	
	1929-1930	779,740	

Location/ Document Type	Years	Roll No.	Comments
Conguaco Conguaco (c/p)			
Expedientes Matrimoniales			
	1880-1884	751,539/1	
	1885-1886	751,539/2	
	1887-1888	751,540	
	1889-1891	751,541	
	1892-1894	751,542	
	1895-1897	751,543	
	1898-1900	751,544	
	1900-1909	748,051	Document damage ODT/OL
	1901-1903	751,545/1-2	
	1904-1906	751,546/1-2	
	1907-1909	751,547	
	1910-1912	751,548/1-2	
	1913-1914	751,549	
	1914-1915	751,550	
	1916-1918	751,551/1-2	
	1919-1920	751,552/1-2	
	1921-1925	779,404	
	1924-1925	779,406	
	1925-1929	779,405	
	1929-1930	779,407	
	1930	779,408	

Location/ Document Type	Years	Roll No.	Comments
El Adelanto El Adelanto (c/p)			
Expedientes Matrimoniales			
	1882	748,044/1/2	
	1890-1899	748,045	Intermittent years
	1910	748,046/1	
	1911	748,049/3	
	1912	748,046/2	
	1913	748,047/1	
	1914	748,047/2	
	1915	748,048/1	
	1916	748,048/2	
	1917	748,048/3	
	1918	748,048/4	
	1919	748,049/1	
	1920	748,049/2	
	1921-1924	779,736	
	1924-1928	779,737	
	1928-1930	779,738	
El Progreso El Progreso (c/p)			
Expedientes Matrimoniales			
	1907	748,144	
Jalpatagua Jalpatagua (c/p)			
Expedientes Matrimoniales			
	1880-1882	751,804/1	
	1883-1885	751,804/2	

Location/ Document Type	Years	Roll No.	Comments
	1886-1889	751,805/1	
	1890-1892	751,805/2	
	1893-1896	751,898/1	
	1896-1899	751,898/2	
	1900-1902	751,899/1	
	1903-1905	751,899/2	
	1906-1909	751,899/3	
	1910-1912	751,900/1	
	1913-1914	751,900/2	
	1915-1917	751,900/3	
	1918-1920	751,901	
	1922	779,457/1	
	1923	779,457/2	
	1924	779,457/3	
	1925	779,458	
	1928	779,459/1	
	1929	779,459/2	
	1930	779,459/3	

Jérez
  Jérez (c/p)

Expedientes Matrimoniales

	1898	747,137/1	
	1900	747,137/2	
	1901	747,137/3	
	1902	747,137/4	
	1903	747,137/5	
	1904	747,137/6	
	1905	747,137/7	
	1907	747,137/8	

Location/ Document Type	Years	Roll No.	Comments
	1908	747,137/9	
	1909	747,137/10	
	1910	747,137/11	
	1911	747,138/1	Poor focus
	1911	747,138/2	No documents filmed
	1912	747,138/3	Poor exposure
	1913	747,138/4	Poor exposure
	1914	747,138/5	
	1915	747,138/6	
	1916	747,138/7	
	1917	747,138/8	
	1918	747,139/1	
	1919	747,139/2	
	1920	747,139/3	
	1921-1930	779,735	

Jutiapa
  Jutiapa (c/cd)

Expedientes Matrimoniales

	1881	748,044/1/1	
	1883	748,044/1/3	
	1884	748,044/1/4	
	1884-1889	748,050	ODT/OL
	1886	748,044/1/5	
	1887	748,044/1/6	
	1889	748,044/1/7	
	1902	748,155/1	
	1903,1905	748,155/2	
	1904	748,155/3	
	1905	748,155/4	

Location/ Document Type	Years	Roll No.	Comments
	1906	748,156/1	
	1907	748,156/2	
	1908	748,157	
	1909	748,158	
	1910	748,159	
	1910	748,160	
	1910	748,161	
	1911	748,162	
	1911	748,163	
	1911	748,147	ODT/OL
	1912	748,164	
	1912	748,165	
	1913	748,166	
	1913	673,054	
	1914	748,037/1-2	
	1915	748,038/1-2	
	1916	748,039	
	1917	748,040/1-2	
	1918	748,041	
	1919	748,042	
	1920	748,043/1-2	
	1921	779,116	
	1921-1922	779,117	
	1922-1923	779,118	
	1923	779,119	
	1924-1925	779,120	
	1924-1925	779,121	
	1925-1926	779,122	
	1926-1927	779,123/1-2	

Location/ Document Type	Years	Roll No.	Comments
Moyuta Moyuta (c/p)			
Expedientes Matrimoniales			
	1884-1889	748,050	ODT/OL
	1900-1909	748,051	Document damage ODT/OL
	1909	748,052	
	1911-1912	748,053	
	1912-1914	748,054	Document damage
	1915	748,055	
	1918	748,056	
	1921-1924	779,401	
	1925-1928	779,402	
	1928-1930	779,403	
Pasaco Pasaco (c/p)			
Expedientes Matrimoniales			
	1881-1899	751,537/1	Intermittent years
	1900-1905	751,537	
	1906,1909	751,538/1	
	1910, 1912-1919	751,538/2	
	1920	751,538/3	
	1921	779,445/1	
	1922	779,445/2	
	1923	779,445/3	
	1923	779,446/1	
	1924	779,446/2	
	1925	779,446/3	

Location/ Document Type	Years	Roll No.	Comments
	1926	779,446/4	
	1927	779,446/5	
	1928	779,446/6	
	1929	779,446/7	
	1929	779,447/1	
	1930	779,447/2	

Zapotitlán
  Zapotitlán (c/ɔ)

Expedientes Matrimoniales

	Years	Roll No.	Comments
	1882-1884, 1886-1889	751,553	Document damage
	1390-1894, 1897-1899	751,554/1-2	
	1900-1901, 1903, 1906-1908	751,555/1	
	1910-1911, 1913	751,555/2	
	1914	751,555/3	
	1915, 1917-1920	751,556	
	1921	779,455/1	Document damage
	1922	779,455/2	
	1923	779,455/3	
	1924	779,455/4	
	1925	779,455/5	
	1926	779,455/6	
	1927	779,455/7	Document damage
	1928	779,456/1-2	
	1929	779,456/3	
	1930	779,456/4	

Location/ Document Type	Years	Roll No.	Comments
Petén La Libertad <u>La Libertad</u> (c/p)			
Causas Matrimoniales			
	1808	745,076/10	Legajo 187
Expedientes Matrimoniales			
	1883, 1885-1889	738,160	
	1889, 1891-1893, 1895-1896	738,161	
	1896-1909	738,162	
	1909-1919	738,163	
	1921	776,060/1	
	1922	776,060/2	
	1923	776,060/3	
	1924	776,060/4	
	1925	776,060/5	
	1926	776,060/6	
	1927	776,060/7	
	1928	776,060/8	
	1929	776,060/9	
	1930	776,061	
Quezaltenango Quezaltenango <u>Quezaltenango</u> (c/cd)			
Expedientes Matrimoniales			
	1920	757,341	
	1925	757,335	
	1925	757,336	

Location/ Document Type	Years	Roll No.	Comments
	1925	757,337	
	1926	757,338	
	1926	757,339	
	1926	757,340	

Sacatepéquez
  Alotenango
    Alotenango (c/p)

Expedientes Matrimoniales

	Years	Roll No.	Comments
	1881-1886	717,075/1	
	1887-1889	717,075/2	
	1890-1894	717,076/1	
	1895-1899	717,076/2	
	1900-1905	717,077	
	1906-1909	717,078	
	1910-1911	717,079	
	1912-1920	717,080	
	1916-1920	717,081	Disordered
	1922	778,463/1	
	1923	778,463/2	
	1924	778,463/3	
	1925	778,463/4	
	1926	778,463/5	
	1927	778,807/1	
	1928	778,807/2	
	1929	778,808/1-2	
	1930	778,808/3	

Location/ Document Type	Years	Roll No.	Comments
Antigua Guatemala Antigua Guatemala (c/cd)			
Expedientes Matrimoniales			
	1854–1906	717,744	Intermittent years
	1882–1885	717,745	
	1885–1889	717,746	
	1889–1900	717,747	
	1890–1893	717,892	Disordered
	1892, 1898–1902	717,893	
	1892–1896	717,891	Disordered
	1894–1898, 1895–1900, 1900–1901, 1905–1906	717,748	
	1902–1905	717,894	
	1905–1907	717,895	
	1907–1910	717,896	
	1910	717,897	
	1910–1912	717,898	
	1913	751,702	
	1914	751,703	
	1915	751,704	
	1916	751,705	
	1917	751,706/1	
	1918	751,706/2	
	1919	751,707	
	1920	751,708	
	1921–1922	779,597	
	1922–1924	779,598	

Location/ Document Type	Years	Roll No.	Comments
	1924-1925	779,599	
	1925-1926	779,600	

Ciudad Vieja
   Ciudad Vieja (c/p)

Expedientes Matrimoniales

	Years	Roll No.	Comments
	1881-1883, 1888	736,588/1	
	1881-1885	717,082/1-2	Document damage
	1886-1889	717,083	
	1889	736,588/2	
	1890-1891	717,084/1	
	1891-1892	717,084/2	
	1893-1896	717,085	
	1896-1898	736,588/3	
	1897-1898	717,086/1	Includes one case dated 1941
	1898-1899	717,086/2	
	1898	736,588/4	
	1900-1903	717,087	
	1903	736,588/5	
	1904	717,088/1	
	1904-1906	717,088/2	
	1907-1909	717,089	
	1909-1910	717,090	
	1910	717,091	
	1910	736,588/6	
	1911-1913	717,092	
	1913-1914	717,093	
	1915	736,588/7	
	1915-1917	717,094	

Location/ Document Type	Years	Roll No.	Comments
	1917	717,095	
	1917-1922	736,588/8	
	1918-1919	717,096	
	1919-1920	717,593	
	1923	778,718/1	
	1924	778,718/2	
	1925	736,588/9	
	1925	778,719/1	
	1926	778,719/2	
	1927	778,720/1	
	1928	778,720/2	
	1929	779,603/1-2	
	1930-1931	779,603/3	

Ciudad Vieja
  San Lorenzo el Cubo (a)

Expedientes Matrimoniales

	1880-1899	717,355	
	1900-1910	717,658	
	1911-1920	717,659	
	1926-1927	779,182/1	
	1928	779,182/2	
	1929	779,182/3	

Jocotenango
  Jocotenango (c/p)

Expedientes Matrimoniales

	1881-1899	717,660/1	
	1904-1918	717,660/2	

Location/ Document Type	Years	Roll No.	Comments
Pastores _Pastores_ (c/p)			
Expedientes Matrimoniales			
	1881–1889	717,666/1	
	1890–1899	717,666/2	
	1900–1909	717,667	Poor focus
	1910–1912	717,668	Indexed
	1913–1920	717,669	Records for 1917 poorly focused Indexed
	1921–1928	779,595	Indexed
	1928–1930	779,596/1-2	Indexed
San Antonio Aguas Calientes _San Antonio Aguas Calientes_ (c/p)			
Expedientes Matrimoniales			
	1879–1884	717,377	
	1885–1889	717,378	
	1890–1892	717,379	
	1893–1895	717,380	
	1896–1900, 1906	717,381	Disordered
	1899–1903	717,382	Disordered
	1904–1909	717,383	
	1910–1911	717,384	
	1912–1915	717,385	
	1916–1920	717,386	
	1923	778,716/1	
	1924	778,716/2	
	1925	778,716/3	

Location/ Document Type	Years	Roll No.	Comments
	1926	778,716/4	
	1927	778,716/5	
	1928	778,717/1-2	
	1929	778,717/3	
	1930	778,717/4	

San Andrés Ceballos (a)

Expedientes Matrimoniales

	1881-1886, 1888-1904	717,501	
	1905-1920	717,502	

San Bartolomé Milpas Altas
  San Bartolomé Milpas Altas (c/p)

Expedientes Matrimoniales

	1880-1889	717,663	
	1890-1898	717,664	
	1901-1920	717,665	
	1921	779,594/1	
	1923-1923	779,594/2	
	1930	779,594/3	

San Lucas Sacatepéquez
  San Lucas Sacatepéquez (c/p)

Actas Matrimoniales

	1880,1885, 1890,1912, 1916,1924, 1943	717,742/4	ODT/OL

Location/ Document Type	Years	Roll No.	Comments

San Miguel Dueñas
San Miguel Dueñas (c/p)

Expedientes Matrimoniales

	Years	Roll No.	Comments
	1880-1885	716,857	
	1885-1891	716,858	
	1892-1903	716,859	
	1903-1910	716,860	
	1910-1914	716,861	
	1914-1920	717,175	
	1920	717,176	
	1921	779,183/1	
	1922	779,183/2	
	1922	779,184/2	ODT/OL
	1923	779,183/3	
	1924	779,183/4	
	1925-1926	779,183/5	

Santa Catarina Barahona
Santa Catarina Barahona (c/v)

Expedientes Matrimoniales

	Years	Roll No.	Comments
	1380-1889	717,503	
	1890-1896, 1898-1899	717,504	
	1900-1904, 1907, 1909-1913	717,505	
	1913-1920	717,506	

Location/ Document Type	Years	Roll No.	Comments
Santa Lucía Milpas Altas Santa Lucía Milpas Altas (c/p)			
Expedientes Matrimoniales			
	1881-1920	717,601/1-2	
Santa María de Jesús Santa María de Jesús (c/p)			
Expedientes Matrimoniales			
	1881-1887	717,177	
	1887-1892	717,178	
	1892-1894	717,179	
	1894-1907	717,180	
	1907-1916	717,181	Disordered
	1916-1921	717,182	Disordered
	1921-1924	778,705/1	
	1925-1927	778,706/1-2	
	1926-1927	778,706/3	
	1929	778,707/1	
	1930	778,707/2	
Santiago Sacatepéquez Santa Maria Cauqué (cas)			
Expedientes Matrimoniales			
	1878-1901	716,855	
	1902-1920	716,856	
Santiago Sacatepéquez (c/p)			
Actas Matrimoniales			
	1885-1886	717,670/1	

Location/ Document Type	Years	Roll No.	Comments
Expedientes Matrimoniales			
	1877-1884	717,670/2	
	1880-1920	717,677	Intermittent years Includes one case dated 1932
	1885-1886	717,670/3	
	1887-1889	717,671/1-2	
	1890-1894	717,671/3	
	1896-1899	717,672/1	
	1900-1904, 1906,1908, 1913-1915	717,672/2	
Sumpango Sumpango (c/p)			
Actas Matrimoniales			
	1880-1889	717,188	ODT/OL
	1892-1900	717,190	ODT/OL
Expedientes Matrimoniales			
	1880-1889	717,188	ODT/OL
	1889-1892	717,189	
	1892-1900	717,190	ODT/OL
	1893-1901	717,191	
	1901-1903	717,192	
	1903-1908	717,193	
	1908-1914	717,194	
	1914-1915	717,195	
	1915-1920	717,196	
	1921	778,708/1	
	1922	778,708/2	
	1923	778,709/1-2	

Location/ Document Type	Years	Roll No.	Comments
	1924–1925	778,709/3	
	1926	778,710/1	
	1927	778,710/2	
	1928	778,711/1-2	
	1929	778,711/3	
	1930	778,712/1-2	

San Marcos
  Comitancillo
    <u>Comitancillo</u> (c/p)

Expedientes Matrimoniales

	Years	Roll No.	Comments
	1884–1886	717,064	
	1886–1890	717,065	
	1891–1893	717,066	
	1893,1895	717,067	
	1896–1897	717,068	
	1897–1898, 1900–1902	717,069	
	1906–1908	717,070	
	1909–1912	717,071	ODT/OL
	1915	717,072	
	1916–1918	717,073	ODT/OL
	1916–1920	717,074	ODT/OL
	1918	717,074	ODT/OL
	1921	778,468/1	
	1922	778,468/2	
	1923	778,468/3	
	1924	778,468/4	
	1925	778,469/1-2	
	1926	778,469/3	

Location/ Document Type	Years	Roll No.	Comments
	1927	778,469/4	
	1928-1929	778,469/5	
	1929	755,749	

El Rodeo
El Rodeo (c/p)

Expedientes Matrimoniales

	1879-1889	714,771/1	
	1890-1899	714,771/2	
	1900-1909	714,796	
	1910-1920	714,797	
	1921-1923	776,319/1	
	1924-1926	776,319/2	
	1926-1927	776,320/1-**3**	
	1928	776,320/4	
	1929	776,320/5	

El Tumbador
El Tumbador (c/p)

Expedientes Matrimoniales

	1883-1895	715,215	
	1895-1899	715,216	
	1921	776,321/1	
	1922	776,321/2	
	1923	776,321/3	
	1924	776,321/4	
	1925	776,321/5	
	1926	776,321/6	
	1927	776,322/1-2	
	1928	776,322/3	

Location/ Document Type	Years	Roll No.	Comments
	1929	776,322/4	
	1930	776,322/5	

Esquipulas Palo Gordo
  Esquipulas Palo Gordo (c/p)

Expedientes Matrimoniales

	1881-1892	715,221	
	1892-1899	715,222	
	1900-1910	715,223	
	1910-1919	715,224	

San Antonio Sacatepéquez
  San Antonio Sacatepéquez (c/p)

Expedientes Matrimoniales

	1898	714,648/1	
	1898-1899	714,648/2	
	1900-1902	714,649	
	1902-1903, 1905-1907	714,650	
	1907-1909	714,651	
	1910-1911	714,652	
	1911-1914	714,653	
	1914-1919	714,654	
	1919	714,655	
	1920	714,656	
	1921	776,323/1	
	1922	776,323/2	
	1923	776,323/3	
	1924	776,323/4	
	1925	776,324/1-2	
	1926	776,324/3	

Location/ Document Type	Years	Roll No.	Comments
	1927	776,324/4	
	1928	776,324/5	
	1929	776,325/1-2	
	1930	776,325/3	

San Cristóbal Cucho
  San Cristóbal Cucho (c/p)

Expedientes Matrimoniales

	Years	Roll No.	
	1882-1888	715,225	
	1888-1892, 1900-1909	715,226	
	1891-1899	716,905	
	1900-1909	716,906	
	1910-1920	716,907	
	1922	778,466/1	
	1923	778,466/2	
	1924	778,466/3	
	1925	778,466/4	
	1926-1930	778,467/1-2	
	1927	778,467/3	
	1928	778,467/4	
	1929	778,467/5	
	1930	778,467/6	

San Marcos
  San Marcos (c/cd)

Expedientes Matrimoniales

	Years	Roll No.	
	1921-1926	778,464	
	1927-1930	778,465	

Location/ Document Type	Years	Roll No.	Comments
San Pedro Sacatepéquez San Pedro Sacatepéquez (c/cd)			
Expedientes Matrimoniales			
	1877-1881	714,657	
	1882, 1884-1891, 1893-1896, 1898-1902	715,219	
	1882-1883	714,659	
	1883, 1890-1891	714,660	
	1884, 1895-1896	716,837	
	1884-1885	716,836	
	1885-1886	716,835	
	1886-1887	714,665	
	1887-1888	714,664	
	1888-1889	714,663	
	1889,1899	714,662	
	1889-1890, 1915	714,661	
	1891-1892, 1896	716,841	
	1892-1893	716,840	
	1893-1894	716,839	
	1894-1895	716,838	
	1896-1899	716,842	
	1899-1900	716,843	
	1900-1902	716,844	
	1902-1904	716,845	
	1902-1913, 1915-1919	715,220	

Location/ Document Type	Years	Roll No.	Comments
	1904-1905	716,846	
	1905-1906	716,847	
	1906-1907	716,848	
	1907-1908	716,849	
	1908-1909	716,850	
	1909-1910	716,851	
	1910	716,852	

San Rafael Pie de la Cuesta
  San Rafael Pie de la Cuesta (c/p)

Expedientes Matrimoniales

	Years	Roll No.	Comments
	1880-1907	715,217	Intermittent years Document damage
	1907-1909, 1911-1917, 1919-1920	715,218/1-2	

Tejutla
  Tejutla (c/v)

Expedientes Matrimoniales

	Years	Roll No.	Comments
	1882-1884, 1887	716,908	
	1887-1889	716,909	Document damage
	1891	716,910/1/1	
	1893	716,911	
	1893-1896	716,912	
	1898-1901	717,059	ODT/OL
	1910-1905	717,060	
	1906-1912	717,061	
	1913-1916	717,062	

Location/ Document Type	Years	Roll No.	Comments

Santa Rosa
  Barberena
    Barberena (c/p)			

Expedientes Matrimoniales			
	1895	748,059/3	ODT/OL
	1905	738,156/1	
	1912-1913	738,156/2	
	1914	738,156/3	
	1915	738,157/1	
	1916	738,157/2	
	1917	738,158/1	
	1918	738,158/2	
	1919	738,159	
Cuilapa Cuilapa (c/cd)			
Actas Matrimoniales			
	1895-1897	738,315	ODT/OL
Expedientes Matrimoniales			
	1880, 1882-1884	738,039/1-2	
	1883	748,057/2	ODT/OL
	1886	748,057/5	ODT/OL
	1886-1889	738,039/3	
	1887	748,057/6	ODT/OL
	1891	748,058/3	ODT/OL
	1891-1896, 1899	738,040	Disordered
	1892	748,058/4	
	1893	748,059/1	ODT/OL

Location/ Document Type	Years	Roll No.	Comments
	1895	748,059/3	ODT/OL
	1896	738,041	
	1896	748,059/4	ODT/OL
	1897	738,315/1/2	
	1897	748,059/5	Document damage ODT/OL
	1898	738,316	
	1900	748,060/3	Document damage ODT/OL
	1900-1904	738,043	
	1904	738,044	
	1904-1907	760,381/1	
	1905	738,042	
	1905	748,061/2	ODT/OL
	1907	760,381/2	
	1908-1920	738,045	
	1920-1922	738,046	Disordered
	1922	738,047	

Guazacapán
  Guazacapán (c/v)

Expedientes Matrimoniales

	Years	Roll No.	Comments
	1868	738,150/1	
	1885	738,150/2	
	1886	738,150/3	
	1887	738,150/4	
	1888	738,150/5	
	1889	738,150/6	
	1890	738,150/7	
	1891	738,150/8	
	1892	738,150/9	

Location/ Document Type	Years	Roll No.	Comments
	1893	738,150/10	
	1894	738,151/1	
	1896	738,151/2	
	1897	738,151/3	
	1898	738,151/4	
	1899	738,151/5	
	1900	738,152/1	
	1901	738,152/2	
	1902	738,152/3	
	1903	738,152/4	
	1904	738,153/1	
	1905	738,153/2	
	1906	738,153/3	
	1907	738,153/4	
	1908	738,153/5	
	1909	738,153/6	
	1910	738,154/1	Poor focus
	1911–1913	738,154/2	
	1914–1916	738,154/3	
	1917–1919	738,155/1	
	1920–1921	738,155/2	
	1923	738,155/3	
	1923, 1925–1930	775,925	
	1925	738,155/4	

Nueva Santa Rosa
  Nueva Santa Rosa (c/p)

Expedientes Matrimoniales

	Years	Roll No.	Comments
	1915–1917	738,317/1	Indexed for 1917 Document damage

Location/ Document Type	Years	Roll No.	Comments
	1918	738,318	Indexed Microfilmer's location (Cuilapa) is in error
	1918	738,319	Microfilmer's location (Cuilapa) is in error
	1919	738,315/2-3	Indexed Document damage
	1920	738,320/1-2	Microfilmer's location (Cuilapa) is in error Indexed

Santa Rosa de Lima
    Santa Rosa de Lima (c/p)

Expedientes Matrimoniales

	Years	Roll No.	
	1885	738,077/1	
	1886	738,077/2	
	1887	738,078/1-2	
	1888	738,079/1-2	
	1889	738,079/3	
	1890	738,080/1-2	
	1891	738,081	
	1892	738,082/1-2	
	1893	738,083/1-2	
	1894	738,084/1-2	
	1895	738,085	
	1896	738,086	
	1897	738,087	
	1898	738,088	
	1899	738,089/1-2	
	1900	738,090	
	1900	738,091	
	1901	738,092	
	1901	738,093	

Location/ Document Type	Years	Roll No.	Comments
	1902	738,094	
	1902	738,095	
	1903	714,024	Document damage
	1905	714,025	
	1905	714,026	
	1906	714,027	
	1907	714,028	
	1907	714,029	
	1908	714,030	
	1908	714,031	
	1909	714,032	
	1910	714,033	
	1910	714,034	Document damage
	1911	714,035	
	1912	714,036/1-2	
	1913	714,037	
	1914-1915	714,038	Document damage
	1915	714,039	
	1915	714,040	
	1916	714,041/1-2	
	1917	714,042/1-2	
	1921-1923	775,926	
	1923	775,927/1	
	1924	775,927/2	Document damage
	1925	775,927/3	
	1925	776,030/1	
	1926	776,030/2	
	1927	776,030/3	
	1927	776,031/1	

Location/ Document Type	Years	Roll No.	Comments
	1928	776,031/2	
	1929	776,031/3	
	1929-1930	776,032	

Taxisco
  Taxisco (c/p)

Expedientes Matrimoniales

	1884,1889 1898,1903, 1910-1912, 1915-1919	738,037	Disordered Document damage
	1918-1921	738,038	
	1920	738,155/5	

Sololá
  Santa Catarina Ixtahuacán
    Santa Catarina Ixtahuacán (c/p)

Actas Matrimoniales

	1877-1886	756,533/1	

Expedientes Matrimoniales

	1881	756,533/2	Indexed on 756,533/1
	1882	756,534/1	
	1883	756,534/2	
	1884	756,534/3	
	1885	756,534/4	
	1909	756,534/5	
	1911	756,535/1-2	
	1912-1913	756,536	
	1914	756,539/1-2	
	1915	756,540/1-2	
	1916	756,541	

Location/ Document Type	Years	Roll No.	Comments
	1917	756,542/1	
	1918	756,542/2	
	1919	756,542/3	
	1920	756,542/4	
	1922-1923	779,663/1	
	1924	779,663/2	
	1925	779,664/1	
	1929	779,664/2	

Santiago Atitlán
  Santiago Atitlán (c/p)

Expedientes Matrimoniales

	Years	Roll No.	Comments
	1881-1887	756,034	
	1887-1891	756,035	
	1891-1896	754,793/1	
	1896-1903	754,794/1	
	1903-1909, 1912, 1915-1920	754,795	
	1921	782,758/1	
	1922	782,758/2	
	1923	782,758/3	
	1924	782,758/4	
	1925	782,758/5	
	1926	782,758/6	
	1927	782,758/7	Document damage
	1928	782,759/1	
	1929	782,759/2	
	1930	782,759/3	

Location/ Document Type	Years	Roll No.	Comments
Sololá Sololá (c/cd)			
Causas Matrimoniales			
	1810	745,076/11	Legajo 204
Expedientes Matrimoniales			
	1915	738,331	ODT/OL
	1921-1923	779,716/1-2	

Suchitepéquez
  Chicacao
    Chicacao (c/p)			

Expedientes Matrimoniales			
	1900-1914	714,043	Indexed ODT/OL
	1914-1920	714,044	Indexed ODT/OL
Patulul Patulul (c/p)			
Actas Matrimoniales			
	1905	738,334/1	ODT/OL
	1914	738,331	ODT/OL
Expedientes Matrimoniales			
	1903	738,335	ODT/OL
	1910-1918	738,164	
	1915	738,331	ODT/OL
	1915	738,332/1	ODT/OL
	1915	738,332/2	ODT/OL
	1916	738,333/1	ODT/OL

Location/ Document Type	Years	Roll No.	Comments
Pueblo Nuevo Pueblo Nuevo (c/p)			
Expedientes Matrimoniales			
	1883,1900, 1907,1912, 1914,1919, 1920	714,072	
Samayac Samayac (c/v)			
Expedientes Matrimoniales			
	1921	776,051/1	
	1922	776,051/2	
	1923	776,051/3	
	1924	776,051/4	
	1925	776,051/5	
	1926	776,051/6	
	1927	776,051/7	
	1928	776,051/8	
	1929	776,051/9	
	1930	776,051/10	
San Bernardino San Bernardino (c/p)			
Expedientes Matrimoniales			
	1881-1898, 1904	714,073	Intermittent years Disordered Document damage
	1904,1906, 1908-1912, 1915,1917	714,074	Disordered
	1917-1919	714,075	

Location/ Document Type	Years	Roll No.	Comments
Santo Domingo Suchitepéquez Santo Domingo Suchitepéquez (c/p)			
Expedientes Matrimoniales			
	1885-1889	738,336	
	1890-1891	713,819	
	1891-1893	713,712	Disordered
	1892-1895	713,713	
	1897-1899	713,714	Document damage
	1901-1905	713,715	
	1905-1908	713,716	
	1908-1909	713,717	
	1910-1911	713,718	Document damage
	1911-1917	713,719	Document damage
	1917-1919	713,720	
	1920	713,721	
	1921	776,049/1	
	1922	776,049/2	
	1923	776,049/3	
	1924	776,049/4	
	1925	776,050/1-2	
	1926	776,050/3	
	1927	776,050/4	
	1928	776,050/5	
Totonicapán San Andrés Xecul San Andrés Xecul (c/p)			
Expedientes Matrimoniales			
	1881-1882	714,084/1	
	1883-1884	714,084/2	

Location/ Document Type	Years	Roll No.	Comments
	1885-1887	714,085/1	
	1888-1889	714,085/2	
	1890, 1892-1893	714,045	
	1893-1895	714,046	
	1895-1896	739,849	
	1897-1900	739,850	
	1900-1910	739,851	
	1910-1913	759,852	
	1913-1920	739,853	
	1921	776,064/1	
	1922	776,064/2	
	1923	776,064/3	
	1924	776,064/4	
	1926	776,064/5	
	1927	776,064/6	
	1928	776,048/1	
	1929	776,048/2	
	1930	776,048/3	

San Francisco el Alto
San Francisco el Alto (c/p)

Expedientes Matrimoniales

	Years	Roll No.	Comments
	1911-1916, 1918-1919	714,142	
	1920	776,062/1	
	1921	776,062/2	
	1922	776,062/3	
	1924	776,062/4	
	1925	776,062/5	
	1926	776,062/6	

Location/ Document Type	Years	Roll No.	Comments
	1927	776,062/7-8	
	1928	776,062/9	
	1929	776,063/1	Includes one case dated 1943
	1930	776,063/2	

Totonicapán
  Totonicapán (c/cd)

Expedientes Matrimoniales

	Years	Roll No.	Comments
	1885	714,086/1-2	
	1888	714,086/3	
	1889	714,086/4-5	
	1891	714,088	
	1891	714,089	
	1891	714,087	
	1892	714,090	
	1892	714,091	Includes one case dated 1902 Document damage
	1892	714,092	
	1892	714,093	
	1893	714,094	
	1893	714,095	Poor focus
	1893	714,096	
	1893-1894	714,094	
	1894	714,097	
	1894	714,098	
	1894	714,099	
	1894	714,100	
	1895	714,101	
	1895	714,102	

Location/ Document Type	Years	Roll No.	Comments
	1895	714,103	
	1895-1896	739,871	
	1896	739,872	
	1896	739,873	
	1897	739,874	
	1897	739,875	
	1898	739,876	
	1898	739,877	
	1899	739,878	
	1899	739,880	
	1900	739,881	
	1900	714,000	
	1900	714,001	
	1901	714,002	Document damage
	1901	714,003	
	1901	714,004	
	1902	714,005	
	1902	714,006	
	1903	714,007	
	1903	714,008	
	1904	714,009	
	1904	714,010	
	1904	714,011	
	1905	714,012/1-2	Document damage
	1905	714,013	
	1906	714,014	
	1906	714,015	
	1906	714,016	
	1907	714,017	

Location/ Document Type	Years	Roll No.	Comments
	1907	714,018	
	1908	714,019	
	1908	714,020	
	1908	714,021	
	1909	714,022	
	1909	714,023	
	1909	714,749	
	1910	714,750	
	1910	714,751	
	1910	714,752	
	1911	714,753/1-2	
	1911-1912	714,754	
	1913	714,755	
	1913	714,756	
	1913	714,757	
	1914	714,758	
	1914	714,759	
	1914	714,760	
	1915	714,761	
	1915-1916	714,762	
	1916	714,763	
	1917	714,764	
	1918	714,765/1-2	
	1919	714,766	
	1919	714,767	
	1920	714,768	
	1920	714,769	
	1921	776,033	
	1921	776,034	

Location/ Document Type	Years	Roll No.	Comments
	1922	776,035	
	1922	776,036	
	1922	776,037	
	1923	776,038	
	1923	776,039	
	1923	776,040	
	1924	776,041	
	1924	776,042	
	1925	776,043	
	1925	776,044	
	1925	776,045	
	1926	776,046	
	1926	776,047	

Zacapa
  Gualán
    Azacualpa (cas)

Expedientes Matrimoniales

	Years	Roll No.	Comments
	1898	748,060/1	
	1899	748,060/2	
	1900	748,060/3	Document damage ODT/OL
	1901	748,060/4	
	1902	748,060/5	
	1930	779,661	

  Gualán (c/v)

Expedientes Matrimoniales

	Years	Roll No.	Comments
	1881	751,734/1	
	1882	751,734/2	
	1883	751,734/3	

Location/ Document Type	Years	Roll No.	Comments
	1885	751,735/1	
	1886	751,735/2	
	1887	751,735/3	
	1888	751,735/4	
	1889	751,736/1-2	
	1890	751,736/3	
	1893	751,737/1	
	1894	751,737/2	
	1895	751,737/3	
	1896	751,737/4	
	1897	751,737/5-6	
	1898	751,737/7	
	1899	751,738/1	
	1900	751,738/2	
	1901	751,739/1	
	1902	751,739/2-3	
	1903	751,740/1	
	1904	751,740/2	
	1905	751,740/3-4	
	1906	751,741/1	
	1907	751,741/2	
	1908	751,741/3	
	1909	751,741/4-5	
	1910	751,742/1	
	1911	751,742/2	
	1912	751,743/1-2	
	1913	751,743/3	
	1914	751,744/1-2	
	1915	751,745	

Location/ Document Type	Years	Roll No.	Comments
	1916	752,068/1-2	
	1917	752,068/3	
	1918	752,069	
	1919	752,070/1	
	1920	752,070/2	
	1921	779,184/1	ODT/OL
	1921-1922	779,184	
	1922	779,184/2	ODT/OL
	1923	779,185/1	
	1924	779,185/2	
	1924	779,186/1	
	1925	779,186/2	
	1925-1927	779,187	
	1927-1929	779,188	
	1930	779,189	

Río Hondo
  Río Hondo (c/p)

Expedientes Matrimoniales

	1921	779,184/1	ODT/OL

Usumatlán
  Usumatlán (c/p)

Expedientes Matrimoniales

	1890	714,770	
	1901	751,733/1	
	1902	751,733/2	
	1903	751,733/3	
	1904	751,733/4	
	1905	751,733/5	

Location/ Document Type	Years	Roll No.	Comments
	1906	751,733/6	
	1907	751,733/7	

Zacapa
  Zacapa (c/cd)

Expedientes Matrimoniales

	Years	Roll No.	Comments
	1880	751,611/1	
	1881	751,611/2	
	1882	751,611/3	
	1883	751,612/1	
	1884	751,612/2	
	1885	751,612/3	
	1886	751,612/4	
	1887	751,613	
	1888	751,614	
	1889	751,615/1	Document damage
	1890	751,615/2	Document damage
	1891	751,616	
	1892	751,617	
	1893	751,618	
	1894	751,619/1	
	1895	751,619/2	
	1896	751,620/1	
	1897	751,620/2	
	1898	751,620/3	
	1899	751,621/1	
	1900	751,621/2	
	1901	751,622	
	1902	751,623	Document damage
	1903	751,624/1	

Location/ Document Type	Years	Roll No.	Comments
	1904	751,624/2	
	1905	751,625/1	
	1906	751,625/2	
	1907	751,626	
	1908	751,627/1	
	1909	751,627/2	
	1910	751,628	
	1911	715,629	
	1912	751,630	
	1913	751,631/1-2	
	1914	751,632/1	
	1915	751,632/2	Indexed
	1916	751,633	
	1917	751,634/1	
	1917-1918	751,634/2	
	1919	751,635/1-2	
	1921	779,164	
	1921	779,165	
	1922	779,166/1-2	
	1923	779,167	
	1923	779,168	
	1924	779,169	
	1924	779,133	
	1925	779,134	
	1925	779,135	
	1926	779,136/1-2	
	1927	779,137/1-2	
	1928	779,172	

Location/ Document Type	Years	Roll No.	Comments
	1929	779,173	
	1930	779,174	

EL SALVADOR
nación

San Salvador
  San Salvador
    San Salvador (cap nl)

Expedientes Matrimoniales

	1809	741,896/10	Legajo 1072

HONDURAS
nación

Colón
    Trujillo (cap de dpto)

Expedientes Matrimoniales

	1803	744,864/1	ODT/OL Legajo 56

Comayagua
    Comayagua (cap de dpto)

Expedientes Matrimoniales

	1772	741,765/4	Legajo 323
	1782-1807	744,864/3	ODT/OL Legajo 371
	1787-1806	744,864/4	ODT/OL Legajo 386
	1795	744,864/5	Legajo 601

Location/ Document Type	Years	Roll No.	Comments

MEXICO
<u>nación</u>

Chiapas
  San Cristóbal las Casas
    <u>San Cristóbal las Casas</u>

Causas Matrimoniales

	1760	741,582/3/2	Legajo 142

NICARAGUA
<u>nación</u>

León
  León
    <u>León</u> (cap de dpto)

Autos de Disensos

	1791-1801	745,072/1	Legajo 450
	1801-1802	745,072/2	Legajo 451

Causas Matrimoniales

	1752	745,814/16	Legajo 5911
	1771	745,071/2	Legajo 117

PERU
<u>nación</u>

  <u>Lima</u> (cap nl)

Actas Matrimoniales

	1694	744,761/8	Document damage ODT/OL Legajo 4691

Location/ Document Type	Years	Roll No.	Comments

Current jurisdictions are unknown or
unavailable for the following areas

Location/ Document Type	Years	Roll No.	Comments
<u>Chalchuapa</u>			Gaz/no. Documents place near Azacualapa, aldea of Quezaltepeque, Chiquimula
Expedientes Matrimoniales			
	1907	748,061/4	
<u>Santa Catarina</u>			Gaz/various. Documents place near San Manuel Chaparrón, Jalapa
Expedientes Matrimoniales			
	1889-1890	751,636/5	
	1899	751,637/3	
	1900	751,637/4	
<u>Santo Domingo</u>			
Expedientes Matrimoniales			
	1885-1889	738,336	

INFORMACIÓN PERSONAL

Location/ Document Type	Years	Roll No.	Comments

GUATEMALA
nación

Capital

Absueltos

	Years	Roll No.	Comments
	1663	746,860/1	ODT/OL Legajo 4681

Calidades

	Years	Roll No.	Comments
	1577	746,864/1	Legajo 4782
	1580-1605	746,857/1	ODT/OL Disordered Legajo 4676
	1600,1615, 1621,1661 1694,1737	746,864/12	ODT/OL Legajo 5923
	1609	746,864/7	Legajo 5452
	1640-1688	746,860/1	ODT/OL Legajo 4681
	1651	746,864/17	Legajo 6071
	1724	746,860/3	ODT/OL Legajo 4682
	1737-1754	746,860/4	ODT/OL Legajo 4683
	1745-1772	746,861/2	ODT/OL Legajo 4685
	1746	745,423/5-6	Legajos 177-178
	1758	746,864/10	Legajo 5553
	1761,1771	745,423/10	Legajo 191
	1763-1769	745,423/12	Legajo 193
	1766	746,864/2	ODT/OL Legajo 4791
	1769	745,423/9	Legajo 190

Location/ Document Type	Years	Roll No.	Comments
	1770,1772	745,423/13	Legajo 194
	1773	745,423/14	Legajo 195
	1776–1778	746,862/1	ODT/OL Legajo 4692
	1777	746,864/3	Legajo 4796
	1782–1786	746,862/7	Legajo 4692
	1783	746,862/1	ODT/OL Legajo 4692
	1785	746,864/4	Legajo 4799
	1788	745,076/2	Legajo 12
	1789–1791	746,862/1	ODT/OL Legajo 4692
	1791	746,864/5	Legajo 4800
	1791–1797	746,862/2	ODT/OL Legajo 4693
	1798	746,863/1	ODT/OL Legajo 4694
	1798	746,864/8	Legajo 5517
	1801	746,864/6,18	Legajos 4802, 6083
	1802–1809, 1811–1812	746,863/2	ODT/OL Legajos 40596–40625
	1809	745,422/7	Legajo 26
	1811	745,422/8	Legajo 28
	1816–1818	745,422/9	Legajo 29
	1818	746,864/9	Legajo 5530
Comisiones			
	1675,1678	746,860/1	ODT/OL Legajo 4681
	1701	741,738	Indexed ODT/OL Legajo 1572

Location/ Document Type	Years	Roll No.	Comments
Hidalguías			
	1774	746,861/2	ODT/OL Legajo 4685
	1775	746,862/1	ODT/OL Legajo 4692
	1783-1792	746,847/2	ODT/OL Legajo 2614
	1789	746,862/1	ODT/OL Legajo 4692
Legitimidades			
	1600-1816	746,861/2	Intermittent years ODT/OL Legajo 4685
	1609,1706, 1772,1794	746,864/12	ODT/OL Legajo 5923
	1638	746,864/11	Legajo 5954
	1651	746,864/16	Legajo 6055
	1659	746,860/2	ODT/OL Legajo 4681
	1667-1680	746,860/1	ODT/OL Legajo 4681
	1718-1780	746,860/3	ODT/OL Legajo 4682
	1721-1738	746,862/2	ODT/OL Legajo 4693
	1754	746,862/1	ODT/OL Legajo 4692
	1754-1780	746,860/4	ODT/OL Legajo 4683
	1766	746,864/2	ODT/OL Legajo 4791
	1778	746,364/13	Legajo 6025
	1797	745,422/4	ODT/OL Legajo 12
	1800-1801	746,863/1	ODT/OL Legajo 4694

Location/ Document Type	Years	Roll No.	Comments
	1802	746,864/19	Legajo 6943
Mercedes y Nombramientos			
	1638-1730	746,843/3	Disordered ODT/OL Legajo 2358
	1645	746,756/28	Legajo 4581
	1668	746,756/13	Legajo 2318
	1675	746,860/1	ODT/OL Legajo 4681
	1701	741,738	Indexed ODT/OL Legajo 1572
	1767	746,755/19	Legajo 25
	1771-1789	746,842/1	Legajo 1754
	1776-1778	746,860/4	ODT/OL Legajo 4683
	1791-1800	746,852/4	Legajo 2649
	1800	746,756/9	ODT/OL Legajo 1943
	1809	746,861/2	ODT/OL Legajo 4685
Méritos y Servicios			
	1542-1604	746,842/5	Legajo 2326
	1548-1625	746,341/6	Legajo 1723
	1561-1564	746,854/3	Legajo 4672
	1564-1565	746,855/1-2	Legajo 4673
	1570-1572	746,855/3	Legajo 4674
	1574	744,761/5	Document damage ODT/OL Legajo 4675
	1574	746,856	Legajo 4675
	1580-1605	746,857/1	Disordered ODT/OL Legajo 4676

Location/ Document Type	Years	Roll No.	Comments
	1582	746,852/9	Legajo 2799
	1584–1598	746,858/1	Document damage ODT/OL Legajo 4677
	1602	746,852/12	Legajo 2808
	1603	746,842/4	Legajo 2313
	1605–1609	746,852/10	Legajo 2801
	1605–1638	746,843/1-2	Legajo 2327
	1607	746,755/33	Legajo 1514
	1607–1622	746,859/1-2	Legajo 4679
	1608	746,852/14	Legajo 2833
	1611	746,864/12	ODT/OL Legajo 5923
	1615	745,422/1	Legajo 1
	1620	745,423/30	Legajo 212
	1621	746,852/11	Legajo 2803
	1621	745,423/3	Legajo 160
	1622–1659	746,859/3	Legajo 4680
	1625–1772	746,841/7	Legajo 1724
	1638–1730	746,843/3	Legajo 2358
	1650–1689	746,860/1	ODT/OL Legajo 4681
	1657	746,841/1	Legajo 1111
	1664–1720	746,852/16	Legajo 2878
	1683	746,842/3	Legajo 2033
	1687	746,860/2	ODT/OL Legajo 4681
	1700	745,423/34	Legajo 295
	1712	744,578/2	Legajo 1
	1725	745,423/4	Legajo 169
	1727	746,852	Illegible Document damage

Location/ Document Type	Years	Roll No.	Comments
	1730-1780	746,860/4	ODT/OL Legajo 4683
	1738	746,841/3	Legajo 1481
	1738-1763	746,846	Legajo 2611
	1744	746,852/19	Legajo 2895
	1746,1803	746,861/2	ODT/OL Legajo 4685
	1749	746,852/17	Legajo 2879
	1753-1763	745,423/18	Legajo 199
	1756-1758	745,423/7	Disordered Legajo 184
	1759-1783	745,423/19	Legajo 200
	1763	745,422/2	Legajo 6
	1770	746,852/13	Legajo 2817
	1771-1773	745,423/11	Legajo 192
	1773	746,844/1	Legajo 2329
	1774	745,423/15,29	Legajos 196, 211
	1774	746,852/2	Legajo 2647
	1774-1798	745,423/22	Legajo 203
	1775-1776	745,423/16	Legajo 197
	1776-1791	745,423/20	Legajo 201
	1776-1796	746,852/8	Legajo 2759
	1776-1803	745,422/5	Legajo 23
	1777	746,841/5	Legajo 1582
	1777-1778	745,423/17	Legajo 198
	1779	745,423/1,32	Legajos 41, 226
	1780	746,861/1	Legajo 4684
	1781	746,862/1	ODT/OL Legajo 4692
	1782	746,847/2	ODT/OL Legajo 2614
	1783	745,422/6	Legajo 24

Location/ Document Type	Years	Roll No.	Comments
	1785	746,852/5	Legajo 2654
	1785-1792	745,423/21	Legajo 202
	1789	745,423/31	Legajo 217
	1792	745,422/4	ODT/OL Legajo 12
	1792	746,852/3,7	Legajos 2648, 2758
	1793	746,848/1	Legajo 2615
	1793-1794	745,423/23	Legajo 204
	1795	744,579/1	Legajo 203
	1795	746,852/6,15	Legajos 2755, 2863
	1797	745,423/33	Legajo 241
	1797	746,848/2-3	Legajo 2616
	1800-1801	744,769	ODT/OL Legajo 21
	1800-1820	746,851	ODT/OL Legajo 2620
	1801	745,423/2	Legajo 43
	1801-1804	746,849/1	Legajo 2617
	1801-1808	745,423/25	Disordered Legajo 206
	1801-1808	746,845	Legajo 2331
	1803	745,423/24	Legajo 205
	1803-1818	745,423/28	Disordered Legajo 208
	1804-1817	745,423/26	Legajo 207
	1805-1808	746,849/2	Legajo 2618
	1806	745,423/35	Legajo 743
	1808	746,850/1	Legajo 2619
	1808-1814	746,850/2	ODT/OL Legajos 2610-2620
	1809	745,423/27	Legajo 208
	1810	746,863/2	ODT/OL Legajos 40596-40625

Location/ Document Type	Years	Roll No.	Comments
	1810–1818	746,842/2	Legajo 1767
	1815?	746,852/1	Illegible Legajo 2640
	1823	746,841/2,4	Legajos 1277, 1493
Pensiones			
	1636	746,755/35	Legajo 1516
	1636	746,756/25	Legajo 4579
	1637	746,756/26	Legajo 4579
	1644	746,755/36	Legajo 1517
	1656	746,755/26	Legajo 825
	1656	746,756/14	Legajo 2318
	1661	746,755/37	Legajo 1519
	1664	746,756/18,21	Legajos 2726, 4569
	1666	746,756/23	Legajo 4569
	1667	746,756/15	ODT/OL Legajo 2318
	1672	746,755/38	Legajo 1520
	1674	746,756/31	Legajo 4583
	1675	746,756/11	Legajo 2162
	1676	746,756/33	Legajo 4583
	1676	746,756/34	Legajo 4584
	1677	746,802/4	Legajo 4587
	1678	746,756/3	Legajo 1571
	1678	746,802/9	Legajo 4591
	1680	746,756/35	Legajo 4584
	1683	746,802/5	Legajo 4587
	1684	746,755/22	Legajo 256
	1685	746,756/37	Legajo 4585
	1686	746,802/6	Legajo 4589
	1687	746,755/40	Legajo 1522

Location/ Document Type	Years	Roll No.	Comments
	1687	746,756/38	Legajo 4585
	1690	746,802/1	Legajo 4586
	1691	746,756/40	Legajo 4586
	1692	746,756/39	Legajo 4586
	1692	746,802/2	Legajo 4586
	1693	746,802/3,7	Legajos 4586, 4540
	1694	746,756/12	Legajo 2163
	1694	746,802/8,10	Legajos 4590-4591
	1700	746,802/11	Legajo 4594
	1701	741,738	Indexed ODT/OL Legajo 1572
	1704	746,802/13	Legajo 4596
	1706	746,802/26	Legajo 4789
	1707	746,802/12,14	Legajos 4596-4597
	1707	746,802/17,18	Legajos 4599,4601
	1709	746,755/41	Legajo 1709
	1709	746,756/5	Legajo 1581
	1710	746,802/15	Legajo 4597
	1712	746,756/4	Legajo 1579
	1713?	746,802/19	Date omitted Microfilmer dates 1713
	1714	746,755/7	Legajo 23
	1714	746,756/6	Legajo 1582
	1717	746,755/42	Legajo 1526
	1717	746,802/16	Legajo 4598
	1718	746,802/20	Legajo 4604
	1723	746,802/21	Legajo 4604
	1726	746,802/22	Legajo 4606
	1728?	746,802	Document damage Legajo 4606

Location/ Document Type	Years	Roll No.	Comments
	1729?	746,802	Document damage Legajo 4607
	1734	746,755/8	Legajo 23
	1735	746,802/25	Legajo 4611
	1736	746,756/10	Legajo 1948
	1737	747,152/1	ODT/OL Legajo 5
	1754	746,755/43	Legajo 1528
	1764	746,755/31	Legajo 1282
	1771	746,756/1	Legajo 1529
	1776	746,755/18	Legajo 27
	1777	746,755/12	Legajo 25
	1778	746,755/9	Legajo 24
	1786	746,756/7	Legajo 1794
	1789	746,755/10	Legajo 24
	1792	746,755/11	Legajo 24
	1795	746,755/15	Legajo 25
	1796	746,755/13	Legajo 25
	1798	746,755/16	Legajo 25
	1800	746,756/9	ODT/OL Legajo 1943
	1800	746,756/17	Legajo 2535
	1801	746,755/23	Legajo 259
	1814	746,851	ODT/OL Legajo 2620
	1815	746,756/8	Legajo 1791
	1815-1821	746,756/2	Legajo 1543
Probanzas de Mayorazgo			
	1624	744,398/3	ODT/OL Legajo 88

Location/ Document Type	Years	Roll No.	Comments
Probanzas de Pobreza			
	1571	744,580/4	ODT/OL Legajo 4674
	1684	746,755/24	Legajo 557
	1759	746,844/2	Legajo 2330
	1798	746,862/2	ODT/OL Legajo 4693
	1814-1816	746,851/1	ODT/OL Legajo 2620
Títulos de Encomienda			
	1637	746,756/27	Legajo 4579
	1638-1730	746,843/3	ODT/OL Legajo 2358
	1640	746,756/19	Legajo 4568
	1643	746,756/20	Legajo 4568
	1664	746,756/22	Legajo 4509
	1667	746,756/15	ODT/OL Legajo 2318
	1667	746,756/16	Legajo 2501
	1668	746,755/1	Legajo 1
	1681	746,756/24	Legajo 4569
	1691	746,755/14	ODT/OL Legajo 25
	1698	746,755/27	Legajo 936
	1700	746,755/2	ODT/OL Legajo 3
	1750	746,755/30	ODT/OL Legajo 1050

Location/ Document Type	Years	Roll No.	Comments
Alta Verapaz San Cristóbal Verapaz (c/v)			
Méritos y Servicios			
	1792	745,422/3	ODT/OL Legajo 9

Chimaltenango
  Chimaltenango
    Chimaltenango (c/cd)			

Mercedes y Nombramientos			
	1797	745,418/1	ODT/OL Legajos 164-166

Huehuetenango
  Huehuetenango
    Huehuetenango (c/cd)			

Méritos y Servicios			
	1791	746,852/20	Legajo 2908
	1813	746,852/22	Legajo 2928

Quezaltenango
  Quezaltenango
    Quezaltenango (c/cd)			

Méritos y Servicios			
	1814-1815	746,851/1	ODT/OL Legajo 2620

Sacatepéquez
  Antigua Guatemala
    Antigua Guatemala (c/p)			

Calidades			
	1818	747,296/15	ODT/OL

Location/ Document Type	Years	Roll No.	Comments
Méritos y Servicios			
	1807	746,852/24	Legajo 2959
	1810	746,853	Legajo 4671
Probanzas de Mayorazgo			
	1857–1860	745,423/36	Legajo 859

San Marcos
  Comitancillo
    <u>Comitancillo</u> (c/p)

Méritos y Servicios			
	1801	746,852/21	Legajo 2919

Suchitepéquez
  Santo Domingo Suchitepéquez
    <u>Santo Domingo Suchitepéquez</u> (c/p)

Comisiones			
	1752	744,763/1	Legajo 182
Méritos y Servicios			
	1775	746,847/1	Legajo 2613

<u>COSTA RICA</u>
nación

San José
  <u>San José</u> (cap nl)

Pensiones			
	1639–1678	741,740	Document damage Legajo 4580

Location/ Document Type	Years	Roll No.	Comments

ECUADOR
nación

Quito (cap nl)

Comisiones

	1755-1757	744,763/2	Legajo 210

EL SALVADOR
nación

El Salvador
  San Salvador
    San Salvador (cap nl)

Comisiones

	1700	741,875/1	Indexed Legajo 1571
	1764	741,894/2	ODT/OL Legajo 188
	1774-1779	741,894/10	ODT/OL Legajo 195

Hidalguías

	1574?	744,761/5	Document damage ODT/OL Legajo 4675

Méritos y Servicios

	1558	746,854/2	Legajo 4671
	1587	741,896/6	Legajo 4677
	1588	741,896/7	Legajo 4677
	1590	741,896/5	Legajo 2326
	1632	741,871/1	ODT/OL Legajo 1557
	1689	741,896/8	Legajo 4651

Location/ Document Type	Years	Roll No.	Comments
	1700	741,875/2	Legajo 1571
	1716	741,896/9	Legajo 4682
	1760	741,894/1	Legajo 185
	1760	745,423/8	Legajo 185
	1765	741,894/2	ODT/OL Legajo 188
	1766	741,894/3	Legajo 188
	1767,1772	741,894/6	Legajo 192
	1768	741,894/7	Legajo 192
	1768	741,895/10	Legajo 197
	1768-1769	741,894/8	Legajo 194
	1769	741,894/4	Legajo 191
	1771	741,894/5	Legajo 192
	1771	741,896/3	Legajo 210
	1773-1774	741,894/9	Legajo 195
	1774	741,895/1	
	1774	741,894/10-13	ODT/OL Legajos 195, 198
	1775	741,895/3-4	Legajos 196, 197
	1776	741,895/5-9	Legajo 197
	1778	741,896/1	Legajo 199
	1779	741,896/2	Legajo 199
	1797	741,896/4	Legajo 1764

Pensiones

| | 1623 | 741,896/11 | Legajo 4568 |

Sonsonate
  Sonsonate
    Sonsonate (c/cd)

Calidades

| | 1769-1775 | 762,299/3 | Legajo 2612 |

Location/ Document Type	Years	Roll No.	Comments
Pensiones			
	1735	744,562/2	ODT/OL Legajo 4066

ESPAÑA
nación

Madrid

Comisiones			
	1746	744,763/5	Legajo 1767
Pensiones			
	1653	744,763/7	Legajo 4580
	1658	744,763/8	Legajo 4580
	1665-1685	744,763/6	Intermittent years Legajo 4569
	1687	744,763/9	Legajo 4585
	1705-1709	744,763/10	Legajo 4599
	1727	744,763/11	Legajo 4607

HONDURAS
nación

Colón
    Trujillo (cap de dpto)

Méritos y Servicios			
	1803	744,864/1	ODT/OL Legajo 56

Comayagua
    Comayagua (cap de dpto)

Calidades			
	1765-1768	762,299/2	Legajo 2612

Location/Document Type	Years	Roll No.	Comments
	1782-1807	744,864/3	ODT/OL Legajo 371
Comisiones			
	1761	744,398/5	ODT/OL Legajo 193
	1774	744,398/6	ODT/OL Legajo 196
Legitimidades			
	1665-1811	744,399	Legajo 215
Méritos y Servicios			
	1556-1557	746,854/1	Legajo 4671
	1624	744,398/4	ODT/OL Legajo 192
	1761	744,398/5	ODT/OL Legajo 196
	1765	762,299/1	Legajo 2612
	1774	741,895/2	Legajo 196
	1782-1807	744,864/3	ODT/OL Legajo 371
	1787-1806	744,864/4	ODT/OL Legajo 386

Cortes
Omoa (c mpl)

Méritos y Servicios			
	1794	744,398/1	ODT/OL Legajo 63
Pensiones			
	1794	744,398/1	ODT/OL Legajo 63

Location/ Document Type	Years	Roll No.	Comments
MEXICO nación			

Campeche
  Campeche
    Campeche (cap del e)			

Calidades			
	1584	744,761/4	Incomplete Document damage Legajo 4618
Pensiones			
	1600?	744,761/6	Document damage Legajo 4678

Chiapas
  San Cristóbal las Casas
    San Cristóbal las Casas			

Hidalguías			
	1608	744,562/3	ODT/OL Legajo 4679
Legitimidades			
	1676	744,580/10	Legajo 4681
Mercedes y Nombramientos			
	1784-1789	744,547/2	ODT/OL Legajo 273
Méritos y Servicios			
	1551	744,580/2	Legajo 4670
	1572-1578	744,579/3	ODT/OL Legajo 354
	1574	744,580/5	Legajo 4675
	1584-1598	746,858/1	Document damage ODT/OL Legajo 4677

Location/ Document Type	Years	Roll No.	Comments
	1587	744,580/6	Illegible Legajo 4675
	1590	744,580/8	Legajo 4677
	1600	746,858/2	ODT/OL Legajo 4678
	1602	744,562/3	ODT/OL Legajo 4679
	1602-1608	744,562/3	ODT/OL Legajo 4679
	1603	744,580/7	Legajo 4676
	1608	744,580/14	Legajo 6934
	1613	744,580/9	Legajo 4679
	1693	744,580/11	Legajo 4682
	1712	744,578/1	Legajo 1
	1741	744,580/1	Legajo 2566
	1772	744,580/12	Legajo 4683
	1782	744,579/2	Legajo 211
	1789	744,580/13	Legajo 4692
Pensiones			
	1574	744,579/3	Document damage ODT/OL Legajo 354
	1643	744,581/3	Incomplete Legajo 4568
	1679	744,581/2	Legajo 1521
	1685	744,581/1	Legajo 256
Probanzas de Mayorazgo			
	1555	744,580/3	Legajo 4671
Probanzas de Pobreza			
	1562	744,579/3	ODT/OL Legajo 354

Location/ Document Type	Years	Roll No.	Comments
Titulos de Encomienda			
	n.d.	744,579/3	ODT/OL Legajo 354

NICARAGUA
nación

León
  León
    León (cap dl)

	Years	Roll No.	Comments
Calidades			
	1729	745,814/8	ODT/OL Legajo 4691
	1756-1759	745,813/1	ODT/OL
	1771	745,814/9	ODT/OL Legajo 4691
Legitimidades			
	1724	745,814/10	Legajo 5923
	1790	745,814/11	Legajo 4797
Mercedes y Nombramientos			
	1596	745,814/3	Legajo 4677
Méritos y Servicios			
	1586	745,814/1	Document damage Legajo 4677
	1597	745,814/4	ODT/OL Legajo 4677
	1730	745,814/7	Legajo 4686
	1757-1758	745,813/1	ODT/OL
Pensiones			
	1659	745,814/15	Legajo 1582

Location/ Document Type	Years	Roll No.	Comments
	1691	745,814/13	Legajo 23
	1695	745,814/12	Legajo 23
	1792	745,814/14	Legajo 24
Probanzas de Mayorazgo			
	1585	745,814/2	Legajo 4677
	1597	745,814/4	ODT/OL Legajo 4677
	1599	745,814/5	Legajo 4678
	1605	745,814/6	Legajo 4678
Probanzas de Pobreza			
	1802	745,817/1	ODT/OL

PERU
nación

Lima (cap nl)

Méritos y Servicios

	1624	744,761/7-8	Document damage ODT/OL Legajo 4680

Pensiones

	1646	744,762/1	Legajo 1521

PUERTO RICO
nación

Pensiones

	1673	744,763/3	Legajo 2318

Location/ Document Type	Years	Roll No.	Comments
Current jurisdictions are unknown or unavailable for the following entries			
Sacatepéquez			Documents fail to specify whether San Juan, San Lucas, San Pedro, or Santiago Sacatepéquez
Probanzas de Pobreza			
	1808–1814	746,850/2	ODT/OL Legajos 2610–2620
San Juan			Gaz/various. Placement on film suggests Huehuetenango
Méritos y Servicios			
	1788	746,852/23	Legajo 2935

POBLACIONES Y TRIBUTOS

Location/ Document Type	Years	Roll No.	Comments
		GUATEMALA nación	
Capital			
Censos			
	1579-1713	744,588/1	Indexed ODT/OL Legajo 443
	1877	747,293	
	1877	744,850	Linea Sur 1ª, 2ª, 3ª, Parroquia de los Remedios y del Calbario only Legajo 88394
	1877	744,851	Linea Sur 9ª, 10ª, Parroquia del Sagrario only Legajo 88395
	1887	744,852	Linea Norte 1ª, 2ª, Parroquia del Sagrario only Legajo 88396
	1877	744,853	Parroquia del Sagrario y de San Sebastián only Legajo 88397
	1877	744,354	Linea 5ª, 6ª, Escuela Politécnica, Parroquia de Jocotenango only Legajo 88398
	1877	744,855	Candelaria, Parroquia del Sagrario, de San Sebastián, y de Militares only Legajo 88399
	1877	747,292/2/2	Parroquia del Sagrario only
	1877	747,292/2/1,3	Parroquia de los Remedios only

Location/ Document Type	Years	Roll No.	Comments
Correspondencia			
	1768	746,866/3/16	
Padrón			
	1778	741,739/1/32	
	1778	741,891/2/24	
	1802	746,827/1/15	
	n.d.	748,134/1/11	Incomplete
Padrón General			
	1735	746,828/3/15	
	1816	741,893	ODT/OL Legajo 1811
	1824	746,871/4/2	
	1824	746,872/1/1	
	1824	746,872/1/5	Barrio del Sagrario only
	1824	746,872/1/6	Document damage
	1824-1825	746,872/1/4	
	1902	748,134/1/8	
Tributos			
	1737	746,828/3/17	
	1740	746,826/1/18	
	1759	746,829/2/9	
	1763	748,127/3/36	
	1788	746,870/3/2	
	1792	745,422/3	ODT/OL Legajo 9
	1794	744,581/4/1	
	1810	744,866/2/2	

Location/ Document Type	Years	Roll No.	Comments

Alta Verapaz
  Cahabón
    Cahabón (c/p)			

Padrón			
	1816	746,827/2/4	
Tributos			
	1791	763,388/6/67	
	1798	773,999/3/98	
	1887	747,294/1/12	
Cobán Cobán (c/cd)			
Padrón			
	1816	746,870/5/3	
Padrón General			
	1816	746,870/5/2	
Tributos			
	1791	763,388/6/66	
	1798	773,999/3/97	
	1887	747,294/1/14	
Chisec Chisec (c/p)			
Tributos			
	1887	747,294/1/13	

Location/ Document Type	Years	Roll No.	Comments
Lanquín			
Lanquín (c/p)			
Padrón			
	1816	746,827/1/16	
Padrón General			
	1821	748,132/3/1	
Tributos			
	1791	763,388/6/68	
	1798	773,999/3/99	
	1887	747,294/1/10	
Panzós			
La Tinta (a)			
Tributos			
	1887	747,294/1/8	
Panzós			
Panzós (c/p)			
Tributos			
	1887	747,294/1/9	
San Cristóbal Verapaz			
San Cristóbal Verapaz (c/v)			Former name San Cristóbal Cahcoh (or Cagcoh)
Padrón			
	1816	746,327/2/2	
Padrón General			
	1741	746,826/1/21	Document damage
	1821	748,132/3/5	

Location/ Document Type	Years	Roll No.	Comments
Tributos			
	1791	763,388/6/71	
	1798	773,999/3/102	
	1887	747,294/1/4	
San Juan Chamelco San Juan Chamelco (c/p)			
Padrón			
	1815	746,870/4/7	
	1816	746,870/4/6	
Padrón General			
	1740	746,828/3/22	Document damage
	1762	763,390/4/17	
	1762	773,996/1/26	
	1765	748,127/4/44	
Tributos			
	1791	763,388/6/70	
	1798	773,999/3/101	
	1887	747,294/1/2	
San Pedro Carchá San Pedro Carchá (c/p)			
Padrón			
	1815	746,870/4/5	
	1816	746,870/4/4	
Padrón General			
	1734	746,825/3/25	

Location/ Document Type	Years	Roll No.	Comments
Tributos			
	1734	746,825/3/24	
	1791	763,388/6/69	
	1798	773,999/3/100	
	1887	747,294/1/3	
Santa Cruz Verapaz Santa Cruz Verapaz (c/p)			
Padrón General			
	1748	747,061/3/10	
	1821	748,132/3/5	
Tributos			
	1748	747,061/3/8	
	1748	747,061/3/9	
	1791	763,388/6/72	
	1798	773,999/3/103	
	1887	747,294/1/1	
Senahú Senahú (c/p)			
Tributos			
	1887	747,294/1/11	
Tactic Tactic (c/p)			
Padrón			
	1815-1817	746,827/1/16	
Padrón General			
	1751	748,125/2/2	

Location/ Document Type	Years	Roll No.	Comments
	1765	746,826/2/12	
	1821	748,133/1/14	
Tributos			
	1791	763,388/6/73	
	1798	773,999/3/104	
	1887	747,294/1/5	
Tamahú Tamahú (c/p)			
Padrón General			
	1821	748,132/3/3	
Tributos			
	1791	763,388/6/74	
	1798	773,999/3/105	
	1887	747,294/1/7	
Tucurú Tucurú (c/p)			
Padrón			
	1816	746,827/2/6	
Padrón General			
	1821	748,133/1/13	
Tributos			
	1791	763,388/6/75	
	1798	773,999/3/106	
	1887	747,294/1/6	

Location/ Document Type	Years	Roll No.	Comments

Baja Verapaz
  Cubulco
    Cubulco (c/v)			

Correspondencia			
	1796	773,999/3/85	
Padrón			
	1815	746,827/2/4	
	1816-1817	746,827/2/3	
Padrón General			
	1732	746,825/3/23	
	1762	746,826/2/10	
	1767	746,866/3/12	
	1813	748,132/2/11	
Tributos			
	1791	763,388/6/63	
	1798	773,999/3/94	
El Chol El Chol (c/p)			
Padrón			
	1816	746,827/2/7	
Padrón General			
	1778	748,128/5/4	
	1820	748,132/3/2	
Tributos			
	1791	763,388/6/76	
	1798	773,999/3/107	

Location/ Document Type	Years	Roll No.	Comments
Granados <u>Saltán</u> (a)			
Padrón General			
	1825	746,825/1/1	
Rabinal <u>Rabinal</u> (c/cd)			
Padrón General			
	1813	748,131/3/16	
	1816	746,870/5/9	
Tributos			
	1791	763,388/6/64	
	1798	773,999/3/95	
Salamá <u>Salamá</u> (c/cd)			
Padrón General			
	1711	746,867/6/1	
	1762	746,866/1/3	
	1762	763,390/4/18	Incomplete
	1762	773,996/1/27	
	1803	747,296/10/1	
	1821	748,133/2/1	
Tributos			
	1791	763,388/6/65	
	1798	773,999/3/96	

Location/ Document Type	Years	Roll No.	Comments
San Jerónimo San Jerónimo (c/p)			
Padrón General			
	1821	748,132/3/4	
San Miguel Chicaj San Miguel Chicaj (c/p)			
Padrón			
	1815	746,827/2/7	
	1816	746,827/2/7	
Padrón General			
	1813	748,131/1/1	Document damage

Chimaltenango
  Acatenango
    Acatenango (c/p)			

Tributos			
	1753	746,869/1/5	
	1754	741,888/1/21	
	1754	741,890/1/5	
	1777	746,827/1/6	
	1792	763,388/7/17	
Nejapa (a)			
Tributos			
	1754	741,888/1/17	
	1754	741,890/1/1	
	1777	746,827/1/6	
	1792	763,388/7/18	

Location/ Document Type	Years	Roll No.	Comments
Comalapa Comalapa (c/p)			
Padrón General			
	1636	747,059/15/1	Document damage
	1718	746,827/4/3	
	1735	747,060/7/3	
	1821	748,129/1/2	
Tributos			
	1731-1736	741,888/3/30	
	1791	763,388/7/27	
Chimaltenango Chimaltenango (c/cd)			
Correspondencia			
	1794	746,827/1/13	
Padrón			
	1778	741,739/1/15	
Padrón General			
	1673	747,059/20/1	Incomplete
Tributos			
	1753	746,826/2/2	
	1792	763,388/7/7	
	1812	747,296/22/17	
	1887	747,295/2/31	

Location/ Document Type	Years	Roll No.	Comments
Parramos Parramos (c/p)			
Tributos			
	1753	746,869/1/32	
	1756	741,888/2/12	
	1756	741,890/1/33	
	1792	763,388/7/20	
Patzicía Patzicía (c/v)			
Padrón			
	1813	748,132/2/8	
Tributos			
	1753	746,869/1/33	
	1756	741,888/2/13	
	1756	741,890/1/34	
	1792	763,388/7/25	
Patzún Patzún (c/v)			
Padrón			
	1810	773,999/11/1-2	
Tributos			
	1752-1770	746,868/3/1	
Pochuta Pochuta (c/p)			
Padrón General			
	1751	741,889/1/22	

Location/ Document Type	Years	Roll No.	Comments
	1751	746,868/2/21	Poor focus

San Andrés Itzapa
San Andrés Itzapa (c/p)

Padrón General

| | 1752 | 746,868/3/12 | |
| | 1756 | 746,869/2/11 | |

Tributos

	1753	746,869/1/34	
	1756	741,888/2/14	
	1756	741,890/1/35	

San Martín Jilotepeque
Pajón (cas de Xesuj)

Tributos

	1753	746,869/1/38	
	1756	741,888/2/19	
	1756	741,890/1/40	

San Martín Jilotepeque (c/v)

Padrón General

| | 1815 | 747,059/12/4 | |
| | 1821 | 747,059/12/7 | |

Tributos

	1753	746,869/1/25	Poor focus
	1755	741,888/2/4	
	1755	741,890/1/25	
	1792	763,388/7/9	

Location/ Document Type	Years	Roll No.	Comments
Semetabaj (cas de Quimal)			
Padrón General			
	1768	746,867/1/8	
Santa Apolonia Santa Apolonia (c/p)			
Tributos			
	1792	763,388/7/23	
Santa Cruz Balanyá Santa Cruz Balanyá (c/p)			
Padrón General			
	1821	748,129/i/1	
Tributos			
	1732	741,888/3/8	
	1792	763,388/7/26	
Tecpán Guatemala Tecpán Guatemala (c/cd)			
Tributos			
	1792	763,388/7/22	
Yepocapa Yepocapa (c/p)			
Tributos			
	1755	741,888/2/3	
	1755	741,890/1/24	
	1777	746,827/1/6	
	1792	763,388/7/19	

Location/ Document Type	Years	Roll No.	Comments

Chiquimula
  Camotán
    Camotán (c/p)			

Correspondencia			
	1750	746,868/2/4	
Padrón			
	1750	741,889/1/8	
	1816	746,829/2/19	
	1818	773,999/17/1	
Padrón General			
	1746	748,130/2/3	Incomplete
	1824	746,821/2/6	
Tributos			
	1747	747,061/1/2	Incomplete
	1750	746,868/2/9	
	1797	746,865/3/52	
	1887	747,295/1/1	
Concepción las Minas Anguiatú (a)			
Padrón General			
	1813	748,131/3/20	
	1825	746,823/1/8	
Ermita (a)			Documents cite as San Juan Jocotán alias Hermita
Padrón General			
	1813	748,131/3/19	

Location/ Document Type	Years	Roll No.	Comments
Tributos			
	1797	746,865/3/51	
Limones (cas de Cruz Calle)			
Padrón General			
	1825	746,823/1/8	
Valeriano (cas de Anguiatú)			
Padrón General			
	1813	748,131/3/21	
Chiquimula (mun)			
Padrón General			
	1825	746,822/1/5	
	1825	746,822/1/6	
Chiquimula (c/cd)			
Correspondencia			
	1750	746,868/2/4	
	1751	746,868/2/15	
	1809	763,389/2/1	
Padrón			
	n.d.	746,828/2/7	
Padrón General			
	1745	747,060/13/11	
	1749	748,128/7/7	Incomplete

Location/ Document Type	Years	Roll No.	Comments
	1750	748,124/2/7	
	1753	747,058/4/1	Document damage
	1754	746,869/1/40	
	1755	748,130/4/1	Incomplete
	1781	741,892/2/1	
	1813	748,131/3/23	
	1817	746,830/1/19	
	1820	763,389/4/1	
	1820	763,389/4/3	Incomplete
	1825	746,823/1/9	
Tributos			
	1741	746,826/1/20	
	1749	748,124/1/5	
	1753-1754	741,890/1/44	
	1791	763,388/6/81	
	1797	746,865/3/46	
	1820	763,389/4/2	
	1825	746,822/1/3	
	1887	747,294/1/42	

San Esteban (a)

Padrón

	1817	748,130/5/6	

Padrón General

	1825	746,822/1/7	

Tributos

	1791	763,388/6/84	
	1797	746,865/3/49	

Location/ Document Type	Years	Roll No.	Comments
	1825	746,822/1/3	

Santa Elena (a)

Padrón

	Years	Roll No.	
	1768-1775	748,128/4/1	
	1816	746,827/2/1	
	1825	746,822/1/3	

Padrón General

	Years	Roll No.	
	1754	741,890/1/42	
	1817	746,830/1/18	
	1825	746,822/1/8	

Tributos

	Years	Roll No.	
	1754	741,888/1/22	
	1754	741,890/1/6	

Esquipulas
Esquipulas (c/v)

Padrón General

	Years	Roll No.	
	1750	748,124/3/4	
	1754	746,868/3/13	
	1764	748,127/4/35	
	1810	746,865/8/1	
	1813	747,059/11/3	
	1820	747,059/12/5	
	1822	746,821/1/1	
	1824	746,821/2/8	

Tributos

	Years	Roll No.	
	1750	748,124/3/3	

Location/Document Type	Years	Roll No.	Comments
	1764	748,128/1/4	
	1791	763,388/6/88	
	1797	746,865/3/53	
	1887	747,294/1/47	

Ipala
  Ipala (c/p)

Padrón

| | 1816 | 746,829/2/17 | |

Padrón General

| | 1741 | 747,060/10/10 | |
| | 1745 | 747,060/13/9 | |

Tributos

	1741	747,060/10/9	
	1791	763,388/6/92	
	1797	746,865/3/57	
	1887	747,294/1/43	

Jocotán
  Jocotán (c/v)

Correspondencia

| | 1750 | 746,868/2/4 | |

Padrón

	1750	741,889/1/9	
	1750	741,889/1/10	
	1768-1775	748,128/5/6	
	1816-1817	746,829/3/5	

Location/ Document Type	Years	Roll No.	Comments
Padrón General			
	1824	746,821/2/5	
Tributos			
	1700	747,060/3/3	
	1750	746,868/2/8	
	1791	763,388/6/85	
	1797	746,865/3/50	
	1887	747,294/1/49	

Olopa
Olopa (c/p)

Tributos			
	1887	747,294/1/50	

Quezaltepeque
Azacualpa (a)

Censo			
	1902	737,251/1/15	
Tributos			
	1837	748,134/1/4	
	1887	747,295/2/10	

Concepción (cas de Estanzuela Abajo)

Padrón General			
	1813	748,131/3/24	

Cubiletes (a)

Padrón General			
	1813	748,131/3/14	

Location/ Document Type	Years	Roll No.	Comments
	1825	746,823/1/3	

Quezaltepeque (c/v)

Correspondencia

	Years	Roll No.	Comments
	1729	747,060/5/4	

Padrón

| | 1768-1775 | 748,128/5/3 | |
| | 1817 | 746,829/2/16 | |

Padrón General

	1741	746,825/3/16	
	1824	746,821/2/12	
	1826	746,823/1/11	

Tributos

	1742	746,825/3/15	
	1753	746,869/1/7	
	1754	741,888/1/23	
	1754	741,890/1/7	
	1791	763,388/6/89	
	1797	746,865/3/54	
	1887	747,294/1/45	

San Marcos (cas de Cubiletes)

Correspondencia

| | 1735 | 747,060/7/1 | |

Location/Document Type	Years	Roll No.	Comments

San Jacinto
  San Jacinto (c/p)

Padrón

| | 1757 | 747,296/7/1 | |
| | 1770-1776 | 748,128/2/2 | |

Padrón General

	1742	747,060/12/10	
	1751	748,124/3/8	
	1817	746,830/1/2	
	1824	746,821/2/2	
	1826	746,823/1/12	

Tributos

	1742	747,060/12/9	
	1751	748,124/3/7	
	1770-1822	746,870/5/8	
	1797	746,865/3/55	
	1887	747,294/1/44	

  Ticanlú (a)

Padrón

| | 1825 | 746,822/1/3 | |

Padrón General

| | 1825 | 746,822/1/9 | |

San José La Arada
  Santa Rosa (a)

Padrón General

| | 1825 | 746,825/2/2 | |

Location/ Document Type	Years	Roll No.	Comments
San Juan Ermita			
San Juan Ermita (c/p)			
Padrón			
	1768-1775	748,128/2/1	
	1816	746,829/2/18	
Padrón General			
	1824	746,821/2/7	
Tributos			
	1791	763,388/6/86	
	1887	747,294/1/48	
El Progreso			
El Progreso			
El Progreso (c/cd)			Former name Guastatoya
Padrón			
	1826	746,824/1/12	
Padrón General			
	1813	748,132/2/2	
	1324	746,822/1/2	
	1826	746,824/1/11	
Tributos			
	1887	747,294/1/19	
Morazán			
Morazán (c/p)			Former name Tocoy
Padrón			
	1821	748,133/1/4	
	1826	746,824/1/13	

Location/ Document Type	Years	Roll No.	Comments
Padrón General			
	1826	746,824/1/14	
San Clemente (a)			
Padrón			
	1826	746,824/1/9	
Padrón General			
	1826	746,824/1/10	
San Agustín Acasaguastlán (mun)			
Padrón General			
	1825	746,822/1/11	
Magdalena (a)			
Padrón			
	1826	746,824/1/15	
Padrón General			
	1750	748,124/2/3	
	1826	746,824/1/16	
Tributos			
	1750	748,124/2/2	
	1825	746,822/1/12	
San Agustín Acasaguastlán (c/p)			
Padrón			
	1826	746,824/1/8	

Location/ Document Type	Years	Roll No.	Comments
Padrón General			
	1700	747,060/3/1	Document damage
	1742	747,060/12/14	
	1750	748,124/2/1	
	1758	748,126/4/24	
	1826	746,824/1/1	
Tributos			
	1742	747,060/12/13	
	1791	763,388/6/109	
	1797	746,865/3/74	
San Antonio la Paz San Antonio la Paz (c/p)			Former name El Valle de San Antonio
Padrón General			
	1813	748,131/3/4	
San Cristóbal Acasaguastlán San Cristóbal Acasaguastlán (c/p)			
Padrón			
	1817	746,829/3/8	
	1825	746,823/1/1	
	1826	746,824/1/3	
Padrón General			
	1741-1742	747,060/12/2	
	1758	748,126/4/23	
	1825	746,823/1/3	
	1826	746,824/1/2	

Location/ Document Type	Years	Roll No.	Comments
Tributos			
	1742	747,060/12/1	
	1791	763,388/6/106	
	1797	746,865/3/71	
Sanarate Sanarate (c/p)			
Padrón			
	1826	746,824/1/6	
	1826	746,824/1/7	
Sansare Sansare (c/p)			
Padrón			
	1826	746,824/2/18	
Padrón General			
	1826	746,824/2/19	
Tributos			
	1887	747,294/1/20	
Escuintla Escuintla (mun)			
Padrón General			
	1831	747,058/10/1	
Tributos			
	1809	763,389/2/2	
Escuintla (c/cd)			Former name Esquintepeque
Correspondencia			
	1795	773,999/3/2	

Location/ Document Type	Years	Roll No.	Comments
Padrón General			
	1748	746,867/4/3	Document damage
	1751	748,124/3/11	
	1760	747,058/4/3	
	1817	746,830/1/8	
	1821	748,132/3/7	
	1825	746,873/1/1	
Tributos			
	1734	747,060/7/2	
	1764	741,871/1	ODT/OL Legajo 264
	1764	748,127/4/26	
	1764	748,127/4/28	
Guanagazapa Guanagazapa (c/p)			
Padrón General			
	1743	747,060/12/15	
	1743	747,060/13/14	
	1756	746,871/1/4	
	1813	748,131/3/12	
	1816	746,870/4/8	
	1836	746,873/1/3	
La Democracia La Democracia (c/p)			Former name Don García
Padrón General			
	1755	741,890/1/46	
	1817	746,830/1/7	

Location/ Document Type	Years	Roll No.	Comments
	1825	746,825/2/5	
Tributos			
	1825	746,825/2/6	
La Gomera Chipilapa (a)			
Padrón General			
	1813	748,131/3/7	
	1817	746,830/1/4	
La Gomera (c/v)			
Padrón General			
	1821	748,133/3/7	
	1836	746,873/1/8	
Texcuaco (a)			
Correspondencia			
	1750	748,124/1/8	
Padrón General			
	1817	746,829/2/17	
	1836	746,873/1/4	
Masagua Masagua (c/p)			
Padrón General			
	1750	746,868/2/12	
	1813	748,131/3/6	
	1817	746,830/1/14	
	1825	746,825/2/3	

Location/ Document Type	Years	Roll No.	Comments
	1836	746,873/1/7	

San Juan Mixtán (a)

Padrón General

	Years	Roll No.	Comments
	1813	748,131/3/11	
	1817	746,830/1/14	
	1836	746,873/1/9	

Santa Lucia Cotzumalguapa
Santa Lucia Cotzumalguapa (c/p)

Correspondencia

	Years	Roll No.	Comments
	1711,1734	747,060/6/1	

Padrón

	1767	748,128/1/2	

Padrón General

	Years	Roll No.	Comments
	1734	746,826/1/2	
	1744	747,061/1/3	
	1744	747,060/13/3	
	1744	747,060/13/6	Documents cite San Cristóbal Cotzumalguapa which DGG describes as incorporated into Santa Lucía Cotzumalguapa in 1772
	1744	747,060/13/7	
	1754	746,869/1/45	
	1755	741,890/1/50	
	1755	748,126/2/1	
	1756	746,869/2/5	Documents cite as San Cristóbal Cotzumalguapa (see above)
	1817	746,830/1/5	

Location/ Document Type	Years	Roll No.	Comments
	1836	746,873/1/10	
Tributos			
	1734	746,826/1/1	
	1735	747,060/7/2	
Siquinalá			
Siquinalá (c/p)			
Padrón General			
	1726	763,388/4/1	
	1744	747,060/13/5	
	1756	741,890/1/54	
	1756	746,865/4/1	
	1817	746,830/1/6	
Tributos			
	1648	747,059/17/1	
Tiquisate			
Santa Ana Mixtán (a)			
Padrón			
	1736	746,826/1/6	
Padrón General			
	1744	747,060/13/10	
	1821	748,133/3/5	
	1836	746,873/1/5	
Tributos			
	1736	746,826/1/5	

Location/ Document Type	Years	Roll No.	Comments
Guatemala			
Tributos			
	1823	746,825/2/1	
	1831	747,058/9/1	
	1893	748,134/1/5	
	1902	748,134/1/6	
Amatitlán Amatitlán (c/cd)			
Correspondencia			
	1678	747,059/9/1	
	1747	748,130/2/4	
Padrón			
	1679	747,059/21/3	
	1781	747,059/1/23	
	1784	747,059/2/1	
Padrón General			
	1731	746,825/3/21	
	1756	746,869/2/2	
	1781	747,049/1/25	
	1813	748,132/2/10	
	1835	746,873/1/3	
Tributos			
	1731	746,825/3/22	
	1756-1757	741,890/1/53	
	1763	748,127/3/42	
	1777	746,827/1/6	

Location/ Document Type	Years	Roll No.	Comments
	1797	746,865/3/60	

Chinautla
Chinautla (c/p)

Padrón

| | 1781 | 747,059/1/19 | |

Padrón General

	1727	746,828/3/3	
	1740	746,826/1/17	
	1817	746,870/5/8	

Tributos

	1753	746,869/1/3	
	1753	746,869/1/30	
	1754	741,888/1/19	
	1754	741,890/1/3	
	1757	741,888/2/10	
	1757	741,890/1/31	
	1763	748,127/3/34	
	1777	746,827/1/6	

Guatemala
Canalitas (a)

Padrón General

| | 1845 | 747,292/1 | |

Mixco
Mixco (c/p)

Padrón General

| | 1777 | 747,059/1/17 | |
| | 1804 | 746,865/7/16 | |

Location/ Document Type	Years	Roll No.	Comments
Padrón General			
	1748	748,128/7/9	
	1756	746,869/2/7	
	1781	747,059/1/18	
	1828	746,872/2/3	
Tributos			
	1753	746,869/1/4	
	1753	746,869/1/26	
	1753	746,869/1/28	
	1754	741,888/1/20	
	1754	741,890/1/4	
	1755	741,888/2/5	
	1755	741,890/1/26	
	1757	741,888/2/8	
	1757	741,890/1/29	
	1763	748,127/3/44	
	1777	746,827/1/6	
	1805	746,865/7/17	

Palencia
  Palencia (c/p)

Padrón General

	1813	748,132/2/6	
	1821	748,133/1/10	

Petapa
  Petapa (c/p)

Padrón

	1781	747,059/1/3	

Location/ Document Type	Years	Roll No.	Comments
Padrón General			
	1781	747,059/1/27	
	1817	746,830/1/20	
Tributos			
	1763	748,127/3/41	
	1777	746,827/1/6	

Santa Inés Petapa (a)

Padrón			
	1781	747,059/1/4	
Padrón General			
	1762	747,059/10/1	
	1763	748,127/4/1	
	1765	748,127/4/45	
Tributos			
	1763	748,127/3/40	
	1764	748,127/3/47	
	1777	746,827/1/6	

San José Pinula
San José Pinula (c/p)

Padrón General			
	1825	746,872/2/1	

San Juan Sacatepéquez
San Juan Sacatepéquez (c/v)

Padrón			
	1732-1734	747,060/6/2	

Location/ Document Type	Years	Roll No.	Comments
	1781	763,388/1/10	
	1818	746,830/2/5	
Padrón General			
	1813	748,132/2/9	
Tributos			
	1732	741,888/3/3	
	1777	746,827/1/6	
	1818-1821	746,870/5/9	

San Pedro Sacatepéquez
   San Pedro Sacatepéquez (c/p)

Padrón

	1818	746,829/3/2	

Padrón General

	1780	747,059/1/16	

Tributos

	1755	741,888/2/5	
	1755	741,890/1/27	
	1756	741,888/2/20	
	1769	746,827/1/5	
	1777	746,827/1/6	

San Raimundo
   San Raimundo (c/p)

Padrón

	1781	747,059/1/7	
	1818	746,830/2/9	

Location/ Document Type	Years	Roll No.	Comments
Padrón General			
	1781	747,059/1/28	
	1813	748,132/2/3	
	1898	748,134/1/4	
	1902	748,134/1/7	
Tributos			
	1777	746,827/1/6	

Santa Catarina Pinula
Santa Catarina Pinula (c/p)

Padrón			
	1778-1781	747,059/1/26	
	1817	747,058/2/1	
Padrón General			
	1781	747,059/1/1	
	1803	746,870/4/2	
Tributos			
	1753	746,869/1/2	
	1753	746,869/1/29	
	1754	741,888/1/18	
	1754	741,890/1/2	
	1757	741,888/2/9	
	1757	741,890/1/30	
	1763	748,127/3/35	
	1763	748,127/3/37	
	1777	746,827/1/6	

Location/ Document Type	Years	Roll No.	Comments
Huehuetenango **Aguacatán** <u>Aguacatán</u> (c/p)			
Padrón General			
	1745	746,829/1/15	
Tributos			
	1812	747,296/22/32	
	1887	747,295/2/40	
<u>Chalchitán</u> (c/v)			Former cabecera municipal
Padrón General			
	1819	747,056/1/12	
Tributos			
	1887	747,205/2/39	
Colotenango <u>Colotenango</u> (c/p)			
Padrón General			
	1819	747,055/1/19	
Tributos			
	1812	747,296/22/27	
Cuilco <u>Cancuc</u> (a)			
Padrón General			
	1816	744,581/8/1	

Location/ Document Type	Years	Roll No.	Comments
Cuilco (c/p)			
Padrón General			
	1780	747,296/16/9-10,13	
	1803	747,296/18/11	
	1810	747,296/20/10	
	1819	747,055/1/10	
	1825	746,820/1/6	
Tributos			
	1812	747,296/22/24	
	1887	747,295/2/24	
Concepción **Concepción** (c/p)			
Padrón General			
	1819	747,055/1/23	
	1819	747,055/1/26	
Petatán (a)			
Padrón General			
	1819	747,055/1/25	
Tributos			
	1812	747,296/22/4	
	1887	747,295/2/46	
Chiantla **Chiantla** (c/v)			
Correspondencia			
	1796	748,130/6/1	

Location/Document Type	Years	Roll No.	Comments
Padrón			
	1738	747,060/8/8	
Padrón General			
	1738	747,060/8/7	
	1803	747,296/18/8	
	1810	747,296/20/8	
	1813	748,131/2/3	
	1819	747,056/1/17	
	1825	746,830/1/3	
Tributos			
	1738	747,060/8/3	
	1739	747,060/8/4	
	1812	747,296/22/31	
	1887	747,295/2/50	

Huehuetenango (mun)

Tributos			
	1887	747,295/2/49	

Huehuetenango (c/cd)

Padrón			
	1738	747,060/8/9	
Padrón General			
	1742	746,867/8/1	
	1803	747,296/18/7	
	1810	747,296/20/6	
	1813	748,131/2/1	

Location/ Document Type	Years	Roll No.	Comments
Tributos			
	1698	746,825/3/9	
	1812	747,296/22/30	
Ixtahuacán Ixtahuacán (c/p)			
Padrón General			
	1748	746,826/1/28	
	1819	747,055/1/17	
Tributos			
	1748	746,826/1/27	
	1812	747,296/22/25	
	1887	747,295/2/53	
Jacaltenango (mun)			
Tributos			
	1887	747,295/2/48	
Jacaltenango (c/p)			
Padrón General			
	1752	746,868/2/27	
	1801	763,388/3/1	
	1803	747,296/18/9	
	1809	747,296/19/2	
	1810	747,296/20/11	
	1819	747,055/1/26	
	1819	747,056/1/1	

Location/ Document Type	Years	Roll No.	Comments
Tributos			
	1812	747,296/22/3	
	1812	747,296/22/6	
San Andrés Huista (a)			
Padrón General			
	1819	747,055/1/13	
San Marcos Huista (a)			
Padrón General			
	1752	746,868/2/26	
	1819	747,055/1/7	
Tributos			
	1812	747,296/22/7	
La Libertad El Trapichillo (a)			
Tributos			
	1887	747,295/2/29	
Malacatancito Malacatancito (c/p)			Former name Santa Ana Malacatán
Padrón General			
	1751	741,889/1/18	
	1751	746,868/2/17	
	1803	747,296/18/1	
	1803	747,296/18/7	
	1810	747,296/20/9	
	1813	748,131/3/2	

Location/ Document Type	Years	Roll No.	Comments
	1819	747,055/1/22	
Tributos			
	1812	747,296/22/28	
	1887	747,295/2/27	
Nentón Nentón (c/p)			
Tributos			
	1887	747,295/2/41	
San Antonio Huista (mun)			
Tributos			
	1887	747,295/2/47	
San Antonio Huista (c/p)			
Padrón General			
	1749	747,061/3/2	
	1810	747,296/20/12	
	1819	747,055/1/12	
San Gaspar Ixchil San Gaspar Ixchil (c/p)			
Padrón General			
	1748	746,867/4/2	
	1819	747,055/1/18	
Tributos			
	1748	746,867/4/1	
	1812	747,296/22/26	

Location/ Document Type	Years	Roll No.	Comments
San Juan Atitán San Juan Atitán (c/p)			
Padrón General			
	1746	746,829/1/6	
	1819	747,055/1/1	
Tributos			
	1756	748,126/3/14	
	1812	747,296/22/16	
	1887	747,295/2/32	Disordered
Santa Isabel (a)			
Tributos			
	1812	747,296/22/15	
San Juan Ixcoy (mun)			
Tributos			
	1887	747,295/2/37	
San Juan Ixcoy (c/p)			
Padrón General			
	1743	746,829/1/3	
	1819	747,055/1/6	
Tributos			
	1812	747,296/22/13	

Location/ Document Type	Years	Roll No.	Comments
San Mateo Ixtatán <u>San Mateo Ixtatán</u> (c/p)			
Padrón			
	1815	746,827/2/5	
	1816	746,827/2/5	
Padrón General			
	1752	746,868/3/7	
	1819	747,056/1/11	
Tributos			
	1812	747,296/22/10	
San Miguel Acatán <u>San Miguel Acatán</u> (c/p)			
Padrón General			
	1819	747,055/1/16	
Tributos			
	1743	746,829/1/2	
	1812	747,296/22/8	
	1887	747,295/2/35	
San Pedro Necta (mun)			
Tributos			
		747,295/2/30	
<u>San Pedro Necta</u> (c/p)			
Padrón General			
	1743	746,826/1/24	
	1752	741,889/1/27	

Location/ Document Type	Years	Roll No.	Comments
	1752	746,868/2/25	
	1819	747,055/1/4	
Tributos			
	1743	746,826/1/23	
	1812	747,296/22/18	

San Sebastián Coatán
San Sebastián Coatán (c/p)

Padrón General

	1819	747,055/1/11	

Tributos

	1812	747,296/22/9	
	1887	747,295/2/34	

San Sebastián Huehuetenango
San Sebastián Huehuetenango (c/p)

Padrón General

	1819	747,056/1/9	

Tributos

	1812	747,296/22/14	
	1887	747,295/2/33	

Santa Ana Huista
Santa Ana Huista (c/p)

Padrón

	1817	748,130/9/3	

Padrón General

	1790	763,386/4/2	
	1810	747,296/20/13	

Location/ Document Type	Years	Roll No.	Comments
	1819	747,056/1/18	
Tributos			
	1735	747,060/6/3	
	1812	747,296/22/5	
	1887	747,295/2/45	
Santa Bárbara Santa Bárbara (c/p)			
Padrón General			
	1748	746,867/3/4	
	1819	747,055/1/14	
Tributos			
	1748	746,867/3/3	
	1812	747,296/22/28	
	1887	747,295/2/26	
Santa Eulalia Santa Eulalia (c/p)			
Padrón			
	1801	747,296/17/1	
Padrón General			
	1819	747,055/1/15	
Tributos			
	1812	747,296/22/11	
	1887	747,295/2/36	

Location/ Document Type	Years	Roll No.	Comments
Santiago Chimaltenango Santiago Chimaltenango (c/p)			
Padrón General			
	1819	747,056/1/10	
Soloma Soloma (c/p)			
Padrón General			
	1752	746,868/3/2	
	1813	748,131/3/1	
	1819	747,055/1/5	
Tributos			
	1812	747,296/22/12	
	1887	747,295/2/38	
Tectitán Tectitán (c/p)			
Padrón General			
	1746	746,867/3/1	
	1752	746,871/1/2	
	1780	747,296/16/16	
	1819	747,055/1/8	
	n.d.	747,296/24/1	
Tributos			
	1812	747,296/22/23	
	1887	747,295/2/44	

Location/ Document Type	Years	Roll No.	Comments
Todos Santos Cuchumatán San Martín (a)			
Padrón			
	1738	748,128/6/5	
Padrón General			
	1738	747,060/8/6	
	1819	747,055/1/20	
Tributos			
	1738	747,060/8/3	
	1739	747,060/8/4	
	1812	747,296/22/2	
	1887	747,295/2/52	
Todos Santos Cuchumatán (c/p)			
Padrón			
	1738	747,060/8/2	
	1738	748,128/6/6	
Padrón General			
	1738	747,060/8/5	Document damage
	1819	747,056/1/5	
Tributos			
	1739	747,060/8/4	
	1812	747,296/22/1	
	1887	747,295/2/51	

Location/ Document Type	Years	Roll No.	Comments
Izabal			
Izabal			
Izabal (c/p)			
Padrón General			
	1833	747,058/7/1	Incomplete
	1844	746,825/2/7,9	
Jalapa			
Jalapa			
Jalapa (c/cd)			
Padrón			
	1826	746,824/2/14	
Padrón General			
	1821	748,133/1/5	Incomplete
Tributos			
	1791	763,388/6/93	
	1797	746,865/3/58	
	1887	747,294/1/15	
Mataquescuintla			
Mataquescuintla (c/v)			
Padrón			
	1828	746,824/2/21	
	1831	747,058/10/6	
Padrón General			
	1743	746,829/1/1	
	1748	747,061/2/2	Incomplete
	1750	748,124/2/10	
	1821	748,133/1/2	

Location/ Document Type	Years	Roll No.	Comments
	1824	746,821/2/4	
	1825	746,823/1/5	
	1828	746,824/2/20	
	1831	747,058/10/5	
Tributos			
	1791	763,388/6/101	
	1797	746,865/3/66	
	1821	748,133/3/10	

San Carlos Alzatate
  San Carlos Alzatate (c/p)

Tributos			
	1887	747,294/1/21	

San Luis Jilotepeque
  San Lucas Jilotepeque (c/p)

Padrón General			
	1824	746,821/2/11	

San Luis Jilotepeque (c/p)

Padrón			
	1826	746,824/2/23	
Padrón General			
	1750	747,061/3/18	
	1826	746,824/2/22	
Tributos			
	1750	747,061/3/17	
	1791	763,388/6/91	
	1797	746,865/3/56	

Location/ Document Type	Years	Roll No.	Comments
	1887	747,294/1/17	

San Manuel Chaparrón
San Manuel Chaparrón (c/p)

Tributos

	Years	Roll No.	Comments
	1887	747,294/1/18	

San Pedro Pinula
San Pedro Pinula (c/p)

Padrón

	Years	Roll No.	Comments
	1767	746,827/3/1	
	1768-1775	748,128/3/2	
	1826	746,824/2/13	

Padrón General

	Years	Roll No.	Comments
	1817	746,830/1/3	
	1826	746,824/2/17	

Tributos

	Years	Roll No.	Comments
	1791	763,388/6/94	
	1797	746,865/3/59	
	1887	747,294/1/16	

Jutiapa
Agua Blanca
Agua Blanca (c/p)

Censo

	Years	Roll No.	Comments
	1902	737,251/1	ODT/OL Legajo 88394

Padrón General

	Years	Roll No.	Comments
	1824	746,821/2/16	

Location/ Document Type	Years	Roll No.	Comments
Tributos			
	1824	746,822/1/1	
	1887	747,295/2/21	
Ojo de Agua (cas de Santa Gertrudis)			
Padrón			
	1826	746,824/2/11	
Padrón General			
	1826	746,824/2/12	
Piñuelas (a)			
Padrón			
	1826	746,824/2/11	
Padrón General			
	1826	746,824/2/12	
Quequexque (a)			
Padrón			
	1826	746,824/2/11	
Padrón General			
	1826	746,824/2/12	
Asunción Mita Asunción Mita (c/v)			
Censo			
	1902	737,251/1/4	Includes literacy list ODT/OL Legajo 88394
	1908	737,250/2	

Location/ Document Type	Years	Roll No.	Comments
Tributos			
	1791	763,388/6/96	
	1797	746,865/3/61	
	1887	747,295/2/20	
Atescatempa Atescatempa (c/p)			
Censo			
	1902	737,251/1	ODT/OL
Padrón			
	1826	746,824/2/5	
Padrón General			
	1750	746,870/1/2	
	1826	746,824/2/6	
Tributos			
	1791	763,388/6/99	
	1797	746,865/3/64	
	1887	747,295/2/19	
Comapa Comapa (c/p)			
Padrón			
	1802-1815	746,829/3/7	
Padrón General			
	1756	741,890/1/60	
	1756	746,869/1/52	
	1813	748,131/3/15	
	1817	746,830/1/13	

Location/ Document Type	Years	Roll No.	Comments
Tributos			
	1887	747,295/2/15	
Sinaca Mecayo (sit arq)			
Padrón General			
	1745	747,058/3/2	
Tributos			
	1745	747,058/3/1	
Conguaco Conguaco (c/p)			
Censo			
	1902	737,251/1	Includes literacy list ODT/OL Legajo 88394
Padrón General			
	1817	746,829/3/8	
Tributos			
	1887	747,295/2/12	
El Adelanto El Adelanto (c/p)			
Censo			
	1902	737,251/1	Includes literacy list ODT/OL Legajo 88394
Tributos			
	1887	747,295/2/17	

Location/ Document Type	Years	Roll No.	Comments
El Progreso El Progreso (c/p)			
Censo			
	1902	737,251/1	Includes literacy list ODT/OL Legajo 88394
Tributos			
	1887	747,295/2/8	
Jalpatagua Azulco (a)			
Censo			
	1902	737,251/1	ODT/OL Legajo 88394
Padrón General			
	1817	746,830/1/11	
	1821	748,133/3/8	
	1825	746,823/1/6	
	1831	747,058/10/4	
Tributos			
	1887	747,295/2/13	
Jalpatagua (c/p)			
Censo			
	1902	737,251/1	Incomplete ODT/OL Legajo 88394
Tributos			
	1887	747,295/2/14	

Location/ Document Type	Years	Roll No.	Comments
Jérez **Jérez** (c/p)			Former name Chingo
Censo			
	1890-1911	737,249/3	Legajo 2
	1897	737,249/7	Legajo 4
	1902	737,251/1	Includes literacy list Incomplete ODT/OL Legajo 88394
Tributos			
	1887	747,295/2/23	
Jutiapa **Canoas** (a)			
Padrón			
	1826	746,824/2/10	
Padrón General			
	1821	748,133/1/12	Document damage
	1826	746,824/2/9	
Jutiapa (c/cd)			
Censo			
	1902	737,251/1	Includes literacy list ODT/OL Legajo 88394
Padrón			
	1769-1775	748,128/1/3	
	1817	748,130/5/4	
	1826	746,824/2/8	

Location/ Document Type	Years	Roll No.	Comments
Padrón General			
	1749	748,124/1/4	
	1756	746,869/2/3	
	1826	746,824/2/7	
Tributos			
	1751	748,124/1/2	
	1791	763,388/6/98	
	1797	746,865/3/63	
	1818	746,870/5/10	
	1887	747,295/2/9	

Moyuta
Moyuta (c/p)

Censo			
	1902	737,251	Includes literacy list ODT/OL Legajo 88394
Padrón General			
	1744	747,060/13/4	
	1756	741,890/1/57	
	1817	746,830/1/12	
	1821	748,133/3/1	
Tributos			
	1887	747,295/2/11	

Location/ Document Type	Years	Roll No.	Comments
Pasaco Pasaco (c/p)			
Censo			
	1902	737,251	Includes literacy list ODT/OL Legajo 88394
Padrón General			
	1817	746,830/1/10	
	1821	748,133/3/2	
	1825	746,823/1/7	
Tributos			
	1765	748,127/4/42-43	
Quesada Quesada (c/p)			
Censo			
	1902	737,251	Incomplete ODT/OL Legajo 88394
Santa Catarina Mita Santa Catarina Mita (c/p)			
Censo			
	1902	737,251/1	Includes literacy list ODT/OL Legajo 88394
Padrón General			
	1817	746,830/1/11	
Tributos			
	1791	763,388/6/97	
	1797	746,865/3/62	

Location/ Document Type	Years	Roll No.	Comments
Yupiltepeque Yupiltepeque (c/p)			
Censo			
	1902	737,251	Includes literacy list ODT/OL Legajo 88394
Padrón			
	1826	746,824/1/18	
Padrón General			
	1817	746,830/1/16	
	1824	746,821/2/9	
	1826	746,824/1/17	
Tributos			
	1791	763,388/6/100	
	1797	746,865/3/65	
	1887	747,295/2/18	
Zapotitlán Zapotitlán (c/p)			
Censo			
	1902	737,251	Includes literacy list ODT/OL Legajo 88394
Padrón			
	1826	746,824/2/2	
Padrón General			
	1824	746,820/1/13-14	
	1826	746,824/2/1	

Location/ Document Type	Years	Roll No.	Comments
Tributos			
	1815	763,386/6/1	
	1887	747,295/2/16	

Petén
  Flores
    Flores (c/cd)
			Former name Petén Itzá

Padrón General			
	1744	763,388/2/1	

Quezaltenango
  Almolonga
    Almolonga (c/p)			

Padrón General			
	1753	748,128/6/1	
	1821	747,057/3/5	
Tributos			
	1753	741,889/2/3	
	1755	741,890/1/48	
	1755	748,126/3/4	
	1790	763,388/6/42	
	1796	773,999/3/40	
Cabricán Cabricán (c/p)			
Padrón General			
	1740-1741	747,060/10/12	
	1821	747,057/2/2	
Tributos			
	1741	747,060/10/11	

Location/ Document Type	Years	Roll No.	Comments
	1757	748,126/4/16	
	1790	763,388/6/58	
	1796	773,999/3/56	
Cajolá Cajolá (c/p)			
Correspondencia			
	1790	763,388/6/1	
Tributos			
	1790	763,388/6/59	
	1796	773,999/3/57	
Camotán Camotán (c/p)			
Tributos			
	1791	763,388/6/87	
Cantel Cantel (c/p)			
Padrón General			
	1821	747,057/1/10	
Tributos			
	1755	748,126/3/9	
	1769	746,827/1/5	
	1790	763,388/6/41	
	1796	773,999/3/39	
Chuijuyub (cas de Xecam)			
Padrón			
	1769	746,827/1/5	

Location/ Document Type	Years	Roll No.	Comments
Coatepeque Coatepeque (c/cd)			
Padrón General			
	1813	741,892/1/12	
Tributos			
	1757	748,126/3/6	
	1757	748,126/4/6	
	1790	763,388/6/39	
	1796	773,999/3/37	
Concepción Chiquirichapa Concepción Chiquirichapa (c/p)			
Padrón General			
	1819	747,055/1/23	
	1821	747,057/1/5	
Tributos			
	1757	748,126/4/11	
	1790	763,388/6/55	
	1796	773,999/3/53	
Olintepeque Olintepeque (c/p)			
Padrón General			
	1748	746,826/1/29	
	1813	748,131/1/8	
	1821	747,057/1/1	
Tributos			
	1755	741,890/1/47	

Location/ Document Type	Years	Roll No.	Comments
	1755	748,136/3/7	
	1769	746,827/1/5	
	1790	763,388/6/53	
	1796	773,999/3/51	

Ostuncalco
  Ostuncalco (c/v)

Padrón

| | 1748 | 746,829/1/9 | Document damage |

Padrón General

| | 1749 | 746,829/1/9 | Document damage |
| | 1821 | 747,057/3/14 | |

Tributos

	1757	748,126/4/8	
	1790	763,388/6/54	
	1796	773,999/3/52	

Quezaltenango
  Quezaltenango (c/cd)

Correspondencia

| | 1795 | 773,999/3/4 | |

Padrón

| | 1778 | 741,739/1/16 | |

Padrón General

	1753	746,868/3/8	
	1759	748,127/1/5	
	1766	748,128/1/1	
	1767	746,827/4/4	

Location/ Document Type	Years	Roll No.	Comments
	1824	746,820/1/4	
Tributos			
	1755	748,126/3/3	
	1767	746,826/2/17	
	1785	746,827/1/11	
	1790	763,388/6/40	
	1790	763,388/6/60	
	1796	773,999/3/38	

San Sebastián (bar de Quezaltenango)

Tributos

	1791	773,996/1/2	
	1791	773,996/1/3	

Salcajá
   Salcajá (c/v)

Padrón General

	1803	747,296/18/4	
	1813	748,131/1/9	

San Carlos Sija
   San Carlos Sija (c/p)

Correspondencia

	1817	748,130/8/1	

Padrón General

	1803	747,296/18/6	
	1810	747,296/20/4	
	1825	746,820/1/5	

Location/ Document Type	Years	Roll No.	Comments
San Martín Sacatepéquez San Martín Sacatepéquez (c/p)			
Padrón General			
	1821	747,057/3/16	
Tributos			
	1757	748,126/4/5	
	1791	763,388/6/56	
	1796	773,999/3/54	
San Mateo San Mateo (c/p)			
Padrón General			
	1821	747,057/1/8	
Tributos			
	1796	773,999/3/43	
San Miguel Sigüilá San Miguel Sigüilá (c/p)			
Padrón General			
	1821	747,057/3/2	
Tributos			
	1757	748,126/4/4	
	1757	748,126/4/21	
	1790	763,388/6/57	
	1796	773,999/3/55	

Location/ Document Type	Years	Roll No.	Comments
Zunil			
Santa María de Jesús (a)			
Padrón General			
	1742	746,826/1/22	
Tributos			
	1796	773,999/3/42	
Zunil (c/p)			
Padrón General			
	1744	746,826/1/25	
	1821	747,057/3/3	
Tributos			
	1755	748,126/3/5	
	1790	763,388/6/43	
	1796	773,999/3/41	
Quiché			
Cunén			
Cunén (c/p)			
Padrón General			
	1819	747,056/1/2	
	1824	746,873/2/3	
Tributos			
	1812	747,296/22/36	
	1887	747,295/1/7	

Location/ Document Type	Years	Roll No.	Comments
Chajul **Chajul** (c/p)			
Padrón General			
	1752	741,889/1/30	
	1752	746,868/2/28	
	1813	748,131/1/5	
	1819	747,056/1/4	
Tributos			
	1812	747,296/22/34	
	1887	747,295/1/8	
Chiché **Chiché** (c/p)			
Tributos			
	1887	747,295/1/5	
Chichicastenango **Chichicastenango** (c/v)			
Padrón General			
	1751	748,124/3/6	
	1768	746,866/3/13	
Tributos			
	1798	746,865/3/32	
	1887	747,295/1/6	
Chinique **Chinique** (c/p)			
Padrón General			
	1825	746,873/2/9	

Location/ Document Type	Years	Roll No.	Comments
Tributos			
	1887	747,295/1/13	
Joyabaj (mun)			
Tributos			
	1887	747,295/2/1	
Joyabaj (c/v)			
Padrón General			
	1768	746,867/1/5	
	1813	747,056/2/1	
Tributos			
	1739	747,060/9/1	
	1798	746,865/3/40	
Nebaj Nebaj (c/p)			
Padrón General			
	1813	748,131/1/3	
	1819	747,059/1/7	
Tributos			
	1812	747,296/22/33	
	1887	747,295/1/9	
Patzité Patzité (c/p)			
Tributos			
	1887	747,295/2/3	

Location/ Document Type	Years	Roll No.	Comments
Sacapulas (mun)			
Tributos			
	1887	747,295/2/7	
Sacapulas (c/p)			
Correspondencia			
	1795	773,999/3/1	
Padrón			
	1810	747,296/20/17	
Padrón General			
	1803	747,296/18/10	
	1810	747,296/20/14	
	1819	747,056/1/3	
	1824	746,873/2/1	
Tributos			
	1795	747,296/12/1	
	1812	747,296/22/38	
San Andrés Sajcabajá **San Andrés Sajcabajá (c/p)**			
Padrón General			
	1767	746,826/2/19	
Tributos			
	1798	746,865/3/38	
	1887	747,295/1/3	

Location/ Document Type	Years	Roll No.	Comments
San Antonio Ilotenango San Antonio Ilotenango (c/p)			
Padrón General			
	1751	748,125/1/8	
	1768	746,867/1/2	
	1821	763,383/1/1	
Tributos			
	1798	746,865/3/36	
	1887	747,295/2/2	
San Bartolomé Jocotenango San Bartolomé Jocotenango (c/p)			
Correspondencia			
	1761	773,999/4/3	
Padrón General			
	1751	746,868/2/16	
	1792	747,296/11/3	Includes tierra util
Tributos			
	1792	747,296/11/3	
	1798	746,865/3/37	
	1887	747,295/2/6	
San Juan Cotzal San Juan Cotzal (c/p)			
Padrón			
	1816	748,130/9/2	
Padrón General			
	1813	748,131/1/4	

Location/ Document Type	Years	Roll No.	Comments
	1819	747,056/1/6	
Tributos			
	1812	747,296/22/35	
	1887	747,295/2/5	
San Pedro Jocopilas San Pedro Jocopilas (c/p)			
Padrón General			
	1768	746,867/1/4	
	1792	747,296/11/2	Incomplete
Tributos			
	1792	747,296/11/1	
	1798	746,865/3/34	
	1887	747,295/1/12	
Santa Cruz del Quiché (mun)			
Tributos			
	1887	747,295/1/10	
	1887	747,295/1/11	
San Sebastián Lemoa (a)			
Padrón General			
	1751	748,125/1/5	
Tributos			
	1798	746,865/3/33	
	1887	747,295/1/4	

Location/ Document Type	Years	Roll No.	Comments
Santa Cruz del Quiché (c/cd)			
Padrón			
	1693	743,128/6/8	
Padrón General			
	1768	746,867/1/9	
	1813	747,056/2/5	
	1816	746,829/2/12	
Tributos			
	1798	746,865/3/35	
Uspantán (mun)			
Tributos			
	1887	747,295/2/4	
Uspantán (c/p)			
Padrón			
	1802	773,999/8/1	
Padrón General			
	1813	748,131/3/3	
	1819	747,055/1/21	
	1824	746,873/2/2	
Tributos			
	1812	747,296/22/37	

Location/ Document Type	Years	Roll No.	Comments
Zacualpa			
Zacualpa (c/p)			
Padrón General			
	1768	746,866/3/14	
	1813	747,056/2/2	
Tributos			
	1798	746,865/3/39	
	1887	747,295/1/2	
Retalhuleu			
Retalhuleu (mun)			
Padrón General			
	1820	748,132/1/1	
Retalhuleu (c/cd)			
Padrón General			
	1748	747,061/3/11	
	1752	748,125/2/8	
	1754	748,126/1/6	
	1759	746,870/1/1	
	1759	746,870/1/3	
	1759	748,127/3/1	
	1813	748,132/1/2	
	1824	746,820/1/11	
	1825	746,820/1/21	
Tributos			
	1763	748,127/4/4	
	1763	748,127/4/9	

Location/ Document Type	Years	Roll No.	Comments
	1796	773,999/3/69	

San Andrés Villa Seca
San Andrés Villa Seca (c/p)

Padrón General

	1748	747,061/3/12	
	1756	748,126/3/10	
	1759	748,127/1/7	
	1759	748,127/1/10	
	1791	748,130/5/1	
	1821	763,389/3/3	
	1825	746,820/1/19	

Tributos

	1757	748,126/3/18	
	1763	748,127/4/13	
	1796	773,999/3/79	

San Felipe
San Felipe (c/v)

Padrón General

| | 1821 | 763,389/3/4 | |

San Martín Zapotitlán
San Martín Zapotitlán (c/p)

Padrón General

	1723	746,828/3/4	
	1748	747,061/1/8	
	1748	748,126/2/7	
	1753	748,125/3/3	
	1753	748,126/1/4	

Location/ Document Type	Years	Roll No.	Comments
	1756	748,126/2/3	
	1759	748,127/3/5	
	1791	748,130/5/2	
Tributos			
	1723	746,828/3/5	
	1749	748,126/2/5	
	1749	748,126/2/6	
	1757	748,126/3/22	
	1763	748,127/4/15	
	1796	773,999/3/77	

San Sebastián
San Sebastián (c/p)

Padrón General

	1754	748,126/1/7	
	1759	748,127/1/9	

Tributos

	1763	748,127/4/10	
	1796	773,999/3/75	

Sacatepéquez
Alotenango
Alotenango (c/p)

Padrón

	1679	747,059/21/2	
	1741	747,060/10/6	
	1781	763,388/1/9	

Padrón General

	1756	741,890/1/59	

Location/ Document Type	Years	Roll No.	Comments
Tributos			
	1738	746,826/1/8	
	1761	748,127/3/12	
	1776	746,827/1/6	
	1792	763,388/7/16	

Antigua Guatemala
Antigua Guatemala (c/p)

Censo			
	1818	747,296/15/1	Ennumerates Spaniards only ODT/OL

Padrón			
	1817	748,130/5/8	

Tributos			
	1806	741,892/1/9	

San Bartolomé Becerra (a)

Padrón General			
	1739	746,826/2/6	

Tributos			
	1739	746,826/2/5	
	1761	748,127/3/28	
	1776	746,827/1/6	

San Cristóbal el Alto (a)

Padrón General			
	1752	748,125/2/7	
	1760	748,127/3/7	

Location/ Document Type	Years	Roll No.	Comments
Tributos			
	1760	748,127/3/11	
	1776	746,827/1/6	
San Cristóbal el Bajo (a)			
Tributos			
	1758	746,829/2/4	
	1776	746,827/1/6	
San Gaspar Vivar (cas de San Juan del Obispo)			
Padrón			
	1781	747,059/1/22	
	1817	748,130/5/9	
Tributos			
	1761	748,127/3/22	
	1776	746,827/1/6	
San Juan del Obispo (a)			
Correspondencia			
	1725	747,060/5/1	
Padrón			
	1781	747,059/1/8	
Padrón General			
	1755	741,890/1/51	
	1755	746,869/1/46	
Tributos			
	1755	741,890/1/52	

Location/ Document Type	Years	Roll No.	Comments
	1761	748,127/3/25	
	1776	746,827/1/6	

San Juan Gascón (a)

Padrón General

	1752	746,868/2/29	

Tributos

	1763	748,127/3/38	
	1777	746,827/1/6	

San Mateo Milpas Altas (a)

Padrón General

	1752	748,125/2/6	
	1755	748,130/2/7	

Tributos

	1763	748,127/3/43	
	1777	746,827/1/6	

San Pedros las Huertas (a)

Correspondencia

	1749	747,061/3/5	

Padrón

	1781	747,059/1/21	
	1788	746,870/3/1	
	1813	773,999/12/1	
	1813	773,999/12/2	
	1817	746,829/2/13	

Location/ Document Type	Years	Roll No.	Comments
Tributos			
	1761	748,127/3/29	
	1776	746,827/1/6	
	1817	763,386/1/4	
Santa Catarina Bobadilla (a)			
Padrón			
	1817	748,130/5/11	
Padrón General			
	1760	748,127/3/10	
Tributos			
	1760	748,127/3/11	
	1776	746,827/1/6	
Santa Inés del Monte Pulciano (a)			
Tributos			
	1758	746,829/2/8	
Ciudad Vieja Ciudad Vieja (c/p)			
Padrón			
	1781	747,059/1/5	
	1817	746,829/2/14	
Padrón General			
	1752	741,889/2/4	
	1752	746,868/2/39	
	1752	747,058/12/1	Document damage
	1762	748,130/2/8	

Location/ Document Type	Years	Roll No.	Comments
Tributos			
	1753	746,868/2/38	
	1762	748,127/3/32	
	1776	746,827/1/6	
San Lorenzo el Cubo (a)			
Tributos			
	1764	748,127/4/38	
Jocotenango **Jocotenango** (c/p)			
Padrón			
	1819	773,996/1/38	
	1821	748,132/2/5	
	1824	746,872/1/3	
Padrón General			
	1739	746,825/3/27	
	1751	741,889/1/17	
	1813	748,132/2/4	
	1824	746,872/1/2	
Tributos			
	1692	747,060/2/1	
	1750	741,889/1/6	
	1750	746,868/2/3	
	1753	746,869/1/35	
	1756	741,888/2/15	
	1756	741,890/1/36	
	1777	746,827/1/8	

Location/ Document Type	Years	Roll No.	Comments
	1819	763,386/5/1	

Magdalena Milpas Altas
  Magdalena Milpas Altas (c/p)

Padrón

| | 1777-1781 | 747,059/1/2 | |

Padrón General

| | 1742 | 747,060/12/6 | |
| | 1768 | 746,866/3/17 | |

Tributos

	1742	747,060/12/5	
	1761	748,127/3/24	
	1777	746,827/1/6	
	1791	763,388/6/110	
	1797	746,865/3/75	

  San Miguel Milpas Altas (a)

Padrón General

| | 1740 | 747,060/10/5 | |

Tributos

| | 1761 | 748,127/3/15 | |
| | 1771 | 747,827/1/6 | |

  Pastores
    Pastores (c/p)

Padrón General

| | 1679 | 747,059/21/4 | Incomplete |

Location/ Document Type	Years	Roll No.	Comments
Tributos			
	1753	746,869/1/37	
	1756	741,888/2/17	
	1756	741,890/1/38	
San Lorenzo el Tejar (a)			
Padrón			
	1817	746,829/3/4	
Tributos			
	1753	746,869/1/36	
	1756	741,888/2/16	
	1756	741,890/1/37	
San Luis las Carretas (a)			
Padrón General			
	1700	746,827/4/1	Document damage
	1755	741,890/1/49	
Tributos			
	1753	746,869/1/31	
	1756	741,890/1/32	
	1756	741,888/2/11	
San Antonio Aguas Calientes **San Andrés Ceballos** (a)			
Padrón			
	1781	747,059	
Padrón General			
	1813	748,132/2/11	

Location/ Document Type	Years	Roll No.	Comments
Tributos			
	1761	748,124/3/22	
	1761	748,127/3/21	
	1764	748,127/4/40	
	1776	746,827/1/6	
	1792	763,388/7/14	
San Antonio Aguas Calientes (c/p)			
Padrón			
	1781	747,059/1/15	
Padrón General			
	1722	746,825/3/18	
	1813	748,132/2/10	
Tributos			
	1723	746,825/3/19	
	1761	748,127/3/17	
	1764	748,127/4/36	
	1776	746,827/1/6	
	1792	763,388/7/13	
Santiago Zamora (a)			
Padrón			
	1781	763,388/1/12	
Padrón General			
	1752	748,125/3/2	
	1761	748,127/3/50	

Location/ Document Type	Years	Roll No.	Comments
	1813	748,132/2/8	
Tributos			
	1761	748,127/3/19	
	1764	748,127/4/37	
	1776	746,827/1/6	
	1792	763,388/7/11	

San Bartolomé Milpas Altas
  San Bartolomé Milpas Altas (c/p)

Tributos			
	1763	748,127/3/39	
	1777	746,827/1/6	

San Lucas Sacatepéquez
  San Lucas Sacatepéquez (c/p)

Padrón

	n.d.	748,134/1/10	

Tributos			
	1670	748,130/2/9	Incomplete
	1761	748,127/3/31	
	1777	746,827/1/6	

San Miguel Dueñas
  San Miguel Dueñas (c/p)

Padrón

	1781	763,388/1/11	

Padrón General

	1761	748,127/3/49	
	1813	748,132/2/7	

Location/ Document Type	Years	Roll No.	Comments
Tributos			
	1761	748,127/3/16	
	1764	748,127/4/41	
	1776	746,827/1/6	
	1792	763,388/7/10	

Santa Catarina Barahona
  Santa Catarina Barahona (c/p)

Padrón General			
	1733	747,059/3/2	
	1813	748,132/2/9	
Tributos			
	1733	747,059/3/1	
	1761	748,127/3/18	
	1764	748,127/4/39	
	1776	746,827/1/6	
	1792	763,388/7/12	

Santa Lucía Milpas Altas
  Santo Tomás Milpas Altas (a)

Padrón			
	1817	746,829/3/3	
Padrón General			
	1753	748,130/2/6	Incomplete
Tributos			
	1761	748,127/3/14	
	1777	746,827/1/6	

Location/ Document Type	Years	Roll No.	Comments
Santa María de Jesús Santa María de Jesús (c/p)			
Padrón General			
	1732	748,128/7/5	
	1776	763,386/4/5	
	1792	773,996/1/8	
	1813	748,132/2/9	
	1821	747,057/3/11	
Tributos			
	1753	746,869/1/18	
	1754	741,888/1/34	
	1754	741,890/1/18	
	1755	748,126/3/6	
	1761	748,127/3/30	
	1776	746,827/1/6	
	1790	763,388/6/44	
Santiago Sacatepéquez Santiago Sacatepéquez (c/p)			
Padrón			
	1818	746,830/2/4	
Tributos			
	1764	748,127/3/46	
	1777	746,827/1/6	
Santo Domingo Xenacoj Santo Domingo Xenacoj (c/p)			
Padrón General			
	1818	746,829/3/2	

Location/ Document Type	Years	Roll No.	Comments
Sumpango			
<u>Sumpango</u> (c/p)			
Padrón			
	1777	746,827/1/7	
	1818	746,830/2/8	
San Marcos			
Comitancillo			
<u>Comitancillo</u> (c/p)			
Correspondencia			
	1796	773,999/3/62	
Padrón General			
	1741	747,060/10/8	
	1821	747,057/3/1	
Tributos			
	1741	747,060/10/7	
	1757	748,126/4/20	
	1790	763,388/6/48	
	1796	773,999/3/46	
Concepción Tutuapa			
<u>Concepción Tutuapa</u> (c/p)			
Tributos			
	1757	748,126/4/19	
	1790	763,388/6/50	
	1796	773,999/3/48	

Location/ Document Type	Years	Roll No.	Comments
Tutuapa (a)			
Padrón General			
	1821	747,057/1/4	
Malacatán Malacatán (c/cd)			
Padrón General			
	1821	747,057/3/15	
Tributos			
	1790	763,388/6/36	
	1796	773,999/3/34	
San Antonio Sacatepéquez San Antonio Sacatepéquez (c/p)			
Padrón General			
	1750	746,868/2/1	
	1821	747,057/2/1	
Tributos			
	1757	748,126/4/9	
	1796	773,999/3/35	
San Cristóbal Cucho San Cristóbal Cucho (c/p)			
Padrón General			
	1821	747,057/1/2	
Tributos			
	1757	748,126/4/14	
	1769	746,827/1/5	

Location/ Document Type	Years	Roll No.	Comments
	1790	763,388/6/38	
	1796	773,999/3/36	

San Miguel Ixtahuacán
  San Miguel Ixtahuacán (c/p)

Padrón General

	1742	747,060/12/12	
	1820	763,386/3/2	
	1821	747,057/3/10	

Tributos

	1742	747,060/12/11	
	1757	748,126/4/18	
	1790	763,388/6/51	
	1796	773,999/3/49	

San Pablo
  San Pablo (c/p)

Padrón

| | 1824 | 746,822/1/4 | |

Padrón General

| | 1821 | 747,057/3/9 | |

San Pedro Sacatepéquez
  San Pedro Sacatepéquez (c/cd)

Padrón General

| | 1817 | 746,830/2/1 | |
| | 1821 | 747,057/1/11 | |

Tributos

| | 1698 | 746,825/3/8 | |

Location/ Document Type	Years	Roll No.	Comments
	1757	748,126/4/12	
	1790	763,388/6/35	
	1796	773,999/3/33	
Sipacapa Sipacapa (c/p)			
Padrón General			
	1729	746,828/3/7	
	1756	748,126/3/11	Incomplete
	1821	747,057/3/12	
Tributos			
	1757	748,126/4/2	
	1757	748,126/4/13	
	1796	773,999/3/50	
Tacaná Tacaná (c/p)			
Padrón General			
	1821	747,057/1/7	
Tributos			
	1757	748,126/4/17	
	1790	763,388/6/34	
	1796	773,999/3/32	
Tajumulco Tajumulco (c/p)			
Padrón General			
	1821	747,057/3/13	

Location/ Document Type	Years	Roll No.	Comments
Tributos			
	1757	748,126/4/1	
	1757	748,126/4/7	
	1790	763,388/6/49	
	1796	773,999/3/47	
Tejutla Tejutla (c/v)			
Padrón General			
	1821	747,057/3/17	
Tributos			
	1757	748,126/4/10	
	1790	763,388/6/46	
	1796	773,999/3/44	

Santa Rosa
  Casillas
    Casillas (c/p)			

Padrón General			
	1821	748,133/1/11	
Tecuaco (cas)			
Padrón			
	1802-1815	746,829/3/7	
	1831	747,058/10/3	
Padrón General			
	1831	747,058/10/2	
	1833	747,058/13/1	Incomplete

Location/ Document Type	Years	Roll No.	Comments
Cuilapa <u>Cuilapa</u> (c/cd)			Former name Cuajiniquilapa
Padrón General			
	1801	747,296/6/1	
	1821	748,133/2/2	
<u>Los Esclavos</u> (a)			
Padrón General			
	1821	748,133/3/4	
	1825	746,823/1/4	
Chiquimulilla <u>Chiquimulilla</u> (c/v)			
Padrón			
	1804	746,865/7/11	
	1805	746,865/7/12	
Padrón General			
	1813	748,131/3/13	
	1816	746,870/5/1	
	1821	748,133/3/11	
	1825	746,825/2/2	
Tributos			
	1735	747,060/7/2	
<u>Nancinta</u> (a)			
Padrón General			
	1744	747,061/3/3	

Location/ Document Type	Years	Roll No.	Comments
	1756	741,890/1/55	
	1816	741,892/1/16	
	1816	746,828/2/2	
	1821	748,133/1/1	Document damage

Sinacantán (a)

Padrón

	1802-1815	746,829/3/7	

Padrón General

	1756	746,871/1/5	
	1813	748,131/3/8	
	1816	741,892/1/17	
	1816	746,828/2/3	

Tributos

	1735	747,060/7/2	
	1752	741,889/1/32	
	1794	763,388/7/43	

Guazacapán
Guazacapán (c/v)

Padrón General

	1667	747,059/19/1	Incomplete
	1753	748,126/1/1	
	1760	747,058/17/1	
	1816	746,870/4/9	
	1825	746,873/1/2	

Tributos

	1735	747,060/7/2	

Location/ Document Type	Years	Roll No.	Comments

Nueva Santa Rosa
Jumaytepeque (a)

Padrón General

1744	747,061/1/1	
1760	746,826/2/7	
1813	748,131/3/9	
1817	746,830/1/1	
1825	746,825/2/2	
1825	746,825/2/4	

San Juan Tecuaco
San Juan Tecuaco (c/p)

Padrón General

1756	741,890/1/55	
1817	746,830/1/9	
1821	748,133/3/3	

Santa María Ixhuatán
Santa Anita (a)

Padrón General

1813	748,131/3/10	

Tributos

1701	747,060/3/5	

Santa María Ixhuatán (c/p)

Padrón General

1652	747,059/18/1	

Location/ Document Type	Years	Roll No.	Comments
Taxisco Tacuilula (sit arq)			
Padrón			
	1744-1748	747,061/1/12	
Padrón General			
	1721	746,829/1/12	
	1743	747,060/13/12	
	1748	746,868/1/1	
	1751	748,125/2/4	
	1756	746,869/2/9	
Tributos			
	1749	746,868/1/2	
Taxisco (c/p)			
Padrón General			
	1753	741,890/1/43	
	1754	746,869/1/41	
	1756	746,869/2/10	
	1759	746,870/1/5	
	1760	746,826/2/6	
	1767	773,996/1/37	
	1813	748,132/3/9	
	1816	763,386/1/1	
	1821	748,132/3/8	
Tepeaco (a)			
Padrón General			
	1725	747,060/5/2	

Location/ Document Type	Years	Roll No.	Comments
	1743	747,060/12/16	Document damage
	1751	748,125/1/2	
	1756	746,869/2/4	
	1760	746,866/1/1	
	1760	773,996/1/20	
	1760	773,996/1/22	
	1767	746,866/3/9	
Tributos			
	1756	748,126/3/12	

Sololá
  Concepción
    Concepción (c/p)
			Former name Concepción
			Quechelaj

Padrón General			
	1756	746,869/2/6	
	1821	747,056/2/11	
Tributos			
	1887	747,294/1/24	
	1887	747,294/1/46	
Panajachel Panajachel (c/p)			
Padrón General			
	1813	747,056/2/17	
	1821	747,056/2/16	
	1825	746,873/2/5	
	1825	746,873/2/17	

Location/ Document Type	Years	Roll No.	Comments
Tributos			
	1738	746,826/1/7	
	1739	746,826/1/12	
	1798	746,865/3/27	
	1887	747,294/1/27	
San Andrés Semetabaj San Andrés Semetabaj (c/p)			
Padrón General			
	1751	748,125/1/9	
	1821	747,056/2/14	
	1825	746,873/2/8	
Tributos			
	1654	748,126/1/5	
	1798	746,865/3/30	
	1887	747,294/1/26	
San Antonio Palopó San Antonio Palopó (c/p)			
Padrón General			
	1751	748,125/1/7	
	1825	746,873/2/7	
Tributos			
	1798	746,865/3/29	
	1887	747,294/1/28	

Location/ Document Type	Years	Roll No.	Comments
San José Chacayá San José Chacayá (c/p)			
Padrón General			
	1751	748,125/2/3	
	1821	747,056/2/15	
	1825	746,873/2/16	
Tributos			
	1798	746,865/3/15	
	1887	747,294/1/25	
San Juan la Laguna San Juan la Laguna (c/p)			
Correspondencia			
	1825	748,134/1/1	
Padrón General			
	1751	748,125/1/12	
	1768	746,827/1/3	
Tributos			
	1798	746,865/3/19	
	1887	747,294/1/30	
San Lucas Tolimán San Lucas Tolimán (c/p)			
Padrón General			
	1768	747,829/2/10	
Tributos			
	1735	746,826/1/3	
	1735	746,826/1/4	

Location/ Document Type	Years	Roll No.	Comments
	1798	746,865/3/23	
	1887	747,294/1/40	

San Marcos la Laguna
San Marcos la Laguna (c/p)

Padrón General

	1751	748,125/1/11	
	1767	746,826/2/13	
	1825	746,873/2/15	

Tributos

| | 1798 | 746,865/3/21 | |
| | 1887 | 747,294/1/32 | |

San Pablo la Laguna
San Pablo la Laguna (c/p)

Padrón General

| | 1767 | 746,826/2/15 | |
| | 1825 | 746,873/2/13 | |

Tributos

| | 1798 | 746,865/3/20 | |
| | 1887 | 747,294/1/35 | |

San Pedro la Laguna
San Pedro la Laguna (c/p)

Padrón General

	1751	748,125/1/10	
	1767	746,866/3/8	
	1813	747,056/2/19	
	1825	746,873/2/14	

Location/ Document Type	Years	Roll No.	Comments
Tributos			
	1798	746,865/3/16	
	1887	747,294/1/31	

Santa Catarina Ixtahuacán
  Santa Catarina Ixtahuacán (c/p)

Tributos			
	1798	746,865/3/41	

Santa Catarina Palopó
  Santa Catarina Palopó (c/p)

Padrón General			
	1768	746,827/1/2	
	1821	747,056/2/18	
	1825	746,873/2/6	
Tributos			
	1798	746,865/3/28	
	1887	747,294/1/29	

Santa Clara la Laguna
  Santa Clara la Laguna (c/p)

Padrón General			
	1767	746,866/3/10	
	1821	747,056/2/10	
Tributos			
	1798	746,865/3/17	
	1887	747,294/1/33	

Location/ Document Type	Years	Roll No.	Comments
Santa Cruz la Laguna Santa Cruz la Laguna (c/p)			
Padrón General			
	1751	741,889/1/21	
	1751	746,868/2/20	
	1751	748,125/1/13	
Tributos			
	1798	746,865/3/13	
	1887	747,294/1/36	
Santa Lucía Utatlán Santa Lucía Utatlán (c/p)			
Padrón General			
	1821	747,056/2/6	
Tributos			
	1798	746,865/3/12	
	1887	747,294/1/38	
Santa María Visitación Santa María Visitación (c/p)			
Padrón General			
	1751	748,125/1/1	
	1751	748,125/1/14	
	1767	746,826/2/18	
Tributos			
	1798	746,865/3/18	
	1887	747,294/1/34	

Location/ Document Type	Years	Roll No.	Comments
Santiago Atitlán			
<u>Santiago Atitlán</u> (c/p)			
Padrón			
	1734	748,128/7/2	
Padrón General			
	1751	748,125/1/6	
	1768	746,826/2/20	
Tributos			
	1743	741,892/1/20	
	1798	746,865/3/22	
	1887	747,294/1/37	
Sololá			
<u>San Jorge la Laguna</u> (a)			
Tributos			
	1798	746,865/3/14	
<u>Sololá</u> (c/cd)			
Padrón General			
	1767	746,866/3/11	
	1887	747,294/1/22	
Tributos			
	1798	746,865/3/11	
	1887	747,294/1/23	

Location/ Document Type	Years	Roll No.	Comments
Suchitepéquez			
Cuyotenango			
<u>Cuyotenango</u> (c/v)			
Padrón General			
	1740	746,826/1/16	
	1748	747,061/1/11	
	1759	748,127/1/3	
	1759	748,127/1/6	
	1791	763,386/4/4	
	1791	773,996/1/1	
	1821	763,389/3/1	
Tributos			
	1757	748,126/3/28	
	1763	748,127/4/11	
	1796	773,999/3/76	
	1887	747,295/2/56	Document damage
Mazatenango			
<u>Mazatenango</u> (c/cd)			
Padrón			
	1777	741,739/1/13	
	1777	741,891/2/5	
Padrón General			
	1749	748,124/1/3,7	
	1753	748,125/3/5	
	1756	748,126/3/15	
	1759	748,127/1/17	
	1759	748,127/3/4	
	1813	748,132/1/3	

Location/ Document Type	Years	Roll No.	Comments
	1813	748,132/1/5	
Tributos			
	1749	748,124/1/6	
	1757	748,126/3/17	
	1763	748,127/4/3	
	1796	773,999/3/70	
	1887	747,295/2/54	Document damage
Tahuexco (a)			
Tributos			
	1887	747,295/2/66	
Patulul			
Patulul (c/p)			
Padrón General			
	1751	748,124/3/5	
	1813	747,056/2/13	
	1821	747,056/2/7	
	1825	746,873/2/10	
Tributos			
	1798	746,865/3/24	
	1887	747,294/1/39	
Samayac			
Samayac (c/v)			
Correspondencia			
	1796	773,999/3/83	
Padrón General			
	1726	746,828/3/2	

Location/ Document Type	Years	Roll No.	Comments
	1752	748,125/2/9	
	1759	748,127/1/18-2/1	
	1778	746,828/1/1	
	1813	748,132/1/2	
	1813	748,132/2/1	
	1825	746,820/1/20	

Tributos

	1726	746,828/3/1	
	1748	747,061/3/6	
	1757	748,126/3/27	
	1763	748,127/4/21	
	1764	748,127/4/23	
	1796	773,999/3/66	
	1887	747,295/2/55	Document damage

San Antonio Suchitepéquez
  Carranza (cas de Nueva Venecia)

Padrón General

	1759	748,127/1/5	

San Antonio Suchitepéquez (c/v)

Padrón General

	1752	748,125/3/1	
	1759	748,127/1/12	
	1768	746,866/3/15	
	1813	748,132/1/4	
	1821	748,133/1/7	

Tributos

	1763	748,127/4/6	

Location/ Document Type	Years	Roll No.	Comments
	1776	748,128/3/1	
	1796	773,999/3/65	
	1821	748,133/1/9	
	1887	747,295/2/58	Document damage

San Bernardino
San Bernardino (c/p)

Padrón General

	1752	748,125/2/5	
	1756	748,126/3/13	
	1759	748,127/3/3	
	1821	748,133/1/8	

Tributos

	1757	748,126/3/23	
	1763	748,127/4/5	
	1796	773,999/3/68	
	1887	747,295/2/67	

San Francisco Zapotitlán
San Francisco Zapotitlán (c/p)

Padrón General

	1759	748,127/1/4	
	1759	748,127/1/7	
	1790	748,130/4/2	
	1813	748,132/1/2	

Tributos

	1757	748,126/3/19	
	1791	773,996/1/4	
	1791	773,996/1/5	

Location/ Document Type	Years	Roll No.	Comments
	1796	773,999/3/63	

San Gabriel
San Gabriel (c/p)

Padrón General

	1748	747,061/1/7	
	1748	747,061/1/10	
	1756	748,126/3/2	
	1790	748,130/4/3	Incomplete
	1820	748,132/1/3	
	1825	746,820/1/16	

Tributos

	1748	747,061/1/6	
	1757	748,126/3/26	
	1763	748,127/4/2	
	1796	773,999/3/71	
	1887	747,295/2/65	

San José el Idolo
San José el Idolo (c/p)

Tributos

	1887	747,295/2/60	

San Lorenzo
San Lorenzo (c/p)

Documents designated as an anexo of Mazatenango, cabecera municipal of Suchitepéquez

Padrón General

	1743	746,871/1/1	

Location/ Document Type	Years	Roll No.	Comments
	1752	746,868/3/6	
	1759	746,870/1/4	
	1759	748,127/3/2	
	1781	747,296/16/7	
	1790	763,386/4/1	
	1819	747,055/1/24	
	1820	748,132/1/3	
	1825	746,820/1/17	
Tributos			
	1757	748,126/3/19	
	1763	748,127/4/22	
	1796	773,999/3/72	
	1812	747,296/22/29	
	1887	747,295/2/62	

San Miguel Panán
  San Miguel Panán (c/p)

Tributos

	1887	747,295/2/64	

San Pablo Jocopilas
  San Pablo Jocopilas (c/p)

Correspondencia

	1796	773,999/3/84	

Padrón General

	1748	747,061/1/9	
	1748	747,061/2/1	
	1748	747,061/2/3	
	1748	747,061/3/4	

Location/ Document Type	Years	Roll No.	Comments
	1752	746,868/3/4	Document damage
	1753	748,125/3/4	
	1759	748,127/1/11	
	1759	748,127/1/14	
	1768	746,867/1/6	
	1813	748,132/1/2	
	1824	746,873/2/4	
Tributos			
	1728	746,828/3/6	
	1739	746,826/1/11	
	1739	746,826/1/13	
	1757	748,126/3/24	
	1763	748,127/4/20	
	1887	747,295/2/61	

Santa Bárbara
Santa Bárbara (c/p)

Padrón General

	Years	Roll No.	Comments
	1751	746,865/3/26	
	1821	747,056/2/9	
	1825	746,873/2/12	
Tributos			
	1798	746,865/3/26	
	1887	747,294/1/41	

Santo Domingo Suchitepéquez
San Miguelito (cas)   Former name San Miguel Solochichas

Padrón General

	Years	Roll No.	Comments
	1740	741,889/1/36	
	1740	741,889/2/2	

Location/ Document Type	Years	Roll No.	Comments
	1740	746,868/2/34	
	1740	746,868/2/37	
	1752	741,889/1/37	
	1752	746,868/2/35	
	1759	748,127/1/15	
	1805	763,389/1/3	
Tributos			
	1741	741,889/1/35	
	1741	741,889/1/38	
	1741	741,889/2/1	
	1741	746,868/2/33	Document damage
	1751	746,868/2/36	Document damage
	1757	748,126/3/21	
	1763	748,127/4/19	

Santo Domingo Suchitepéquez (c/p)

Tributos

	1887	747,295/2/59	Document damage

Santo Tomás la Unión
  Santo Tomás la Unión (c/p)   Former name Santo
                                         Tomás Perdido

Tributos

	1887	747,295/2/63	

Totonicapán
  Momostenango
    Momostenango (c/v)

Padrón General

	1803	747,296/18/6	
	1810	747,296/20/5	

Location/ Document Type	Years	Roll No.	Comment
	1813	748,131/2/2	
	1818	747,055/1/3	
	1824	746,820/1/1	
Tributos			
	1812	747,296/22/40	

San Andrés Xecul
San Andrés Xecul (c/p)

Correspondencia

	1801	748,130/8/4	

Padrón General

	1813	748,131/1/7	
	1818	747,055/1/2	

San Bartolo
San Bartolo (c/p)

Padrón General

	1758	748,126/4/22	
	1819	747,056/1/8	

Tributos

	1812	747,296/22/41	

San Cristóbal Totonicapán
San Cristóbal Totonicapán (c/v)

Correspondencia

	1813	748,130/8/3	

Padrón

	1813	748,131/1/10	

Location/ Document Type	Years	Roll No.	Comments
Padrón General			
	1803	747,296/18/5	
	1810	747,296/20/3	
	1813	748,131/1/6	
	1819	747,056/1/14	
Tributos			
	1812	747,296/22/42	

San Francisco el Alto
San Francisco el Alto (c/p)

Padrón			
	1815	748,130/9/1	
Padrón General			
	1749	746,829/1/11	
	1812	747,296/22/43	
	1818	746,830/2/2	
Tributos			
	1749	746,829/1/11	Document damage

Santa María Chiquimula
Santa María Chiquimula (c/p)

Padrón General			
	1749	748,124/1/1	
	1818	746,830/2/6	
	1818	748,130/9/4	
Tributos			
	1812	747,296/22/39	

Location/ Document Type	Years	Roll No.	Comments
Totonicapán (mun)			
Padrón General			
	1825	746,820/1/2	
Tototonicapán (c/cd)			
Censo			
	1813	747,296/23/1	Incomplete
Correspondencia			
	1795	773,999/3/5	
	1801	763,388/3/2	
Padrón			
	1796	746,865/5/4	
	1796	746,865/6/1	
Padrón General			
	1749	748,124/3/1	
	1760	746,870/1/6	
	1803	747,296/18/3	
	1810	747,296/20/2	
Tributos			
	1690	747,060/1/1	Illegible
	1750	748,124/3/2	
	1798	746,865/5/5	
	1798	746,865/6/2	Duplicate of 746,865/5/5
	1803	745,419/10	ODT/OL Legajo 1334

Location/ Document Type	Years	Roll No.	Comments
Zacapa			
Cabañas			
Cabañas (c/p)			Former name San Sebastían Chimalapa
Padrón			
	1817	746,829/3/10	
	1825	746,823/1/1	
	1826	746,824/1/5	
Padrón General			
	1825	746,823/1/2	
	1826	746,824/1/4	
Tributos			
	1791	763,388/6/107	
	1797	746,865/3/72	
	1813	748,131/3/22	
Estanzuela			
Estanzuela (c/p)			
Padrón General			
	1826	746,823/1/14	
Gualán			
Gualán (c/v)			
Padrón			
	1841	747,058/8/3	
Padrón General			
	1760	748,127/3/9	
	1797	747,296/14/1	

Location/ Document Type	Years	Roll No.	Comments
	1817	746,830/1/17	
	1821	748,133/1/3	
	1824	746,822/1/10	
	1839	747,058/8/1	
	1841	747,058/8/2	
Tributos			
	1761	773,996/1/24	
	1791	763,388/6/105	
	1797	746,865/3/70	

Río Hondo
Río Hondo (c/p)

Padrón General

	1826	746,823/1/15	

Usumatlán
Usumatlán (c/p)

Padrón General

	1742	747,060/12/4	
	1750	748,124/3/9	
	1758	748,126/4/25	
	1826	746,823/1/16	

Tributos

	1742	747,060/12/3	
	1751	748,124/3/10	
	1791	763,388/6/108	
	1797	746,865/3/73	
	1821	763,383/2/14	

Location/ Document Type	Years	Roll No.	Comments
Zacapa			
San Pablo (a)			
Padrón			
	1817	748,130/5/5	
Padrón General			
	1752	748,124/2/6	
	1756	748,126/2/4	
Tributos			
	1761	773,996/1/21	
	1761	773,996/1/23	
	1791	763,388/6/104	
	1797	746,865/3/69	
Santa Lucía (a)			
Padrón General			
	1756	746,869/2/1	
Zacapa (c/cd)			
Padrón			
	1817	746,829/2/15	
	1824	746,822/1/4	
Padrón General			
	1750	748,124/2/11	
	1756	748,126/3/1	
	1821	748,130/1/1	Document damage
	1825	746,823/1/3	

Location/ Document Type	Years	Roll No.	Comments
Tributos			
	1750	746,868/2/5	
	1753	746,869/1/39	
	1757	741,890/1/41	
	1791	763,388/6/103	
	1797	746,865/3/68	
	1824	746,822/1/4	

EL SALVADOR
nación

Ahuachapán
  Ahuachapán
    Ahuachapán (c/cd)

Padrón General

	1813	763,382/1/1	

Tributos

	1791	741,887/4/5	
	1791	763,388/6/6	
	1796	741,887/5/1	

Concepción de Ataco (c/v)

Censo

	1821	763,383/2/16	

Padrón General

	1813	763,382/1/2	

Tributos

	1791	741,887/4/7	
	1791	763,388/6/8	

Location/ Document Type	Years	Roll No.	Comments
	1796	741,887/5/3	
	1796	733,999/3/10	
Apaneca Apaneca (c/v)			
Padrón General			
	1821	763,383/3/1	
Tributos			
	1791	741,887/4/21	
	1791	763,388/6/22	
	1796	741,887/5/17	
	1796	773,999/3/24	
Atiquizaya Atiquizaya (c/cd)			
Padrón General			
	1821	763,383/3/5	
Guaymango Guaymango (c/p)			
Padrón General			
	1821	763,383/2/5	
Tributos			
	1791	741,887/4/9	
	1791	763,388/6/10	
	1791	763,388/6/13	
	1796	741,887/5/5	
	1796	773,999/3/12	

Location/ Document Type	Years	Roll No.	Comments
Jujutla Jujutla (c/p)			
Padrón General			
	1821	763,383/2/6	
Tributos			
	1791	741,887/4/10	
	1791	763,388/6/11	
	1796	741,887/5/6	
	1796	773,999/3/13	
San Pedro Puxtla San Pedro Puxtla (c/v)			
Padrón General			
	1821	763,383/1/9	
	1821	763,383/2/2	
Tributos			
	1791	741,887/4/17	
	1791	763,388/6/18	
	1796	741,887/5/13	
	1796	773,999/3/20	
Tacuba Tacuba (c/v)			
Padrón General			
	1813	763,382/1/3	
Tributos			
	1791	741,887/4/6	
	1791	763,338/6/7	

Location/ Document Type	Years	Roll No.	Comments
	1796	741,887/5/2	
	1796	773,999/3/9	

Cabañas
  Guacotecti
    Guacotecti (c/v)			

Tributos			
	1790	741,887/3/51	
	1803	741,887/6/50	
Ilobasco Ilobasco (c/cd)			
Tributos			
	1790	741,887/3/71	
	1803	741,887/6/70	
Sensuntepeque Sensuntepeque (c/cd)			
Tributos			
	1790	741,887/3/50	
	1803	741,887/6/49	

Cuscatlán
  Cojetepeque
    Cojutepeque (c/cd)			

Padrón General			
	1813	763,381/1/1	
Tributos			
	1790	741,887/3/70	
	1803	741,887/6/69	

Location/ Document Type	Years	Roll No.	Comments
San Bartolomé Perulapán San Bartolomé Perulapán (c/v)			
Padrón General			
	1813	763,382/1/13	
Tributos			
	1790	741,887/3/73	
	1803	741,887/6/72	
San José Guayabal San José Guayabal (c/v)			
Tributos			
	1790	741,887/3/81	
	1803	741,887/6/80	
San Pedro Perulapán San Pedro Perulapán (c/cd)			
Padrón General			
	1813	763,382/1/12	
Tributos			
	1790	741,887/3/72	
	1803	741,887/6/71	
Suchitoto Suchitoto (c/cd)			
Tributos			
	1790	741,887/3/75	
	1803	741,887/6/74	

Location/ Document Type	Years	Roll No.	Comments
Tenancingo Tenancingo (c/v)			
Tributos			
	1790	741,887/3/76	
	1803	741,887/6/75	

Chalatenango
  Arcatao
    Arcatao (c/v)			

Tributos			
	1790	741,887/3/54	
	1803	741,887/6/53	
Citalá Citalá (c/v)			
Tributos			
	1790	741,887/3/57	
	1803	741,887/6/56	
Chalatenango Chalatenango (c/cd)			
Padrón General			
	1746	763,386/7/1	
Tributos			
	1790	741,887/3/52	
	1803	741,887/6/51	

Location/ Document Type	Years	Roll No.	Comments
Tejutla			
Tejutla (c/cd)			
Padrón General			
	1813	763,382/1/4	
Tributos			
	1790	741,887/3/56	
	1803	741,887/6/55	
La Libertad			
Antiguo Cuscatlán			
Antiguo Cuscatlán (c/v)			Also known as Nuevo Cuscatlán
Padrón General			
	1756	741,890/1/58	
	1813	763,381/3/8	
Tributos			
	1790	741,887/3/28	
	1803	741,887/6/27	
Comasagua			
Comasagua (c/v)			
Padrón General			
	1821	763,383/1/3	
Tributos			
	1790	741,887/3/26	
	1803	741,887/6/25	

Location/ Document Type	Years	Roll No.	Comments
Chiltiupán Chiltiupán (c/p)			
Padrón General			
	1821	763,383/1/4	
Tributos			
	1790	741,887/3/23	
	1803	741,887/6/22	
Huizúcar Huizúcar (c/v)			
Padrón General			
	1813	763,381/3/7	
Tributos			
	1790	741,887/3/29	
	1803	741,887/6/28	
Jayaque Jayaque (c/cd)			
Padrón General			
	1813	763,381/3/13	
Nuevo Cuscatlán Nuevo Cuscatlán (c/p)			See Antiguo Cuscatlán
Quezaltepeque Quezaltepeque (c/cd)			
Padrón General			
	1813	763,382/1/7	
Tributos			
	1790	741,887/3/55	

Location/ Document Type	Years	Roll No.	Comments
	1803	741,887/6/54	

Sacacoya
Sacacoya (c/p)

Tributos

| | 1790 | 741,887/3/14 | |
| | 1803 | 741,887/6/13 | |

San Juan Opico
San Juan Opico (c/cd)

Padrón General

| | 1813 | 763,381/3/10 | |

Tributos

| | 1790 | 741,887/3/82 | |
| | 1803 | 741,887/6/81 | |

San Pablo Tacachico
San Pablo Tacachico (c/p)

Padrón General

| | 1813 | 763,381/3/11 | |

Tributos

| | 1790 | 741,887/3/12 | |
| | 1803 | 741,887/6/11 | |

Tamanique
Tamanique (c/p)

Tributos

| | 1790 | 741,887/3/25 | |
| | 1803 | 741,887/6/24 | |

Location/ Document Type	Years	Roll No.	Comments
Teotepeque <u>Teotepeque</u> (c/v)			
Tributos			
	1790	741,890/3/21	
	1803	741,887/6/21	
Tepecoyo <u>Tepecoyo</u> (c/pv)			
Padrón General			
	1813	763,381/3/12	
Tributos			
	1790	741,887/3/13	
	1803	741,887/6/12	
Municipio unknown <u>Ateos</u>			
Tributos			
	1790	741,887/3/20	
	1803	741,887/6/19	
La Paz Cuyultitán <u>Cuyultitán</u> (c/v)			
Tributos			
	1790	741,887/3/41	
	1803	741,887/6/40	
Olocuilta <u>Olocuilta</u> (c/cd)			
Tributos			
	1790	741,887/3/40	
	1803	741,887/6/39	

Location/ Document Type	Years	Roll No.	Comments
San Francisco Chinameca <u>San Francisco Chinameca</u> (c/p)			
Tributos			
	1732	746,867/7/1	
	1732	741,888/3/6	
	1790	741,887/3/35	
	1803	741,887/6/34	
San Juan Nonualco <u>San Juan Nonualco</u> (c/cd)			
Padrón General			
	1813	763,381/1/3	
Tributos			
	1790	741,887/3/48	
	1803	741,887/6/47	
San Juan Talpa <u>San Juan Talpa</u> (c/v)			
Tributos			
	1790	741,887/3/42	
	1803	741,887/6/41	
San Juan Tepezontes <u>San Juan Tepezontes</u> (c/v)			
Tributos			
	1790	741,887/3/36	
	1803	741,887/6/35	

Location/ Document Type	Years	Roll No.	Comments
San Miguel Tepezontes San Miguel Tepezontes			
Tributos			
	1790	741,887/3/37	
	1803	741,887/6/36	
San Pedro Masahuat San Pedro Masahuat (c/cd)			
Tributos			
	1790	741,887/3/34	
	1803	741,887/6/33	
San Pedro Nonualco San Pedro Nonualco (c/cd)			
Padrón General			
	1813	763,381/1/4	
Tributos			
	1790	741,887/3/47	
	1803	741,887/6/46	
Santa María Ostuma Santa María Ostuma (c/v)			
Tributos			
	1790	741,887/3/49	
	1803	741,887/6/48	
Santiago Nonualco Santiago Nonualco (c/cd)			
Padrón General			
	1813	763,381/1/2	

Location/ Document Type	Years	Roll No.	Comments
Tributos			
	1790	741,887/3/43	
	1803	741,887/6/42	
Tapalhuaca 　Tapalhuaca (c/p)			
Tributos			
	1790	741,887/3/39	
	1803	741,887/6/38	
Zacatecoluca 　Zacatecoluca (c/cd)			
Padrón General			
	1783	741,887/1/1	
	1783	763,385/1/1	
Tributos			
	1783	763,385/1/2	
	1790	741,887/3/44	
	1803	741,887/6/43	
La Unión 　Anamorós 　　Anamorós (c/v)			
Padrón General			
	1813	763,384/1/1	
	1820	763,384/3/12	
Tributos			
	1790	741,887/3/97	
	1803	741,887/6/96	

Location/ Document Type	Years	Roll No.	Comments
El Sauce El Sauce (c/v)			
Padrón General			
	1813	763,384/1/4	
	1820	763,384/3/10	
Intipucá Intipucá (c/v)			
Tributos			
	1790	741,887/3/122	
	1803	741,887/6/121	
Lislique Lislique (c/v)			
Padrón General			
	1813	763,384/1/3	
	1820	763,384/3/1	
Tributos			
	1790	741,887/3/98	
	1803	741,887/3/97	
Meanguera del Golfo Meanguera del Golfo (c/p)			
Padrón General			
	1820	763,384/1/14	
	1820	763,384/3/2	

Location/ Document Type	Years	Roll No.	Comments
Pasaquina			
Pasaquina (c/cd)			
Padrón General			
	1813	763,384/1/6	
Polorós			
Polorós (c/v)			
Padrón General			
	1813	763,384/1/2	
	1820	763,384/3/4	
Tributos			
	1790	741,887/3/99	
	1803	741,887/6/98	
Santa Rosa de Lima			
Santa Rosa de Lima (c/cd)			
Padrón General			
	1813	763,384/1/5	
	1820	763,384/3/3	
Yayantique			
Yayantique (c/p)			
Tributos			
	1790	741,887/3/123	
	1803	741,887/6/122	
Municipio unknown			
Cacaopera			
Padrón General			
	1820	763,384/3/5	

Location/ Document Type	Years	Roll No.	Comments
Tributos			
	1790	741,887/3/111	
	1803	741,887/6/110	
Morazán Arambala Arambala (c/p)			
Padrón General			
	1820	763,384/1/10	
Tributos			
	1790	741,887/3/106	
	1803	741,887/6/105	
Municipio unknown Chilanga			
Padrón General			
	1820	763,384/3/8	
Tributos			
	1790	741,887/3/92	
	1803	741,887/6/91	
Gualococte			
Padrón General			
	1820	763,384/3/14	
Tributos			
	1790	741,887/3/103	
	1803	741,887/6/102	

Location/ Document Type	Years	Roll No.	Comments
Guatajiagua			
Padrón General			
	1820	763,384/1/19	
	1820	763,384/2/1	
Jocoro			
Tributos			
	1790	741,887/3/117	
	1803	741,887/6/116	
Lolotiquillo			
Padrón General			
	1820	763,384/3/11	
Tributos			
	1790	741,887/3/93	
	1803	741,887/6/92	
Osicala			
Padrón General			
	1820	763,384/1/15	
	1820	763,384/3/15	
Tributos			
	1790	741,887/3/109	
	1803	741,887/6/108	

Location/ Document Type	Years	Roll No.	Comments
Perquin			
Padrón General			
	1820	763,384/1/11	
Tributos			
	1790	741,887/3/105	
	1803	741,887/6/104	
San Francisco Goterra (cap)			
Padrón General			
	1820	763,384/3/16	
	1820	763,384/3/19	
Tributos			
	1790	741,887/3/91	
	1803	741,887/6/90	
San Simón			
Padrón General			
	1820	763,384/3/7	
	1820	763,384/3/18	
Tributos			
	1790	741,887/3/102	
	1803	741,887/6/101	
Sensembra			
Padrón General			
	1820	763,384/3/6	

Location/ Document Type	Years	Roll No.	Comments
Tributos			
	1790	741,887/3/94	
	1803	741,887/6/93	
Torola			
Padrón General			
	1820	763,384/3/13	
Tributos			
	1790	741,887/3/104	
	1803	741,887/6/103	
Yamabal			
Padrón General			
	1820	763,384/3/9	
Tributos			
	1790	741,887/3/95	
	1803	741,887/6/94	
Yoloaiquin			
Padrón General			
	1820	763,384/3/17	
Tributos			
	1790	741,887/3/110	
	1790	741,887/3/116	
	1803	741,887/6/109	
	1803	741,887/6/115	

Location/ Document Type	Years	Roll No.	Comments
San Miguel Ciudad Barrios Amapala (cas)			
Tributos			
	1790	741,887/3/121	
	1803	741,887/6/120	
Ciudad Barrios (c/cd)			Former name Cacaguatique
Tributos			
	1790	741,887/3/101	
	1803	741,887/6/100	
Comacarán Comacarán (c/p)			
Tributos			
	1790	741,887/3/118	
	1803	741,887/6/117	
Chinameca Chinameca (c/cd)			
Padrón General			
	1732	741,888/3/7	
	1732	746,867/7/2	
	1813	763,384/1/8	
Tributos			
	1790	741,887/3/89	
	1803	741,887/6/88	

Location/ Document Type	Years	Roll No.	Comments
Lolotique Lolotique (c/v)			
Tributos			
	1790	741,887/3/90	
	1803	741,887/6/89	
Moncagua Moncagua (c/v)			
Tributos			
	1790	741,887/3/113	
	1803	741,887/6/112	
Quelepa Quelepa (c/v)			
Tributos			
	1790	741,887/3/112	
	1803	741,887/6/111	
Sesori Sesori (c/cd)			
Tributos			
	1790	741,887/3/100	
	1803	741,887/6/99	
Uluazapa Uluazapa (c/v)			
Tributos			
	1803	741,887/6/118	

Location/ Document Type	Years	Roll No.	Comments

San Salvador
  Apopa
    Apopa (c/cd)			

Padrón General			
	1813	763,382/1/6	
Tributos			
	1790	741,887/3/64	
	1803	741,887/6/63	
Ayutuxtepeque Ayutuxtepeque (c/p)			
Tributos			
	1790	741,887/3/67	
	1803	741,887/6/66	
Cuscatancingo Cuscatancingo (c/p)			
Padrón General			
	1755	741,887/8/2	
Tributos			
	1790	741,887/3/61	
	1803	741,887/6/60	
El Paisnal El Paisnal (c/p)			
Padrón General			
	1813	763,382/1/9	

Location/ Document Type	Years	Roll No.	Comments
Guazapa Guazapa (c/cd)			
Padrón General			
	1813	763,382/1/8	
Tributos			
	1790	741,887/3/63	
	1803	741,887/6/62	
Ilopango Ilopango (c/cd)			
Tributos			
	1790	741,887/3/60	
	1803	741,887/6/59	
Mejicanos Mejicanos (c/cd)			
Tributos			
	1791	763,388/6/15	
	1796	773,999/3/17	
Nejapa Nejapa (c/cd)			
Padrón General			
	1813	763,382/1/5	
Tributos			
	1790	741,887/3/65	
	1803	741,887/6/64	

Location/ Document Type	Years	Roll No.	Comments
Panchimalco Panchimalco (c/v)			
Padrón General			
	1813	763,381/3/6	
Tributos			
	1790	741,887/3/30	
	1803	741,887/6/29	
Santiago Texacuangos Santiago Texacuangos (c/v)			
Tributos			
	1790	741,887/3/33	
	1803	741,887/6/32	
Soyapango Soyapango (c/cd)			
Tributos			
	1790	741,887/3/59	
	1803	741,887/6/58	
Tonacatepeque Tonacatepeque (c/cd)			
Tributos			
	1790	741,887/3/58	
	1790	741,887/3/15	
	1803	741,887/6/14	
	1803	741,887/6/57	

Location/ Document Type	Years	Roll No.	Comments

San Vicente
  Apastepeque
    Apastepeque (c/cd)			

Padrón General			
	1755	746,869/1/48	
	1756	741,890/1/56	
Tributos			
	1790	741,887/3/77	
	1803	741,887/6/76	
San Cayetano Istepeque San Cayetano Istepeque (c/v)			
Tributos			
	1790	741,887/3/79	
	1803	741,887/6/78	
Tecoluca Tecoluca (c/cd)			
Tributos			
	1790	741,887/3/46	
	1803	741,887/6/45	

Santa Ana
  Coatepeque
    Coatepeque (c/cd)			

Padrón General			
	1755	741,890/1/45	
Tributos			
	1790	741,887/3/11	
	1803	741,887/6/10	

Location/ Document Type	Years	Roll No.	Comments
Chalchuapa			
<u>Chalchuapa</u> (c/cd)			
Tributos			
	1790	741,887/3/8	
	1803	741,887/6/7	
Masahuat			
<u>Masahuat</u> (c/p)			Placement on film suggests this location over Masagua, Escuintla
Padrón General			
	1750	741,889/1/14	
	1821	763,383/2/1	
Tributos			
	1790	741,887/3/38	
	1803	741,887/6/37	
Metapán			
<u>Conchagua</u>			
Tributos			
	1790	741,887/3/120	
	1803	741,887/6/119	
<u>Metapán</u> (c/cd)			
Padrón General			
	1755	741,887/8/1	
	1755	746,867/2/2	
	1787	741,887/2/1	
	1787	746,865/4/2	
	1813	763,381/3/9	

Location/ Document Type	Years	Roll No.	Comments
Tributos			
	1787–1789	741,887/3/1	
	1790	741,887/3/4	
	1803	741,887/6/3	
Santa Ana Santa Ana (c/cd)			
Padrón General			
	1714	746,827/4/2	
	1813	763,381/2/1	
	1813	763,381/3/1	
Texistepeque Texistepeque (c/cd)			
Tributos			
	1790	741,887/3/5	
	1803	741,887/6/4	
Sonsonate Caluco Caluco (c/p)			
Padrón General			
	1821	763,383/2/3	
Tributos			
	1791	741,887/4/8	
	1791	763,383/6/9	
	1796	741,887/5/4	
	1796	773,999/3/11	

Location/Document Type	Years	Roll No.	Comments
Cuisnahuat			
Cuisnahuat (c/p)			
Tributos			
	1790	741,887/3/17	
	1803	741,887/6/16	
Izalco			
Izalco (c/cd)			
Padrón General			
	1813	763,381/3/3	
	1813	763,381/3/4	
Tributos			
	1791	741,887/4/15	
	1791	741,887/4/25	
	1791	763,388/6/16	
	1791	763,388/6/26	
	1796	741,887/5/11	
	1796	741,887/5/22	
	1796	773,999/3/18	
	1796	773,996/3/28	
Juayúa			
Juayúa (c/cd)			
Padrón General			
	1821	763,383/3/2	
Tributos			
	1796	741,887/5/19	

Location/ Document Type	Years	Roll No.	Comments
Nahuizalco Nahuizalco (c/cd)			
Padrón General			
	1813	763,381/3/2	
	1821	763,383/3/4	
Tributos			
	1791	741,887/4/18	
	1791	763,388/6/19	
	1796	741,887/5/14	
	1796	773,999/3/21	
Nahulingo Nahulingo (c/p)			
Padrón General			
	1755	747,058/16/1	
	1821	763,383/2/4	
Tributos			
	1791	741,887/4/11	
	1791	763,388/6/12	
	1796	741,887/5/7	
	1796	773,999/3/14	
Salcoatitán Salcoatitán (c/p)			
Padrón General			
	1821	763,383/3/3	

Location/ Document Type	Years	Roll No.	Comments
San Antonio del Monte San Antonio del Monte (c/p)			
Tributos			
	1791	741,887/4/24	
	1791	763,388/6/25	
	1796	741,887/5/21	
	1796	773,999/3/27	
Santa Catarina Masahuat Santa Catarina Masahuat (c/p)			
Tributos			
	1791	741,887/4/19	
	1791	763,388/6/20	
	1796	741,887/5/15	
	1796	773,999/3/22	
Sonsonate Sonsonate (c/cd)			
Padrón General			
	1821	763,383/2/7	
Tributos			
	1794	763,386/9/1	
Sonzacate Sonzacate (c/cd)			
Padrón General			
	1821	763,383/2/13	
Tributos			
	1791	741,887/4/13	

Location/ Document Type	Years	Roll No.	Comments
	1791	763,388/6/14	
	1796	741,887/5/9	
	1796	773,999/3/16	

Usulatán
  Ereguayquín
    Ereguayquín (c/p)

Tributos

| | 1790 | 741,887/3/114 | |
| | 1803 | 741,887/6/113 | |

  Jiquilisco
    Jiquilisco (c/cd)

Tributos

| | 1790 | 741,887/3/83 | |
| | 1803 | 741,887/6/82 | |

  Jucuapa
    Jucuapa (c/cd)

Tributos

| | 1790 | 741,887/3/88 | |
| | 1803 | 741,887/6/87 | |

  Jucuarán
    Jucuarán (c/v)

Tributos

| | 1790 | 741,887/3/115 | |
| | 1803 | 741,887/6/114 | |

Location/ Document Type	Years	Roll No.	Comments
Usulatán			
Usulatán (c/cd)			
Tributos			
	1791	741,887/3/84	
	1803	741,887/6/83	
Municipio unknown			
Tecapa			
Padrón General			
	1813	763,384/1/9	
Tributos			
	1790	741,887/3/86	
	1803	741,887/6/85	

Departamentos and municipios for the following
could not be located

Mizata			
Tributos			
	1790	741,889/3/18	
	1803	741,887/6/17	
Remedios			
Tributos			
	1790	741,887/3/85	
	1803	741,887/6/84	
San Carlos			Gaz/various
Padrón General			
	1820	763,384/1/18	

Location/Document Type	Years	Roll No.	Comments
San Fernando			Gaz/various
Padrón General			
	1820	763,384/1/17	
San Jacinto			Gaz/various
Padrón General			
	1813	763,381/3/5	
Tributos			
	1790	741,887/3/27	
	1803	741,887/6/26	
Santa Lucía			Gaz/various
Padrón General			
	1746	746,867/2/1	

HONDURAS
nación

Location/Document Type	Years	Roll No.	Comments
Comayagua **Comayagua**			
Tributos			
	1755	763,386/8/1	
	1806	763,386/4/6	
Humuya			Former name Tambla
Tributos			
	1753	746,869/1/9	
	1754	741,888/1/25	
	1754	741,890/1/9	

Location/ Document Type	Years	Roll No.	Comments
Siquatepeque			
Tributos			
	1753	746,869/1/13-15	
	1754	741,888/1/29	
	1754	741,888/1/30	
	1754	741,890/1/13	
	1754	741,890/1/14-15	
Cortes Omoa			
Padrón General			
	1777	741,739/1/6	
	1777	741,891/1/3	
	1777	744,866/5/6	
	1825	746,825/2/8	
San Pedro Sula (cap)			
Tributos			
	1782	744,866/4/2	
	1782	744,866/4/5	
	1783	744,866/4/1	
Gracias Gualcince			
Padrón General			
	1821	747,059/12/6	

Location/ Document Type	Years	Roll No.	Comments
La Paz <u>Similatón</u>			
Tributos			
	1753	746,869/1/11	
	1754	741,888/1/27	
	1754	741,890/1/11	
Santa Bárbara <u>Petoa</u>			
Padrón General			
	1703	763,390/1/1	
Tegucigalpa <u>Reitoca</u>			
Padrón General			
	1750	746,868/2/13	
<u>Tegucigalpa</u> (cap nac)			
Correspondencia			
	1809	741,892/1/11	
Padrón			
	1777	741,891/2/1	
	1777	744,866/5/9	
Tributos			
	1737	746,828/3/18	

Location/ Document Type	Years	Roll No.	Comments
Yoro			
Agualteca			
Tributos			
	1813	747,059/12/1	
Olanchito			
Tributos			
	1767	746,827/1/9	
	1813	747,059/12/1	
Yoro (cap)			
Tributos			
	1767	746,827/1/9	

Departamentos for the following could
not be located

Candelaria			Gaz/various
Padrón General			
	1782	744,866/4/4	
Guaimaca			
Tributos			
	1796	773,999/3/15	
Jaitique			
Tributos			
	1754	741,888/1/26	

Location/ Document Type	Years	Roll No.	Comments
Sonaguera			Documents place in Yoro near Olanchito
Tributos			
	1813	747,059/12/1	
Trinidad			Documents place near San Pedro Sula, Cortes
Tributos			
	1813	747,059/12/2	
		MEXICO nación	
Chiapas Acacoyagua Acacoyagua (c/p)			
Padrón General			
	1765	746,826/2/11	
Acala Acala (c/v)			
Tributos			
	1794	763,388/7/78	
Acapetagua Soconusco			
Padrón General			
	1765	747,059/5/1	
Tributos			
	1806	763,386/9/2	

Location/ Document Type	Years	Roll No.	Comments
Amatán <u>Amatán</u> (c/p)			
Tributos			
	1794	763,388/7/74	
Amatenango de la Frontera <u>Amatenango de la Frontera</u> (c/p)			Until 1882 within the jurisdiction of Cuilco, Huehuetenango
Padrón General			
	1752	746,868/3/3	
	1780	747,296/16/15	
	1819	747,059/1/13	
	1825	746,820/1/8	
Tributos			
	1794	763,388/7/45	
	1812	747,296/22/20	
Comitán de Domínguez <u>Comitán de Domínguez</u> (c/cd)			
Tributos			
	1794	763,388/7/61	
Chalchihuitán <u>Chalchihuitán</u>			
Tributos			
	1794	763,388/7/41	

Location/ Document Type	Years	Roll No.	Comments
Chamula Chamula (c/p)			
Tributos			
	1794	763,388/7/35	
Chiapas Chiapilla (c/p)			
Tributos			
	1794	763,388/7/79	
Chilón Chilón (c/v)			
Tributos			
	1794	763,388/7/55	
Guaquitepec			
Tributos			
	1794	763,388/7/53	
Ishuatán Ishuatán			
Tributos			
	1817	746,829/3/11	
Mazapa de Madero Mazapa (c/p)			Until 1882 within the jurisdiction of Cuilco, Huehuetenango
Padrón General			
	1746	746,825/3/13	
	1752	746,871/1/3	
	1780	747,296/16/17	

Location/ Document Type	Years	Roll No.	Comments
	1819	747,056/1/15	
	1825	746,820/1/10	
Tributos			
	1748	746,825/3/14	
	1812	747,296/22/22	
Motozintla Motozintla de Mendoza (c/cd)			Until 1882 within the jurisdiction of Cuilco, Huehuetenango
Padrón General			
	1746	747,061/1/4	
	1752	746,868/3/5	
	1780	747,296/16/11,14	
	1780	747,296/16/12	
	1819	747,055/1/9	
	1825	746,820/1/7	
Tributos			
	1746	747,061/1/5	
	1780	747,296/16/12	
	1812	747,296/22/21	
Ocosingo Cancuc			
Tributos			
	1794	763,388/7/51	
Ococingo (c/v)			
Tributos			
	1794	763,388/7/57-58	

Location/ Document Type	Years	Roll No.	Comments
Ocozocoautla de Espinosa			
Ocozocoautla de Espinosa (c/cd)			
Padrón General			
	1721	747,058/14/1	
	1741	747,048/14/3	
	1742	747,058/14/2	
Palenque			
Palenque (c/v)			
Tributos			
	1794	763,388/7/83	
Sabanilla			
Moyos			
Tributos			
	1794	763,388/7/71	
Simojovel de Allende			
Simojovel de Allende (c/cd)			
Tributos			
	1794	763,388/7/76	
Socoltenango			
Socoltenango (c/p)			
Tributos			
	1794	763,388/7/66	
Tapachula			
Tapachula (c/p)			
Tributos			
	1806	773,996/1/14	

Location/ Document Type	Years	Roll No.	Comments
Tenejapa Tenejapa (c/p)			
Tributos			
	1794	763,388/7/48	
Teopisca Teopisca (c/v)			
Tributos			
	1794	763,388/7/44	
Tonalá Tonalá (c/cd)			
Padrón General			
	1765	744,961/7/1	
Tributos			
	1806	773,996/1/15	
Tumbalá Tumbalá (c/p)			
Tributos			
	1794	763,388/7/82	
Tuxtla Tuxtla Gutiérrez (c/cd)			
Padrón General			
	1765	744,961/6/2	
Venustiano Carranza Aguacatenango			
Tributos			
	1794	763,388/7/46	

Location/ Document Type	Years	Roll No.	Comments
Yajalón Yajalón (c/v)			
Tributos			
	1794	763,388/7/60	
Municipio unknown Belén			
Padrón General			
	1821	763,363/1/6	
Platanós			
Tributos			
	1794	763,388/7/77	
San Felipe			
Tributos			
	1794	763,388/7/80-81	
Santa María Magdalena de Tectitán			Until 1882 within the jurisdiction of Cuilco, Huehuetenango
Padrón General			
	1825	746,820/1/9	

Location/ Document Type	Years	Roll No.	Comments
Tabasco Tenosique Usumacinta			Until 1882 within the Jurisdiction of Petén
Padrón General			
	1818	746,830/2/10	
Tributos			
	1812	747,296/22/19	

Estados and municipios for the following
could not be located

Aguatepec			IMHA places in Istmo de Tehuantepec
Tributos			
	1680	747,059/21/5	
Bachajón			IMAH places in Istmo de Tehuantepec
Tributos			
	1794	763,388/7/56	
Chenalhó			
Tributos			
	1794	763,388/7/40	
Ixtacalco			IMAH and NAPRM place in México, D.F., México
Tributos			
	1794	763,388/7/36	

Location/ Document Type	Years	Roll No.	Comments
Pinola			IMAH places in Istmo de Tehuantepec
Tributos			
	1794	763,388/7/64	
San Pedro Custepeques			Juarros places in Ciudad Real, Chiapas
Padrón General			
	1755	746,869/1/42	
Sibacá			IMAH places in Istmo de Tehuantepec
Tributos			
	1794	763,388/7/59	

NICARAGUA
nación

Location/ Document Type	Years	Roll No.	Comments
Boaco 　Boaco (cap)			
Correspondencia			
	1730	748,124/2/8	
Padrón			
	1815	763,380/2/1	
	1815	763,380/2/2	
	1816	763,387/3/18	
	1816	763,387/3/20	
Padrón General			
	1701	763,385/2/2	
	1701	773,995/1/2	

Location/ Document Type	Years	Roll No.	Comments
	1718	763,390/2/4	
	1755	763,380/1/2	
Tributos			
	1701	763,385/2/1	
	1701	773,995/1/1	
Carazo Diramba			
Padrón			
	1817	763,387/3/40	
Padrón General			
	1663	745,817/2/2	
	1663	763,386/10/2	
Jinotepe (cap)			
Padrón			
	1817	763,387/3/41	
Chinandega Chichigalpa			
Padrón General			
	1768	744,866/6/1	
	1768	747,058/5/2	
	1798	763,387/4/5	
	1817	763,387/3/23	
Tributos			
	1708	773,995/1/14	
	1757	763,385/4/10	
	1757	763,387/1/10	

Location/ Document Type	Years	Roll No.	Comments
Chinandega			
Correspondencia			
	1776	744,866/5/3	
Padrón			
	1777	741,739/1/3	
Padrón General			
	1751	763,380/1/8	
	1768	747,058/5/1	
	1798	763,387/4/3	
	1817	763,387/3/22	
Tributos			
	1708	773,995/1/14	
	1757	763,385/4/8	
	1757	763,387/1/8	
El Viejo			
Correspondencia			
	1753	763,380/1/9	
Padrón			
	1777	741,739/1/1	
Padrón General			
	1768	747,058/5/3-6/1	
	1798	763,387/4/2	
	1817	763,387/3/21	

Location/ Document Type	Years	Roll No.	Comments
Posoltega			
Correspondencia			
	1776	744,866/5/2	
Padrón			
	1777	741,739/1/2	
	1816	763,387/4/20	
	1816	763,387/4/21	
Padrón General			
	1663	745,817/2/6	
	1663	763,386/10/6	
	1676	745,817/2/4	
	1676	763,386/10/4	
	1735	763,390/4/13	
Tributos			
	1676	745,817/2/5	
Realejo			
Correspondencia			
	1776	744,866/5/1	
Padrón			
	1777	741,739/1/4	
Chontales **Comalapa**			
Correspondencia			
	1730	748,124/2/8	

Location/ Document Type	Years	Roll No.	Comments
Juigalpa (cap)			
Padrón			
	1816	763,387/3/16	
Padrón General			
	1755	763,380/1/4	
Teustepe			
Correspondencia			
	1730	748,124/2/8	
Padrón			
	1816	763,387/3/19	
Padrón General			
	1718	763,390/2/3	
	1719	763,390/2/7	
	1755	763,380/1/15	
Tributos			
	1719	763,390/2/6	
Esteli			
Achuapa			
Tributos			
	1796	773,999/3/8	
Granada			
Diriomo			
Padrón			
	1817	763,387/3/31	

Location/ Document Type	Years	Roll No.	Comments
Granada (cap)			
Padrón			
	1778	741,759/1/23	
	1778	741,891/2/15	
Tributos			
	1671	745,817/2/3	
	1671	763,386/10/3	
	1704	773,995/1/4	
	1707	773,995/1/7	
	1708	773,995/1/9	
	1708-1709	773,995/1/10	
	1709	773,995/1/16	
	1710	773,995/1/17	
	1711	773,995/1/18	
	1746	773,996/1/11	
Nandaime			
Padrón			
	1817	763,387/3/42	
Jinotega **Jinotega** (cap)			
Padrón			
	1816	763,387/3/11-12	
Padrón General			
	1717	763,390/2/2	

Location/ Document Type	Years	Roll No.	Comments
León			
El Areo			
Padrón General			
	1821	763,383/1/2	
León (c/cd)			
Tributos			
	1708	773,995/1/12	
Momotombo			
Padrón			
	1817	763,387/3/25	
Quezalguaque			
Padrón			
	1816	763,387/4/18	
Padrón General			
	1619	748,128/6/18	
	1719	763,390/2/5	
	1719	763,390/3/1	
	1751	763,380/1/6	
Tributos			
	1735	763,390/4/3	
Telica			
Padrón			
	1816	763,387/4/19	

Location/ Document Type	Years	Roll No.	Comments
Padrón General			
	1751	763,380/1/7	
Tributos			
	1735	763,390/4/11	
Managua			
Managua (cap nl)			
Padrón			
	1817	763,387/4/6	
Tributos			
	1760	763,387/1/5	
Mateare			
Padrón General			
	1816	763,387/4/9	
Tributos			
	1754	741,888/1/35	
	1754	741,890/1/19	
Masaya			
Masatepe			
Padrón			
	1817	763,387/3/368	
Masaya (cap)			
Correspondencia			
	1733	763,390/4/1	

Location/ Document Type	Years	Roll No.	Comments
Padrón			
	1817	763,387/3/27-30	
Nandasmo			
Padrón			
	1817	763,387/3/367	
Nindiri			
Padrón			
	1817	763,387/3/34	
Tributos			
	1754	741,888/1/37	
	1754	741,890/1/21	
Matagalpa			
Matagalpa (cap)			
Correspondencia			
	1737	763,390/4/14	
Padrón			
	1778	741,891/2/12	
	1816	763,387/3/1	
	1817	763,387/4/8	
Padrón General			
	1700	763,380/3/2	Incomplete
	1755	763,380/1/13	
Tributos			
	1708-1709	773,995/1/11	

Location/ Document Type	Years	Roll No.	Comments
	1754	741,888/1/36	
	1754	741,890/1/20	
Muy Muy			
Padrón			
	1816	763,387/3/6	
Pelón			
Padrón General			
	1703	745,817/3/1	
San Ramón			
Padrón			
	1816	763,387/3/2	
Sebaco			
Padrón			
	1816	763,387/3/8	
Tributos			
	1764	773,996/1/28	
Nueva Segovia **Mosonte**			
Padrón			
	1816	763,387/4/27	
Padrón General			
	1676	745,817/2/7	
	1676	763,386/10/7	
	1741	746,866/3/2	

Location/ Document Type	Years	Roll No.	Comments
	1796	763,387/2/1	
Palacaguina			
Padrón General			
	1741	763,380/3/1	
Telpaneca			
Padrón			
	1816	763,387/4/28	
Tributos			
	1754	741,888/2/2	
	1754	741,890/1/23	
	n.d.	763,385/4/5	
Tepeaco			
Padrón General			
	1760	763,390/4/15	
Totogalpa			
Padrón			
	1816	763,387/4/26	
Padrón General			
	1741	746,366/3/1	
	1796	763,387/4/1	
Tributos			
	1794	763,388/7/33	

Location/ Document Type	Years	Roll No.	Comments
Yalaguina			
Padrón			
	1816	763,387/4/25	
Rivas San Jorge			
Correspondencia			
	1795	763,386/9/4	
Padrón			
	1816	763,387/4/11	
Tola			
Padrón			
	1816	763,387/4/16	

Departamentos for the following
could not be located

Location/ Document Type	Years	Roll No.	Comments
Balana			
Correspondencia			
	1662	748,130/2/2	
Candelaria			Gaz/various
Padrón General			
	1755	763,380/1/14	
	1772	746,870/2/1	Document damage

Location/ Document Type	Years	Roll No.	Comments
Espinal			
Padrón General			
	1824	746,821/2/15	
Jalteba			
Tributos			
	1694	748,128/6/2	
	1694	748,128/6/3	
San Bartolomé			
Tributos			
	1735	763,390/4/12	
San José			Gaz/various
Padrón			
	1816	763,387/4/13	
Trinidad			Documents place in Nueva Segovia, Nicaragua
Padrón General			
	1737	763,385/4/1	
	1737	763,387/1/1	
Tributos			
	1717	763,390/2/1	

Location/ Document Type	Years	Roll No.	Comments
	Current jurisdictions are unknown or unavailable for the following entries		
Abangasca			Placement on film suggests Nicaragua
Padrón General			
	1676	763,386/10/5	
Aculguaca, Santiago			Documents place in San Salvador
Tributos			
	1790	741,887/3/68	
	1803	741,887/6/67	
Achuapas			Documents place in Jutiapa near Canoas (Jutiapa)
Padrón			
	1826	746,824/2/3	
Padrón General			
	1790	763,388/1/1	
	1821	748,133/1/12	
	1826	746,824/2/4	
Aguacatepéquez, San Pedro			Documents and Juarros place in Escuintla
Padrón General			
	1744	747,060/13/13	
	1760	746,826/2/8	

Location/ Document Type	Years	Roll No.	Comments
Aguazapam, Santo Domingo			Placement on film suggests San Salvador, possibly Ahuachapan (El Salvador)
Tributos			
	1791	763,388/6/17	
Alavarez, San Lorenzo			
Padrón General			
	1750	746,868/2/14	
Aloteca, San Juan			Documents place in Esquintepeque provincia
Padrón General			
	1744	748,128/8/1	
Altopeque			Documents place in Chiquimula, near San Cristóbal Acasaguast-lán (El Progreso)
Padrón General			
	1825	746,823/1/8	
	1826	746,823/1/10	
Amatitán, San Cristóbal			Documents and Juarros place in Sacatepéquez near current-day Amatitlán, Guatemala. Possibly Palín (Escuintla)
Padrón			
	1828	746,872/2/2	

Location/ Document Type	Years	Roll No.	Comments
Tributos			
	1750	746,868/2/7	
	1763	748,127/3/33	
	1767	746,827/1/6	
Amatitlán, Santa Domingo			Documents and Juarros place in Chiquimula within the circuito of Jalapa
Padrón			
	1767	746,827/3/1	
	1767	746,827/3/1	
	1817	746,829/2/20	
	1826	746,824/2/16	
Padrón General			
	1826	746,824/2/15	
Tributos			
	1791	763,388/6/95	
Analco, San Sebastián			Documents and Juarros (499) place in San Vicente district, San Salvador province
Tributos			
	1790	741,887/3/45	
	1803	741,887/6/44	
Arante			Placement on film suggests San Salvador
Padrón General			
	1820	763,384/1/13	

Location/ Document Type	Years	Roll No.	Comments
<u>Astatega Baca</u>			Documents place in Nicaragua
Tributos			
	1735	763,390/4/5	
<u>Asunción</u>			Gaz/various
Padrón			
	1816	746,829/3/9	
<u>Atempa, San Juan</u>			Documents and Juarros place in San Salvador
Padrón General			
	1755	741,889/1/19	
	1755	746,868/2/18	
<u>Atepan, San Juan</u>			Documents place in San Salvador district, San Salvador province
Tributos			
	1790	741,887/3/6	
	1803	741,887/6/5	
<u>Atiquipaque</u>			Documents place in Nicaragua
Padrón General			
	1635	748,130/2/1	
<u>(El) Bajo Extramuros, San Ipstoval</u>			Documents designate only as a "barrio de esta ciudad Sacatepé-quez"
Tributos			
	1764	748,127/4/32	

Location/ Document Type	Years	Roll No.	Comments
Barrio del Abajo			Placement on film suggests San Salvador
Padrón General			
	1813	763,382/1/11	
Barrio del Angel			Documents place in Sonsonate, El Salvador
Padrón General			
	1821	763,383/2/10	
Tributos			
	1791	741,887/4/20	
	1791	763,388/6/21	
	1796	741,887/5/16	
	1796	773,999/3/23	
Barrio de Arriba			Placement on film suggests San Salvador
Padrón General			
	1813	763,382/1/10	
Barrio de Custitali			Placement on film suggests Nicaragua
Tributos			
	1794	763,388/7/32	
Barrio de Mexicanos			
Tributos			
	1794	763,388/7/30	

Location/ Document Type	Years	Roll No.	Comments
Barrio del Pilar			
Padrón General			
	1821	763,383/2/8	
Barrio de San Marcos			Documents place in Quezaltenango
Padrón General			
	1821	747,057/3/4	
Barrio de Santa Cruz			Documents place in Ciudad de Cuatemala
Tributos			
	1758	746,829/2/3	
Barrio Veracruz			Placement on film suggests México
Padrón General			
	1821	763,383/2/9	
Bovos, San Antonio			Documents place in Quezaltenango
Padrón General			
	1821	747,057/1/6	
Cabrera, San Lucas			
Tributos			
	1758	746,829/2/2	

Location/ Document Type	Years	Roll No.	Comments
Cacaluta, San Julián			Documents place in El Salvador
Tributos			
	1790	741,887/3/16	
	1803	741,887/6/15	
Cacauterique, Santiago			Documents place in Honduras
Tributos			
	1753	746,869/1/12	
	1754	741,888/1/28	
	1754	741,890/1/12	
Calpul de San Francisco			Documents designated as anexo of Sacapulas, (El Quiché)
Padrón General			
	1797	747,296/13/1	
Calpul de Santo Tomás			Documents place in El Quiché, anexo of Sacapulas (El Quiché)
Padrón General			
	1797	747,296/13/2	
Camsapán			Documents place in Nicaragua near Teustepe (Nicaragua)
Padrón			
	1816	763,387/3/13	
	1816	763,387/3/15	
	1816	763,387/3/17	

Location/ Document Type	Years	Roll No.	Comments
Cancus, San Juan			Juarros places in Ciudad Real, Chiapas
Padrón			
	1816	746,827/1/17	
Candelaria Baca			Documents place in Nicaragua
Tributos			
	1735	763,390/4/8	
Capola, Santa Cruz			Documents place in Quezaltenango
Padrón General			
	1821	747,057/3/6	
Cárdenas, San Diego de			Documents place in Suchitepéquez
Padrón General			
	1759	748,127/1/4	
Carmona, San Bartholomé			Documents place in Sacatepéquez
Padrón General			
	1760	748,127/3/8	
Tributos			
	1761	748,127/3/26	
(Las) Carretas, San Juan			Documents place in Chimaltenango, possibly Las Carretas, caserío of San Martín Jilotepeque (Chimal- tenango)

Location/ Document Type	Years	Roll No.	Comments
Padrón General			
	1755	746,869/1/44	
Castillo de San Felipe del Golfo			Documents place in Honduras
Padrón			
	1778	741,739/1/29	
	1778	741,891/2/21	
Catacsafa ?			Name illegible
Padrón General			
	1813	748,131/1/2	
Cazisco, San Miguel			Placement on film suggests Escuintla
Padrón General			
	1767	746,866/1/5	
Comaltea, San Juan			Documents place in Nicaragua
Padrón General			
	1743	746,866/3/4	
Cometa, Santa María Magdalena			Placement on film suggests México
Tributos			
	1794	763,388/7/68	
Concepción			Documents and Juarros place in Escuintla

Location/ Document Type	Years	Roll No.	Comments
Censo			
	1821	763,383/2/16	
Padrón General			
	1756	746,869/2/6	
Cucumbal			Name illegible
Padrón General			
	n.d.	747,296/24/2	
Cururu, San Lerma			Documents and Juarros place in Honduras
Tributos			
	1753	746,869/1/16	
	1754	741,888/1/32	
	1754	741,890/1/16	
Cutacutasta, San Marcos			Documents place in San Salvador
Tributos			
	1790	741,887/3/32	
	1803	741,887/6/31	
Chamolpan			Documents place in Nicaragua within jurisdiction of El Viejo
Tributos			
	1757	763,385/4/6	
	1757	763,387/1/6	

Location/ Document Type	Years	Roll No.	Comments
Chapón, San Juan ?			Name illegible
Padrón General			
	1752	741,889/1/31	
Chapuluca			Documents place in Honduras
Tributos			
	1754	741,888/4/31	
Chiamiquín, Santa Catalina			Documents place in Verapaz
Padrón General			
	1821	748,132/3/6	
Chiconguezar, San Pedro			Documents place in El Salvador
Tributos			
	1790	741,887/3/7	
	1790	741,887/3/8	
	1803	741,887/6/6	
Chicuanguescoi, San Pedro			Juarros places in San Salvador
Padrón General			
	1736	747,060/8/1	
Chilum, Santo Domingo			Documents and Juarros place in Ciudad Real
Padrón General			
	1760	746,866/1/2	
	1761	763,390/4/16	

Location/ Document Type	Years	Roll No.	Comments
	1761	773,996/1/25	
Chiquimucelo, San Pedro			Juarros places in Ciudad Real
Tributos			
	1794	763,388/7/69	
Chuaxac, Santo Tomás			Documents place in Suchitepéquez
Padrón General			
	1752	741,889/1/34	
	1752	746,868/2/32	
	1759	748,127/1/16	
Tributos			
	1703	747,060/4/1	
	1757	748,126/3/20	
	1763	748,127/4/18	
Dixiox			Placement on film suggests Nicaragua
Padrón			
	1817	763,387/3/35	
Doctrinas de San Miguel			
Tributos			
	1734	741,888/3/13	
El Sagrario			Documents place in Ciudad de Guatemala, a parroquia

Location/ Document Type	Years	Roll No.	Comments
Padrón General			
	1813	747,059/11/1	
Ermita, Santa Elena			Documents place in Chiquimula, possibly Santa Elena, aldea of Chiquimula municipio
Tributos			
	1791	763,388/6/83	
	1797	746,865/3/48	
Escobar, San Miguel			Documents place in Sacatepéquez
Padrón			
	1781	747,059/1/6	
	1817	748,130/5/10	
Padrón General			
	1740	747,060/10/4	
	1761	748,127/3/48	
Tributos			
	1740	747,060/10/3	
	1761	748,127/3/23	
	1776	746,827/1/6	
Escuintenango, Santiago			Juarros places in Ciudad Real
Tributos			
	1794	763,388/7/67	

Location/ Document Type	Years	Roll No.	Comments
Espírito Santos Extramuros			
Tributos			
	1758	746,829/2/6	
Fila			Documents place near San Francisco Petalcingo which Juarros places in Ciudad Real
Tributos			
	1794	763,388/7/84	
Goayucoco			Documents place in Sonsonate
Padrón General			
	1821	763,383/1/8	
Guadalupe			Documents place in Guatemala (municipio)
Padrón General			
	1813	747,059/11/2	
	1813	747,296/4/1	
Guaimoco, San Silvestre			Documents and Juarros place in Zonzonate district, Zonzonate province
Tributos			
	1791	741,887/4/12	
	1796	741,887/5/8	

Location/ Document Type	Years	Roll No.	Comments
Gualtereo			Placement on film suggests Nicaragua
Tributos			
	1757	763,385/4/7	
	1757	763,387/1/7	
Guaquistlán, Santa María			Documents place in Sacatepéquez
Tributos			
	1764	748,127/3/45	
Guarumal			Placement on film suggests El Salvador
Padrón General			
	1821	763,383/1/7	
Guatagias, Santiago			Documents place in San Salvador
Tributos			
	1790	741,887/3/96	
	1803	741,887/6/95	
Guatepeque, Santiago			Documents place in Quezaltenango
Padrón General			
	1821	747,057/1/3	
Guaxiquiro, San Gaspar de los Santos Reyes			Documents place in Honduras
Tributos			
	1754	741,890/1/8	

Location/ Document Type	Years	Roll No.	Comments
Gueitiupán, Asunción			Juarros places in Chiapas
Tributos			
	1794	763,388/7/72	
Gueitiupán, San Pedro			Juarros places in Chiapas
Tributos			
	1794	763,388/7/75	
Gueitiupán, Santa Catarina			Juarros places in Chiapas
Tributos			
	1794	763,388/7/73	
Guelosingo			Juarros places in Chiapas
Padrón General			
	1755	741,889/1/33	
	1775	746,868/2/31	
Guimago			Documents place in Escuintla
Padrón General			
	1676	747,059/21/1	Incomplete
Guistlán, San Francisco			Documents place in Chiapas
Padrón General			
	1765	773,996/1/29	

Location/ Document Type	Years	Roll No.	Comments
Guistlán, Santiago			Placement on film suggests México
Tributos			
	1794	763,388/7/37	
Guistega			Documents place in Nicaragua
Tributos			
	1735	763,390/4/4	
Guixalda			Placement on film suggests Nicaragua
Padrón General			
	1719	763,385/3/2	
Tributos			
	1719	763,385/3/1	
Guizapan, Santo Domingo			Documents place in Chiapas
Tributos			
	1791	741,887/4/16	
	1796	741,887/5/12	
	1796	773,999/3/19	
Ibaninaron, Santo Domingo			
Padrón General			
	1755	746,869/1/47	
Isbuatlán, Santa Ana de			Documents place in Escuintla

Location/ Document Type	Years	Roll No.	Comments
Padrón General			
	1700	747,060/3/6	
	1701	747,060/3/4	
Isumatán, San Juan			
Tributos			
	1817	746,829/3/9	
Istiquipaque, Santa Ana			Documents place in Escuintla
Correspondencia			
	1745	747,060/13/2	
Padrón General			
	1817	746,829/3/10	
Itala			Placement on film suggests Chiquimula
Padrón General			
	1824	746,821/2/10	
Ixlamá, San José			Documents place in Quezaltenango
Padrón General			
	1821	747,057/3/7	
Izapa, San Andrés			Documents and Juarros place in Chimaltenango
Tributos			
	1792	763,388/7/21	

Location/ Document Type	Years	Roll No.	Comments
Jacaltenango, San Andrés			Juarros places in Huehuetenango, possibly San Andrés Huista, aldea of Jacaltenango (Huehuetenango)
Tributos			
	1812	747,296/22/8	
Jacaltenango, San Marcos			Juarros places in Huehuetenango, possibly San Marcos Huista aldea of Jacaltenango (Huehuetenango)
Padrón General			
	1752	741,889/1/29	
Jalata			Placement on film suggests Nicaragua
Padrón			
	1817	763,387/3/39	
Jilotepeque			Documents fail to indicate whether San Luis (Jalapa) or San Martín (Chimaltenango)
Padrón General			
	1756	746,869/2/8	
Jilotepeque, San Jacinto			Documents place in Chimaltenango
Tributos			
	1792	763,388/7/8	

Location/ Document Type	Years	Roll No.	Comments
Juayuba, Santa Lucía			Documents and Juarros place in Sonsonate
Tributos			
	1791	741,887/4/23	
	1791	763,388/6/24	
	1796	773,999/3/26	
Juenatique			Placement on film suggests San Salvador
Padrón General			
	1820	763,384/1/12	
Jutiapilla, San Cristóbal			Documents and Juarros place in San Salvador
Tributos			
	1790	741,887/3/80	
	1803	741,887/6/79	
La Candelaria Extramuros, Nuestra Señora de			Documents designate only as a "barrio de esta ciudad Saca- tepéquez"
Tributos			
	1764	748,127/4/33	
La Canónica, Santa Isabel			Placement on film suggests Totonicapán
Padrón General			
	1819	747,056/1/16	
La Costilla, San Francisco			Documents place in Sololá

Location/ Document Type	Years	Roll No.	Comments
Padrón General			
	1751	748,125/1/3	
La Habana			Documents designate as a barrio of Ciudad de Guatemala
Padrón General			
	1796	747,296/2/1	
	1805	747,296/1/1	
Lamianguera, Santa Catarina			Placement on film suggests San Salvador
Tributos			
	1790	741,887/3/108	
Lapaluta, Santisima Trinidad			Placement on film suggests México
Tributos			
	1794	763,388/7/62	
Las Cañas, Valle de			Gaz/various
Padrón General			
	1813	748,131/3/5	
Las Carranzas, Santa Isabel			
Padrón General			
	1714	746,827/4/2	
Las Misericordias, Nuestra Señora de			Placement on film suggests México
Tributos			
	1794	763,388/7/70	

Location/ Document Type	Years	Roll No.	Comments
Lavorio, San Nicolás			Documents place in León, Nicaragua within the jurisdiction of San Pedro Metapa
Padrón			
	1816	763,387/3/3	
	1816	763,387/3/14	
	1816	763,387/4/10	
	1816	763,387/4/22	
	1817	763,387/4/23	
Linazega, San Juan de			Placement on film suggests Nicaragua
Padrón General			
	1755	763,380/1/1	
Lindega, San Francisco			Documents place in Subtiaba
Tributos			
	1735	763,390/4/6	
Lisaguina			Placement on film suggests Nicaragua
Padrón General			
	1755	763,380/1/1	
Los Leprosos, San Juan de			Documents and Juarros place in Sololá
Padrón General			
	1751	741,889/1/20	

Location/ Document Type	Years	Roll No.	Comments
	1751	746,868/2/19	
	1821	747,056/2/8	
	1825	746,873/2/11	
Tributos			
	1798	746,865/3/25	
Los Matorrales			Name illegible, poor focus Documents place in Nicaragua
Tributos			
	1753	746,869/1/19-24	
Los Reyes, San Gaspar			Documents place in Honduras
Tributos			
	1753	746,869/1/8	
Los Santos Inocentes			
Padrón General			
	1756	746,869/1/50	
Llamapa, San Francisco			Documents place in Soconusco
Padrón General			
	1765	773,996/1/30	
Llamapa, San Juan			Documents place in Soconusco
Padrón General			
	1765	744,961/6/1	

Location/ Document Type	Years	Roll No.	Comments
Llanos			Placement on film suggests México-- IMAH places in Sinaloa only
Tributos			
	1794	763,388/7/65	
Maelen, Trinidad			Documents place in Quezaltenango
Padrón General			
	1821	747,057/3/8	
Malaguina			Placement on film suggests Nicaragua
Padrón			
	1816	763,387/3/7	
Padrón General			
	1755	763,380/1/12	
Mastagua, San Bartolomé			
Padrón General			
	1765	747,059/6/1	
Metapa, San Pedro			Documents and Juarros place in León, Nicaragua
Tributos			
	1708	773,995/1/13	
Metapa, Santiago			Documents and Juarros place in San Salvador

Location/ Document Type	Years	Roll No.	Comments
Padrón General			
	1755	741,887/8/1	
Mexicanos			Juarros places in Ciudad Real
Padrón General			
	1821	763,383/2/12	
Mexicanos, Asunción			Documents and Juarros place in San Salvador
Tributos			
	1790	741,887/3/66	
	1803	741,887/6/65	
Mexicanos, Santa Isabel			Documents and Juarros place in Sonsonate
Tributos			
	1791	741,887/4/14	
	1796	741,887/5/10	
Milbay, Santa Ana			
Padrón			
	1818	746,830/2/7	
Misiones			Documents place in Sololá
Correspondencia			
	1825	748,134/1/2	
Mitontic, San Miguel			Placement on film suggests México

Location/ Document Type	Years	Roll No.	Comments
Tributos			
	1794	763,388/7/42	
Momostenango, San Lorenzo			Placement on film suggests Sacatepéquez
Padrón			
	1781	747,059/1/13	
Monrroy, San Lorenzo			Documents place in Sacatepéquez and pro- vide an alias of San Lorenzo Aguacaliente which Juarros places in Chimaltenango
Padrón General			
	1753	748,127/1/1	
	1761	748,127/3/51	
	1813	748,132/2/12	
Tributos			
	1761	748,127/3/20	
	1776	746,827/1/6	
	1792	763,388/7/15	
Montezroso, Santa Lucía			Documents place in Sacatepéquez
Tributos			
	1761	748,127/3/13	
	1777	746,827/1/6	

Location/ Document Type	Years	Roll No.	Comments
<u>Nag'te</u>			Placement on film suggests Nicaragua, possibly Nagarote, Nicaragua
Padrón			
	1817	763,387/3/24	
<u>Naito, San Francisco</u>			
Padrón General			
	1750	741,889/1/15	
<u>Namotiva, San Juan</u>			Juarros places in Granada, Nicaragua
Padrón			
	1817	763,387/3/33	
<u>Napualapa (or Nagualapa), San Juan</u>			Name illegible Documents place in Suchitepéquez
Padrón General			
	1759	748,127/1/11	
Tributos			
	1700	747,060/3/2	
	1763	748,127/4/16	
<u>Niquinohomo</u>			Juarros places in Granada, Nicaragua
Padrón			
	1817	763,387/3/36	
<u>Nolasco, San Pedro</u>			Documents place in Huehuetenango near Santa Ana Huista

Location/ Document Type	Years	Roll No.	Comments
Padrón General			
	1749	747,061/3/2	
Tributos			
	1749	747,061/3/1	
Ojo de Agua			Documents place in Escuintla
Padrón			
	1817	746,829/3/1	
Ochina, San Miguel			Name illegible
Padrón			
	1748	746,829/1/8	Document damage
Onfreque			
Tributos			
	1767	746,827/1/9	
Ortalanos, Santa Inéz			
Tributos			
	1721	746,825/3/17	
Paleca, San Miguel			Documents and Juarros place in San Salvador, San Salvador
Tributos			
	1790	741,887/3/62	
	1803	741,887/6/61	

Location/ Document Type	Years	Roll No.	Comments
<u>Palo Gordo</u>			Placement on film suggests Sol 0lá
Padrón General			
	1821	747,056/2/20	
<u>Panim, San Bernabe</u>			Placement on film suggests Sacatepéquez
Tributos			
	1792	763,388/7/24	
<u>Pasíjala (or Paquixala), Nuestra Señora de la Concepción</u>			Name illegible Documents place in Solalá
Padrón General			
	1768	746,827/1/1	
Tributos			
	1798	746,865/3/31	
<u>Patululen</u>			Name illegible Possibly Patulul, Suchitepéquez, or Retalhuleu, Retalhuleu
Padrón			
	1693	748,128/6/9	
<u>Perulapám, San Martín</u>			Documents and Juarros place in San Salvador, San Salvador
Padrón General			
	1813	763,382/1/14	

Location/ Document Type	Years	Roll No.	Comments
Tributos			
	1790	741,887/3/74	
	1803	741,887/6/73	
Petalcingo, San Francisco			Juarros places in Ciudad Real, Chiapas-- documents place near Fila
Tributos			
	1794	763,388/7/85	
Pocapa, San Pedro			Name illegible
Padrón General			
	1639	747,059/16/1	Incomplete
Popocatepeque, Nuestra Señora de la Asunción			Documents place in Escuintla
Tributos			
	1735	747,060/7/2	
Popoyoapa			Documents place in Nicaragua
Padrón			
	1816	763,387/4/12	
Posolteguilla			Documents and Juarros place in Subtiava, Nicaragua
Padrón General			
	1719	763,390/3/3	
Tributos			
	1719	763,390/3/3	

Location/ Document Type	Years	Roll No.	Comments
Puebla			Placement on film suggests Nicaragua
Padrón			
	1816	763,387/4/15	
Pueblo Grande			Documents place in Nicaragua within the jurisdiction of Chinandega
Padrón			
	1816	763,387/3/4	
Quastepe			Documents place in Nicaragua
Padrón			
	1817	763,387/4/7	
Tributos			
	1754	741,888/1/38	
	1754	741,888/2/1	
	1754	741,890/1/22	
Quezaltenango, San Felipe			Documents place in Suchitepéquez, possibly San Felipe (Retalhuleu)
Padrón General			
	1748	747,061/2/4	
	1759	748,127/1/8	
Tributos			
	1763	748,127/4/14	
	1796	773,999/3/78	

Location/ Document Type	Years	Roll No.	Comments
Quezalcoatitán, San Miguel			Documents and Juarros place in Sonsonate
Tributos			
	1791	741,887/4/22	
	1791	763,388/6/23	
	1796	741,887/5/18	
	1796	773,999/3/25	
Quiapastlán			
Tributos			
	1750	746,868/2/6	
Quiaquistlán, Santa María			Documents place in Sacatepéquez
Padrón General			
	1752	746,826/2/1	
Tributos			
	1777	746,827/1/6	
Retalhuleu, San Antonio			Documents and Juarros place in Suchitepéquez, possibly Retalhuleu, cabecera municipal in Retalhuleu
Padrón General			
	1752	748,127/3/6	
	1755	748,126/2/2	
Tributos			
	1763	748,127/4/7	
	1796	773,999/3/73	

Location/ Document Type	Years	Roll No.	Comments
Ruiz de Contreras, Don Fernando			Documents place in Suchitepéquez
Padrón General			
	1759	748,127/1/3	
Sacatepéquez, Santa Catarina			Documents and Juarros place in Santa Catarina Sacatepéquez in Suchitepéquez near San Antonio Retalhuleu
Padrón General			
	1791	763,388/6/2	
	1825	746,820/1/18	
Tributos			
	1791	773,996/1/6-7	
	1796	773,999/3/74	
Sacatepéquez, Santa Isabel			
Padrón			
	1803	773,999/9/1	
Saco			Placement on film suggests San Salvador
Padrón General			
	1813	763,384/1/7	
	1820	763,384/1/16	
Sadina			
Padrón General			
	1824	746,820/1/12	

Location/ Document Type	Years	Roll No.	Comments
Saguayapa			Documents and Juarros place in San Salvador
Tributos			
	1790	741,887/3/78	
	1803	741,887/6/77	
Sahloh, San Antonio			Name illegible Documents provide alias of Pahuri and place in Sacatepéquez
Tributos			
	1777	746,827/1/6	
Salaguina, Santa Ana			Documents place in Nicaragua within the jurisdiction of Palacaguina
Padrón General			
	1739	763,385/4/3	
	1739	763,387/1/3	
	1743	746,866/3/5	
	1746	746,866/3/6	
	1747	746,866/3/7	
Tributos			
	1739	763,385/4/4	
	1739	763,387/1/4	
Salto de Agua			
Padrón General			
	1813	748,131/1/2	

Location/ Document Type	Years	Roll No.	Comments
Sambo, Santiago			Documents and Juarros place in Suchitepéquez within jurisdiction of Samayac (Suchitepéquez)
Padrón General			
	1729	746,828/3/9	
	1729	746,828/3/11	
	1729	746,828/3/12	Incomplete
	1753	748,126/1/3	
	1759	748,127/1/2	
	1790	763,386/4/3	
	1813	748,132/1/2	
	1818	746,830/2/3	
	1824	746,820/1/15	
Tributos			
	1729	746,828/3/8	
	1729	746,828/3/10	
	1757	748,126/3/25	
	1763	748,127/4/8	
	1796	773,999/3/64	
Samianguera, Santa Catarina			Documents place in San Salvador
Tributos			
	1803	741,887/6/107	
San Andrés			Documents place in Huehuetenango within jurisdiction of Jacaltenango

Location/ Document Type	Years	Roll No.	Comments
Padrón General			
	1746	747,061/3/14	
Tributos			
	1744	747,060/13/1	
	1887	747,295/2/43	
San Andrés Deán			Documents and Juarros place in Sacatepéquez
Tributos			
	1753	746,869/1/27	
	1755	741,888/2/7	
	1755	741,890/1/28	
	1761	748,127/3/27	
	1776	746,827/1/6	
San Antonio			
Padrón General			
	1821	763,383/2/11	
San Antonio Abad Extramuros			
Tributos			
	1758	746,829/2/7	
San Blas			Documents place in Nicaragua
Tributos			
	1735	763,390/4/10	
San Cristóbal			Documents place in Sacatepéquez near Santa María de Jesús

Location/ Document Type	Years	Roll No.	Comments
Padrón General			
	1813	748,132/2/9	
San Felipe			Documents place in Chimaltenango
Tributos			
	1756	741,888/2/18	
	1756	741,890/1/39	
San Felipe			Documents and Juarros place in Ciudad Real
Padrón General			
	1765	773,996/1/31	
San Francisco			Documents designate as barrio of Ciudad de los Guatemaltecos
Padrón General			
	1719	746,825/3/7	
Tributos			
	1719	746,825/3/4	
	1719	746,825/3/6	
San Francisco			Documents cite as barrio of Ciudad de los Méxicanos. Juarros places Méxicanos in Ciudad Real
Padrón General			
	1719	746,825/3/5	

Location/ Document Type	Years	Roll No.	Comments
Tributos			
	1695–1717	746,825/3/3	
San Francisco			Documents place in Suchitepéquez
Tributos			
	1887	747,295/2/57	Document damage
San Gaspar			Documents place in Huehuetenango
Tributos			
	1887	747,295/2/25	
San George			Documents place in Sololá
Padrón General			
	1751	748,125/1/4	
San Jacinto			Juarros places in Chiquimula
Padrón General			
	1754	746,868/3/11	
Tributos			
	1791	763,388/6/90	
San José			Documents and Juarros place in Chiquimula, possibly San José la Arada (Chiquimula)
Padrón			
	1817	748,130/5/7	
	1825	746,822/1/3	

Location/ Document Type	Years	Roll No.	Comments
Tributos			
	1791	763,388/6/82	
San Josef			Documents and Juarros place in Chiquimula
Padrón General			
	1742	747,060/12/8	
	1750	741,889/1/13	
	1750	746,868/2/11	
	1768-1775	748,128/5/2	
Tributos			
	1742	747,060/12/7	
	1750	741,889/1/11-12	
	1750	746,868/2/10	
	1797	746,865/3/47	
San Juan _____			Name illegible Possibly Moyuta, Jutiapa
Padrón General			
	1755	746,869/1/49	
San Juan Bautista			Documents place in Nicaragua
Tributos			
	1735	763,390/4/7,9	
San Lorenzo			Documents place in Quezaltenango, anexo of Almolonga

Location/ Document Type	Years	Roll No.	Comments
Padrón General			
	1750	741,889/1/16	
	1764	748,127/3/52	
Tributos			
	1887	747,295/2/28	
San Lucas Evangelista			Documents place in Nicaragua, anexo of Totolapa
Tributos			
	1794	763,388/7/34	
San Luis de la Real Corona			Documents place in San Salvador
Tributos			
	1790	741,887/3/10	
	1803	741,887/6/9	
San Luis de la Real Corona			Documents place in Suchitepéquez
Padrón General			
	1753	746,868/3/10	
	1759	748,127/1/13	
Tributos			
	1763	748,127/4/17	
San Marcos			Documents place in Huehuetenango
Tributos			
	1887	747,295/2/42	

Location/ Document Type	Years	Roll No.	Comments
San Martín			Documents place in Suchitepéquez
Padrón General			
	1821	763,389/3/2	
Tributos			
	1747	746,829/1/7	
San Mateo			Placement on film suggests Huehuetenango
Padrón General			
	1750	741,889/1/4	
Tributos			
	1790	763,388/6/45	
San Miguel			Gaz/various Juarros/various
Tributos			
	1701-1713	746,825/3/11	
San Nicolás			Documents place in Chiquimula
Padrón General			
	1826	746,823/1/13	
Sansaria			Documents and Juarros place in Acasaquastlán within the jurisdiction of San Agustín Acasaguastlán (El Progreso)
Tributos			
	1813	748,131/3/17	

Location/ Document Type	Years	Roll No.	Comments
Santa Ana Extramuros			Documents designate only as a "barrio de esta ciudad Sacatepéquez"
Tributos			
	1758	746,829/2/5	
	1764	748,127/4/30	
Santa Barbarita			Documents place in Honduras, near Petoa
Tributos			
	1813	747,059/12/3	
Santa Castana			Documents place in El Quiché, near Santa Cruz del Quiché
Padrón General			
	1813	747,056/2/4	
Santa Catarina			Placement on film suggests Nicaragua
Padrón			
	1817	763,387/3/32	
Santa Catarina			Gaz/various
Padrón General			
	1714	746,827/4/2	Document damage
	1821	748,133/1/6	
Santa Catarina			Documents designate as anexo of Almolonga
Padrón General			
	1764	748,127/3/52	

Location/ Document Type	Years	Roll No.	Comments
Santa Catarina			Documents place in Sacatepéquez near Santa María de Jesús
Padrón General			
	1813	748,132/2/9	
Santa Catarina			Placement on film suggests Chiquimula
Padrón General			
	1824	746,821/2/3	
Santa Catarina			Documents place in Jutiapa
Tributos			
	1887	747,295/2/22	
Santa Cruz			Gaz/various
Padrón			
	1816	746,827/2/1	
Tributos			
	1769	746,827/1/5	
Santa Cruz Extramuros			Documents designate only as a "barrio de esta ciudad Sacatepéquez
Tributos			
	1764	748,127/4/34	
Santa Elena			Placement on film suggests Sacatepéquez

Location/ Document Type	Years	Roll No.	Comments
Padrón General			
	1754	741,888/2/21	
Santa Elena			Documents place in Chiquimula
Tributos			
	1753	746,869/1/6	
Santa Inés Extramuros			Documents designate only as a "barrio de esta ciudad Sacatepéquez"
Tributos			
	1764	748,127/4/29	
Santa Isabel Extramuros			Documents designate only as a "barrio de esta ciudad Sacatepéquez"
Tributos			
	1758	746,829/2/1	
	1764	748,127/4/31	
Santa Lucía			Placement on film suggests Chiquimula
Padrón			
	1825	746,822/1/4	
Padrón General			
	1742	747,060/11/2	
Tributos			
	1742	747,060/11/1	
	1791	763,388/6/102	

Location/Document Type	Years	Roll No.	Comments
	1791	763,388/6/113	
	1797	746,865/3/67	
Santa Lucía			Documents place in San Salvador
Padrón General			
	1746	741,887/6/2	
Tributos			
	1748	741,887/7/3	
Santa Lucía			Documents place in Quezaltenango
Padrón General			
	1756	748,128/6/16	
Tributos			
	1757	748,126/4/3	
Santa Lucía			Documents place in Sololá
Padrón General			
	1821	747,056/2/12	
San Seoro			Name illegible
Tributos			
	1767	746,827/1/9	
Santa Rosa			Gaz/various
Padrón			
	1788	747,296/9/1	
	1806–1815	746,829/3/6	

Location/ Document Type	Years	Roll No.	Comments
Padrón General			
	1817	746,829/3/12	
Santa Rosa			Documents place in Chiquimula
Tributos			
	1837	748,134/1/3	
Santiago			Gaz/various
Padrón General			
	1714	746,827/4/2	Document damage
Santo Domingo			Documents place in Huehuetenango, within jurisdiction of Mazatenango
Padrón			
	1802	773,999/8/2	
Santo Domingo			Documents place within the barrio de Capuchinas in Ciudad de Guatemala
Padrón General			
	1796	747,296/3/1	
Santo Tomás			Gaz/various
Padrón General			
	1846	746,825/2/10	
Sapotal			Placement on film suggests Nicaragua

Location/ Document Type	Years	Roll No.	Comments
Padrón			
	1816	763,387/4/14	
Sapotán, San Isabel			Documents and Juarros place in San Salvador
Tributos			
	1790	741,887/3/19	
	1803	741,887/6/18	
Sapotitlán, Niño Jesús			Documents place in San Salvador
Tributos			
	1803	741,887/6/86	
Sayatitán, Asunción			Documents place in México
Tributos			
	1794	763,388/7/63	
Sena, San Bernardino de			Documents place in Suchitepéquez
Padrón General			
	1748	747,061/3/13	
	1748	748,130/2/5	Incomplete
Sicapa, San Bartolomé			Documents place in Quezaltenango
Padrón General			
	1729	746,828/3/9	
Tributos			
	1790	763,388/6/52	

Location/ Document Type	Years	Roll No.	Comments
Sierra de Canales			Documents place in Sacatepéquez
Tributos			
	1819	763,386/3/1	
Sinacameca, Santo Domingo			Documents place in San Salvador
Padrón General			
	1756	741,887/9/1	
	1764	748,127/4/24-25	
Sintalapa, Santo Domingo			Juarros places in Tuxtla
Tributos			
	1769	746,827/1/4	
Solingalpa			Placement on film suggests Nicaragua
Padrón			
	1816	763,387/3/5	
Padrón General			
	1755	763,380/1/11	
Subtiava			Documents and Juarros place in Nicaragua; designate as capital of Subtiava partido
Padrón General			
	1735	763,390/4/2	
	1757	763,380/1/5	

Location/ Document Type	Years	Roll No.	Comments
	n.d.	741,892/1/23	
	n.d.	746,828/2/4	Document damage
Taitique, Nuestra Señora de la Concepción			Documents place in Honduras
Tributos			
	1753	746,869/1/10	
	1754	741,890/1/10	
Talnictepeque, San Luis			Documents place in San Salvador
Tributos			
	1790	741,887/3/24	
	1803	741,887/6/23	
Techoncho, San Miguel			Documents and Juarros place in San Salvador
Padrón General			
	1746	741,887/7/1	
	1790	741,887/3/53	
	1803	741,887/6/52	
Tenango			Documents place in Quezaltenango, designate as anexo of Tejutla (San Marcos)
Padrón General			
	1741	744,866/7/1	
	1741	747,060/10/1	
Tributos			
	1741	747,060/10/2	
	1742	744,866/7/2	

Location/ Document Type	Years	Roll No.	Comments
	1757	748,126/4/15	
	1790	763,388/6/47	
	1794	763,388/7/52	
	1796	773,999/3/45	
Tencoa			Juarros places in Comayagua, Honduras
Tributos			
	1767	746,827/1/9	
Tenescatlán, Santa María Magdalena			Placement on film suggests México
Tributos			
	1794	763,388/7/39	
Teotepeque, San Pedro			Placement on film suggests México IMAH and NAPRM place in Guerreo only
Padrón General			
	1821	763,383/1/5	
Tepala, San Ildefonso			
Padrón General			
	1750	748,124/2/9	
Tepesomoto			Documents and Juarros place in Nueva Segovia, Nicaragua
Padrón			
	1816	763,387/4/24	

Location/ Document Type	Years	Roll No.	Comments
Padrón General			
	1713	745,817/3/2	
	1713	763,390/1/2	
	1719	763,390/3/4	
Teuaco			Placement on film suggests Nicaragua
Padrón General			
	1755	763,380/1/3	
Teultepeque, San Martín			
Tributos			
	1794	763,388/7/50	
Teultepeque, Santo Tomás			
Tributos			
	1794	763,388/7/49	
Texacuangos, Santo Tomás			Documents and Juarros place in San Salvador
Tributos			
	1790	741,887/3/31,33	
	1803	741,887/6/30	
Texincal, San Sebastián			Documents and Juarros place in San Salvador
Tributos			
	1790	741,887/3/69	
	1803	741,887/6/68	

Location/ Document Type	Years	Roll No.	Comments
Theosoatega			Placement on film suggests Nicaragua
Tributos			
	1757	763,385/4/9	
	1757	763,387/1/9	
Thesmottán, Santa María Magdalena			
Padrón General			
	1743	747,059/4/2	
Tributos			
	1743	747,059/4/1	
Ticamayi			Placement on film suggests Honduras
Padrón General			
	1781	744,866/4/3	
Titala, San Pedro			Placement on film suggests México
Tributos			
	1794	763,388/7/54	
Tittelpaneca, San Juan			Documents place in Nicaragua within the jurisdiction of Nueva Segovia
Padrón General			
	1662	763,386/10/1	
	1737	763,385/4/2	
	1737	763,387/1/2	

Location/ Document Type	Years	Roll No.	Comments
	1772	745,817/2/1	
	1796	763,387/2/2	
Tonaga			Documents place in Nicaragua within the jurisdiction of Acoyapa
Padrón			
	1816	763,387/3/10	
Toniguisca			Documents place in Nicaragua within the jurisdiction of Acoyapa
Padrón			
	1816	763,387/3/9	
Tozuaco, San Juan			Placement on film suggests Nicaragua
Padrón General			
	1726	763,390/3/5	
Uluazam, San Pedro			Placement on film suggests San Salvador
Tributos			
	1790	741,887/3/119	
Upatoro, San Juan			Documents place in Comayagua
Tributos			
	1754	741,890/1/17	
Utzamiximuleu, San Matheo			Documents place in Quezaltenango

Location/ Document Type	Years	Roll No.	Comments
Tributos			
	1755	748,126/3/8	
Valle de las Casillas			
Padrón General			
	1824	746,821/2/13	
Valle de las Castillas			Placement on film suggests El Quiché
Padrón General			
	1813	747,056/2/3	
Valle de Limoes			Placement on film suggests Chiquimula
Padrón General			
	1813	748,131/3/18	
Valle de San Lorenzo			Placement on film suggests Quezaltenango
Padrón General			
	1821	747,057/1/9	
Valle de Trapiche			Possibly Trapiche Grande, aldea of Chuarrancho, Guatemala
Padrón General			
	1824	746,821/2/14	
Villa de Nicaragua			Documents and Juarros place in Nicaragua

Location/ Document Type	Years	Roll No.	Comments
Correspondencia			
	1778	741,891/2/17	
Padrón			
	1778	741,739/1/25	
Xalteca			
Padrón General			
	1692	763,386/10/8	
Xicalapa, Santa Ursula			Documents place in El Salvador
Tributos			
	1790	741,887/3/22	
	1803	741,887/6/21	
Xiquimala			
Padrón General			
	1821	748,133/3/6	
Xolotepeque, Santa Marta			Placement on film suggests México
Tributos			
	1794	763,388/7/38	
Ychanqueque, San Francisco			Documents place in Escuintla
Padrón General			
	1739	746,826/1/15	

Location/ Document Type	Years	Roll No.	Comments
Tributos			
	1739	746,826/1/14	
Ynutil			Documents place in Chiquimula
Padrón General			
	1824	746,821/2/1	
Ypatoro, San Juan			Documents place in Honduras
Tributos			
	1753	746,869/1/17	
	1754	741,888/1/33	
Ypuscatepeque, San Pedro			Documents place in Sacatepéquez within the jurisdiction of Alotenango
Padrón General			
	1756	746,869/1/51	
Ysala, Asunción			Placement on film suggests El Salvador
Padrón General			
	1821	763,383/3/6	
Ysquan			Placement on film suggests Jutiapa
Padrón General			
	1821	748,133/3/9	

Location/ Document Type	Years	Roll No.	Comments
Ysguatán, Santa María de Todos Santos			Documents and Juarros place in Escuintla
Padrón General			
	1744	747,060/13/8	
	1753	748,126/1/2	
	n.d.	748,128/6/4	
Yucuaitique, San Gaspar			Documents place in San Salvador
Tributos			
	1790	741,887/3/107	
	1803	741,887/6/106	
Zacapa, San Juan			Juarros places in Chiquimula
Padrón General			
	1599	747,059/13/1	Incomplete
Zapotitlán, Niño Jesús			Placement on film suggests El Salvador
Tributos			
	1790	741,887/3/87	
Zapotitlán, San Juan			Documents place in Suchitepéquez
Tributos			
	1763	748,127/4/12	
Zerillo			Placement on film suggests Nicaragua Documents designate as barrio

Location/ Document Type	Years	Roll No.	Comments
Tributos			
	1794	763,388/7/31	

Information Recorded in Native Indian Language

Padrón			
		748,130/5/12	Placement on film suggests ca. 1820
		748,130/5/13	Placement on film suggests ca. 1820
		748,130/5/14	Placement on film suggests ca. 1820
Padrón General			
		747,058/1/1	Placement on film suggests ca. 1820

Information For Which Location Is Illegible

Padrón			
	1749	747,061/3/16	Document damage
Tributos			
	1698	746,825/3/10	
	1737	746,828/3/16	
	1739	746,828/3/19	
	1752	746,868/2/24	Document damage

Information For Which Location Is Omitted

Correspondencia			
	1734	746,828/3/14	
	1795	773,999/3/3	

Location/ Document Type	Years	Roll No.	Comments
	1796	773,999/3/88	
	1796	773,999/3/89	
	1797	773,999/6/1	
	1801	773,999/7/1	
	1816	773,999/13/1	
	1817	773,999/14/1	
	1817	773,999/15/1	
	1817	773,999/16/1	
	1819	773,999/18/1	
Padrón			
	1749	747,296/8/1	
	1807	748,130/7/1	
	1813	748,130/8/2	
Padrón General			
	1729	747,060/5/3	Incomplete
	ca. 1740	748,130/2/10	Consists of several sets of unidentified, disordered records
	1750	741,889/1/5	
	1750	746,868/2/2	
	1750	748,124/2/4	
	1750	748,124/2/5	
	1753	748,128/7/1	
	1781	747,059/1/20	
	1809	747,296/19/1	
	1813	748,131/3/25	
	1819	747,296/5/1	
	1836	746,873/1/6	Placement on film suggests Escuintla

Location/ Document Type	Years	Roll No.	Comments
Tributos			
	1688-1691	746,828/2/6	
	1725-1738	746,826/1/10	Document damage
	1738	746,826/1/9	Document damage
	1739	746,828/3/21	
	1739-1745	741,892/1/19	
	1744	741,892/1/21	
	1746	746,826/1/26	
	1748	747,061/3/7	
	1749	747,061/3/15	
	1752-1753	741,889/1/25	
	1752-1753	741,889/1/26	
	1754	741,892/1/24	
	1775-1777	747,059/1/24	
	1791	747,059/7/2	
	1813	741,892/1/13	
	1815	741,892/1/14	
	1816	741,892/1/15	
	1818	748,130/5/15	

Information For Which Both Location
And Dates Are Omitted

Padrón			
		748,134/1/9	Possibly capital
		746,828/2/7	Document damage
		748,130/5/14	Disordered Incomplete
		748,130/5/16	Incomplete

Location/ Document Type	Years	Roll No.	Comments
Padrón General			
		747,058/15/1	Incomplete
		748,128/6/7	Incomplete
		748,128/6/10	Incomplete
		748,128/6/11	Incomplete
		748,128/6/12	Incomplete
		748,128/6/13	Incomplete
		748,128/6/14	Incomplete
		748,128/6/15	Incomplete
		748,128/7/3	Incomplete
		748,128/7/4	
		748,128/7/6	Incomplete
Tributos			
		746,829/1/10	

The following lists refer to filmed documentation summarizing
population and tribute statistics. Locations provided
are those appearing on the documents, rather than
current-day designations, in order to avoid
misrepresentation of territory involved.

Guatemala (reino)

Censo

	Years	Roll No.	
	1825	746,871/3/1	

Correspondencia

	Years	Roll No.	
	1759	773,999/3/2	
	1795	773,999/3/6	

Location/ Document Type	Years	Roll No.	Comments
Padrón			
	1779	741,739/1/33	
	1779	741,891/2/25	
	1816	741,893	ODT/OL Legajo 1811
	n.d.	741,892/1/25	
Tributos			
	1701	741,738	ODT/OL Legajo 1572
	1715–1716	746,825/3/12	
	1729	746,828/3/11	
	1729	746,828/3/13	
	1730	746,825/3/20	
	1737	746,828/3/21	
	1739	746,828/3/23	
	1750	746,825/3/26	
	1754	746,826/2/3	
	1755	746,826/2/4	Document damage
	1794	746,870/5/12	
	1796	741,892/1/3	
	1800	741,892/1/10	
	1804	747,059/8/1	
	1816	746,865/9/3	

Chiapas (prov)

Location/ Document Type	Years	Roll No.	Comments
Correspondencia			
	1665	747,058/11/1	
	1752	741,889/1/24	
	1824	746,871/4/1	

Location/ Document Type	Years	Roll No.	Comments
Padrón			
	1778	741,739/1/17	
	1778	741,739/1/22	
	1778	741,891/2/14	
Tributos			
	1698	746,828/2/5	
	1716	746,825/3/11	
	1741	747,058/14/3	
	1744	746,829/1/4	
	1749	748,128/6/17	
	1751	746,868/2/23	Document damage
	1751	746,868/2/30	Poor focus
	1794	773,996/1/18	
	1794	773,996/1/19	
	1795	763,386/9/3	
	1796	773,996/1/16	
	1796	773,996/1/17	
	1811	746,865/8/2	
Comayagua (prov)			Also known as Honduras
Padrón			
	1777	741,739/1/9	
	1777	741,891/2/6	
	1778	741,739/1/14	
Tributos			
	1751-1752	744,866/3/3	
	1752-1753	744,866/3/1	
	1753	744,866/3/2	

Location/ Document Type	Years	Roll No.	Comments
	1754	741,888/1/24	
	1767	746,827/1/9	
	1801-1802	746,865/7/1	
	1801-1803	744,866/1/1	
	1803	744,866/1/2	
	1803	746,865/7/2	
	1806	744,866/2/1	
	1806	773,996/1/9	
Costa Rica (prov)			
Padrón			
	1777	741,739/1/11	
	1777	741,891/2/3	
	1777	744,866/5/11	
Chimaltenango (prov)			
Correspondencia			
	1766	773,999/5/1	
Padrón			
	1777	741,891/2/7	
Tributos			
	1767	746,826/2/16	
	1767-1768	773,996/1/34	
	1790	763,388/7/4	
	1791	763,388/7/1	
	1791	763,388/7/5	
	1792	763,388/7/3	
	1792	763,388/7/29	

Location/ Document Type	Years	Roll No.	Comments
	1793	763,388/7/2	
	1793	763,388/7/6	
	1805	741,892/1/7	
Chiquimula (prov)			Also known as Acasa- guastlán
Correspondencia			
	1796	773,999/3/86	
Padrón			
	1768–1775	748,128/5/1	
	1778	741,739/1/27	
	1778	741,891/2/19	
	1804–1805	746,865/1/3	
	1825	748,822/1/5	
Tributos			
	1640	748,128/6/19	
	1731–1732	741,888/3/14	
	1732	741,888/1/1	
	1732	741,888/1/2	
	1732	741,888/1/3	
	1732	741,888/3/4	
	1733	741,888/1/4	
	1733	741,888/1/5	
	1733	741,888/1/6	
	1733	741,888/3/11	
	1733–1734	741,888/3/15	
	1734	741,888/1/7	
	1734	741,888/1/8	
	1734	741,888/1/9	

Location/ Document Type	Years	Roll No.	Comments
	1734	741,888/1/10	
	1734	741,888/3/16	
	1735	741,888/1/11	
	1735	741,888/1/12	
	1736	741,888/1/13	
	1736	741,888/1/14	
	1736	741,888/1/15	
	1736	741,888/1/16	
	1748	748,128/7/8	
	1750	741,889/1/7	
	1754	746,869/1/1	
	1757	748,126/3/16	
	1758	748,128/8/2	
	1767	746,826/2/14	
	1791	763,388/6/79	
	1791	763,388/6/80	
	1791	763,388/6/111	
	1791	763,388/6/112	
	1796-1797	746,865/3/44	
	1797	746,865/3/45	
	1797	746,865/3/76	
	1797	746,865/3/77	
	1802	746,865/7/7	
	1802	746,865/7/8	
	1802-1805	741,892/1/5	
	1813	746,828/2/1	
	1816	746,870/5/6	
	1818	763,386/2/1	

Location/ Document Type	Years	Roll No.	Comments
Escuintla (prov)			Also known as Guazacapán
Correspondencia			
	1796	773,999/3/90	
	1797	773,999/3/91	
Padrón			
	1755	746,869/1/43	
	1778	741,739/1/19	
	1778	741,891/2/11	
Tributos			
	1731-1732	741,888/3/14	
	1732	741,888/3/5	
	1733-1734	741,888/3/15	
	1734	741,888/3/16	
	1735	741,888/3/29	
	1756	747,058/4/2	
	1767	746,866/1/4	
	1767-1768	773,996/1/36	
	1790	763,388/6/27	
	1790	763,388/6/28	
	1790	763,388/6/29	
	1801	746,865/6/7	
	1801	746,865/6/8	
	1805	741,892/1/7	
	1817	763,386/1/3	
	1817-1820	746,870/5/7	

Location/ Document Type	Years	Roll No.	Comments
Nicaragua (prov)			
Correspondencia			
	1754	763,380/1/10	
	1777	741,891/2/2	
	1777	744,866/5/10	
Padrón			
	1741	746,866/3/3	
	1777	741,739/1/8	
	1777	741,739/1/10	
	1777	741,891/1/1	
	1777	741,891/1/5	
	1777	744,866/5/4	
	1777	744,866/5/8	
	1778	741,739/1/20	
	1778	741,739/1/24	
	1778	741,739/1/26	
	1778	741,891/2/16	
	1778	741,891/2/18	
Tributos			
	1701	773,995/1/3	
	1702-1709	773,995/1/6	
	1708	773,995/1/15	
	1710	773,995/1/5	
	1804	763,387/4/5	
	1816	763,387/3/26	

Location/ Document Type	Years	Roll No.	Comments
Petén Itzá (prov)			
Padrón			
	1778	741,739/1/28	
	1778	741,891/2/20	
Quezaltenango (prov)			
Padrón			
	1777	741,891/2/8	
	1778	741,891/2/9	
	1804-1805	746,865/1/2	
Tributos			
	1732	741,888/3/9	
	1734	741,888/3/21	
	1790-1791	763,388/6/32	
	1791	747,059/7/4	
	1791	763,388/6/33	
	1791	763,388/6/61	
	1791	763,388/6/62	
	1795-1796	746,865/3/3	
	1796	746,865/3/4	
	1796	746,865/3/5	
	1796	773,996/3/58	
	1796	773,999/3/59	
	1796	773,999/3/60	
	1796	773,999/3/61	
	1801	746,865/6/5	
	1801	746,865/6/6	
	1805	741,892/1/6	

Location/ Document Type	Years	Roll No.	Comments
Sacatepéquez			Also known as Amati- tanes y Sacatepéquez
Padrón			
	1758	746,869/2/12	
	1778	741,739/1/31	
	1778	741,891/2/23	
	n.d.	741,892/1/25	
	1820	748,130/5/11	
	1820	748,130/5/12	
Tributos			
	1700–1702	741,892/1/22	
	1739	746,828/3/20	Incomplete
	1752	746,868/3/9	
	1761	748,127/3/37	
	1767	773,996/1/32	Incomplete
	1768	773,996/1/33	Incomplete
	1779	741,892/1/18	
	1790	763,388/5/4	
	1790	763,388/6/37	
	1796–1799	746,865/5/1	
	1800	746,865/5/2	
	1800	746,865/5/3	
	1802–1804	746,865/7/13	
	1804	746,865/7/14	
	1804	746,865/7/15	
	1804	746,870/4/1	
	1804	773,999/10/1	
	1806	741,892/1/8	
	1814	746,865/9/1	

Location/ Document Type	Years	Roll No.	Comments
	1814	746,865/9/2	
	1819	763,386/2/2	
San Salvador (prov)			
Censo			
	1821	763,383/2/15	
Correspondencia			
	1757	773,999/4/1	
Padrón			
	1778	741,739/1/30	
	1778	741,891/2/22	
Tributos			
	1734	741,888/3/12	
	1788–1789	741,887/3/2	
	1790	741,887/3/3	
	1790	741,887/3/9	
	1790	763,388/5/2	
	1800–1802	741,887/6/1	
	1800–1802	746,865/7/3	
	1803	741,887/6/2	
	1803	741,887/6/8	
	1803	746,865/7/4	
	1821	763,383/3/7	
Soconusco (prov)			
Padrón			
	1777	741,739/1/12	
	1777	741,891/2/4	

Location/ Document Type	Years	Roll No.	Comments
	1777	744,866/5/12	
Tributos			
	1799	744,961/5/1	
	1799	744,961/5/2	
	1806	773,996/1/12	
	1806	773,996/1/13	
Sololá (prov)			Also known as Atitán
Correspondencia			
	1676	746,825/3/1	
	1796	773,999/3/87	
Padrón			
	1777	741,891/1/2	
	1777	741,739/1/5	
	1777	744,866/5/5	
	1802	746,827/1/15	
Tributos			
	1731-1732	741,888/3/14	
	1733-1734	741,888/3/15	
	1734	741,888/3/16	
	1787	748,128/5/5	
	1791	746,865/4/3	
	1791	747,059/7/3	
	1795	746,865/3/43	
	1795-1797	746,865/3/9	
	1798	746,865/3/10	
	1798	746,865/3/42	
	1802	746,865/7/9	

Location/ Document Type	Years	Roll No.	Comments
	1802	746,865/7/10	
	1811	746,870/4/3	
	1816	763,386/1/2	
Sonsonate (prov)			
Correspondencia			
	1796	773,999/3/7	
Padrón			
	1777	741,739/1/7	
	1777	741,891/1/4	
	1777	744,866/5/7	
Tributos			
	1790–1791	741,887/4/2	
	1790–1791	763,388/6/4	
	1790–1791	763,388/6/5	
	1791	741,887/4/1	
	1791	741,887/4/3	
	1791	741,887/4/4	
	1791	763,388/6/3	
	1795–1796	741,887/5/24	
	1795–1796	746,865/3/2	
	1795–1796	773,999/3/30	
	1796	741,887/4/23	
	1796	741,887/5/25	
	1796	746,865/3/1	
	1796	773,999/3/29	
	1796	773,999/3/31	

Location/ Document Type	Years	Roll No.	Comments
Suchitepéquez (prov)			
Padrón			
	1813-1815	746,865/2/1	
Tributos			
	1731-1732	741,888/3/14	
	1733-1734	741,888/3/15	
	1734	741,888/3/16	
	1739	746,828/3/20	Incomplete
	1767-1768	773,996/1/35	
	1791	747,059/7/1	
	1791	763,388/6/30	
	1791	763,388/6/31	
	1796	746,865/3/6	
	1796	746,865/3/7	
	1796	746,865/3/8	
	1796	773,999/3/80	
	1796	773,999/3/81	
	1796	773,999/3/82	
	1803	763,389/1/2	
	1805	763,389/1/1	
	n.d.	746,870/5/11	
Totonicapán (prov)			Also known as Huehue- tenango
Padrón			
	1607	747,059/14/1	
	1778	741,739/1/18	
	1778	741,891/2/10	
	1804	746,865/1/1	

Location/ Document Type	Years	Roll No.	Comments
Tributos			
	1676	746,825/3/2	
	1734	741,888/3/22	
	1734	741,888/3/23	
	1734-1736	741,888/3/25	
	1735	741,888/3/17	
	1735	741,888/3/24	
	1736	741,888/3/18	
	1736	741,888/3/26	
	1737	741,888/1/19	
	1737-1738	741,888/3/27	
	1738	741,888/3/20	
	1744-1749	741,889/1/2	
	1748	741,889/1/3	
	1749	741,889/1/1	
	1765	748,127/4/38	
	1778	747,296/16/1	
	1779	747,296/16/5-6	
	1781	747,296/16/2	
	1782	747,296/16/8	
	1783	747,296/16/4	
	1784	747,296/16/3	
	1790	763,388/5/1	
	1791	747,059/7/5	
	1800-1801	746,865/6/3	
	1801	746,865/6/4	
	1803	747,296/18/2	
	1810	747,296/20/1	

Location/ Document Type	Years	Roll No.	Comments
Verapaz (prov)			
Correspondencia			
	1792	745,422/3/2	
Padrón			
	1778	741,739/1/21	
	1778	741,891/2/13	
Tributos			
	1732	741,888/3/1	
	1732-1733	741,888/3/10	
	1733	741,888/3/2	
	1734	741,888/3/28	
	1735	746,828/3/12	
	1735	746,828/3/14	
	1735	746,828/3/15	
	1735-1736	746,828/3/18	
	1736	746,828/3/13	
	1736	746,828/3/16	
	1736	746,828/3/17	
	1767	746,826/2/9	
	1790	763,388/5/3	
	1790	763,388/6/78	
	1792	763,388/6/77	
	1796-1797	773,999/3/92	
	1798	773,999/3/93	
	1798	773,999/3/108	
	1798	773,999/3/109	
	1801-1802	746,865/7/5	

Location/ Document Type	Years	Roll No.	Comments
	1802	746,865/7/6	
	1811	746,865/8/3	
	1817	746,870/5/5	
	1817	748,130/5/3	
	1817	763,386/1/5	
	1818	746,871/1/6	
	1838	746,825/1/2	

PROTOCOLOS

Location/ Document Type	Years	Roll No.	Comments
GUATEMALA nación			
Capital			
	1541–1565	738,008	Juan de León
	1543	737,639	
	1553–1584	753,591/3	
	1550–1598	717,517	Juan Martinez de Soría
	1553–1554	753,591/2	Antonio García
	1560	753,591/2	Juan de León
	1568	738,009	Luis Azetuno y Guzmán
	1568	737,268	
	1568–1762	744,881	
	1569	736,323	
	1572–1574	736,322	
	1574	736,321	
	1577–1579	736,324	
	1579	736,320	
	1580–1584	736,316	
	1580–1584	736,317	
	1581	736,319	
	1582	736,318	
	1589	736,315	
	1570	736,325	S. Pablo de Escobar
	1575	738,023/2	Pedro de Grijalva
	1577–1697	753,591/4	
	1584–1586	738,024/1	
	1602	738,024/2	
	1603	744,862	
	1575–1761	737,595	Joseph de Asurdia
	1577	753,591/3	Alonzo M. Peralta
	1583	737,252	Cristóbal Azetuno de Guzmán
	1584,1586	737,253	
	1584,1590	737,254	
	1586	744,861/1	
	1602	737,257	
	1602	737,258	
	1602–1603, 1605	737,259	
	1603–1800	744,883	
	1603–1604	737,260	

Location/ Document Type	Years	Roll No.	Comments
(cont)	1604-1605	737,262	
	1604	744,863	
	1604	737,261	
	1605-1606	737,263	
	1607-1608	737,264	
	1608-1609	737,265	
	1613-1614	737,266	
	1584	753,591/2	Francisco Morales
	1590	717,516	Fernando Niño
	1591	737,255	
	1592	737,256	
	1592-1593	716,868/1	Miguel de Monteverde
	1593-1605	714,804	Diego Jacomé
	1595-1599	738,022/2	Sebastián Gudiel
	1604-1614	737,666	
	1615-1619,	737,667	
	1624-1626,	737,668	
	1631,		
	1633-1641		
	1632-1640	737,669/1-2	
	1597-1621	753,559	Pedro Valles de Quexo
	1598	737,642	Marcos Díaz
	1601-1609	744,727/2	Alonzo Rodrígues
	1607-1608,	744,728	
	1615,1617		
	1612-1613	737,267/2	
	1613-1614,	744,729	
	1616		
	1617-1633	744,735	
	1622-1623	744,731	
	1622-1627	744,732	
	1624	744,733	
	1625	744,734	
	1627-1628	737,267/1	
	1602	744,861/2	Francisco de Vega
	1602-1603,	738,022	
	1620-1623		
	1608	736,784/4	Francisco de Vega
	1609-1610	756,022/5	
	1609	747,047	Francisco de Vallejo
	1610	747,048	
	1611,1640	746,754/1	
	1611-1613	747,049	
	1613-1616	747,050	
	1620-1623	747,051	
	1622	747,052	
	1625	747,053	

Location/ Document Type	Years	Roll No.	Comments
(cont)	1634	746,750	
	1636–1637	746,751	
	1639–1641	746,753	
	1613–1614	741,713/2	Joán Palomino
	1634–1641	741,714	
	1615–1617	737,279	Juan Bravo de Lagunas
	1617,1619	737,280	
	1616–1762	753,590	
	1620–1621, 1623	737,281	
	1618–1619	737,546/2-3	Pedro de Caviedes
	1622	737,547	
	1622	737,548	
	1624	737,549	
	1626	737,550	
	1626–1629	737,552	
	1627	737,551	
	1630–1636	737,614	
	1630–1640	737,617	
	1631	737,553	
	1632	737,612	
	1633	737,613	
	1635	737,615	
	1636–1639	737,616	
	1618–1620	737,659	Pedro de Estrada
	1619–1623	737,658	
	1621–1622	738,014	
	1624–1628	738,013	
	1631–1637	738,012	
	1634–1638	738,011	
	1639	738,010/2	
	1640	736,779	
	1620–1623	737,640/1-2	Hernando Delgadillo
	1630–1633	737,640/3	
	1622–1628	737,634/2	Felipe Díaz
	1636	737,630	
	1636–1639	737,631	
	1637–1639	737,632	
	1642	736,635	
	1639–1640	737,633	
	1624–1629	737,282	Gaspar de Gallegos
	1644–1646	738,309	
	1648	737,673	
	1650	737,674	
	1653	737,675	
	1654	737,676	
	1655–1659	737,677	
	1655–1659	738,028	

Location/ Document Type	Years	Roll No.	Comments
	1624–1631	736,618	Gerónimo de Castro
	1628–1629	736,619	
	1630	736,620/1	
	1631–1632	736,612	
	1624–1633	753,591/1-2	Luis Ballejo
	1625–1626	737,277	Juan Beltrán
	1626–1629	737,601/1	Francisco de Carvajal
	1627–1645	737,607/1	
	1647–1649	737,607/2	
	1651,	737,608	
	1654–1659		
	1660–1665	737,609	
	1629–1635	746,244	Juan Francisco Santos
	1638–1640	746,245/1	
	1631	753,591/3	Domingo Escobar
	1631–1632,	736,330/1	Gaspar de Armas
	1637		
	1632	741,713/1	Fernán Pérez
	1632	717,511/2	Juan Martínez Telles
	1633–1634	717,513	
	1633	717,512	
	1636–1638	717,514	
	1632–1770	744,882	
	1633	714,810	Marcos de Ledesma
	1636	714,812	
	1640–1641	714,811	
	1634–1637	744,742	Sebastían Ramírez
	1638–1639	744,743	
	1640–1641	744,744	
	1645–1646	744,745	
	1650–1651,	744,746	
	1653		
	1654–1656	744,747	
	1657–1659	744,748	
	1641,1644	736,758	Felipe Díaz (el mayor)
	1646	736,759	
	1646	736,760	
	1648	736,761	
	1648	736,762	
	1648	736,763	
	1690	736,764	
	1692–1693	736,765	
	1694–1697,	736,766	
	1699		

Location/ Document Type	Years	Roll No.	Comments
(cont)	1700-1701	736,767	
	1642	753,583/1	Juan Zerrano
	1642-1656	738,017	Diego Escobar
	1643	716,874/3	Francisco Muñoz
	1648-1649	716,875	
	1650-1652	716,876	
	1667-1670	716,877	
	1670-1677	716,878/1	
	1645	753,591/3	Gerónimo Figueroa
	1645-1651	738,097	Luis de Andino Lozano
	1653-1654	738,098	
	1656-1657	736,599	
	1658,1666	736,600	
	1669	736,601	
	1670	736,602	
	1671	736,603	
	1672	736,604	
	1673,1675	736,605	
	1677-1680	744,750	
	1679-1681	736,607	
	1646	753,591/3	Fernando Figueroa
	1650-1653	737,610/1-2	Jacinto de Castañeda
	1651	756,022/2	Juan de Medina
	1651-1653	716,900	Luis Marín
	1654	716,901	
	1656	716,902	
	1657-1661, 1676	716,904	
	1658	716,903	.
	1653	737,643/1	Estebán de Dávila
	1655	737,644	
	1657	737,645	
	1658	738,117	
	1659	738,118	
	1660	738,120	
	1665	737,653	
	1665	737,654	
	1666	736,772	
	1666	736,768	
	1667	736,769	
	1667-1668	736,770	
	1669	736,771	
	1669	737,638	

Location/ Document Type	Years	Roll No.	Comments
	1654	737,643/2	Esteban de Dávila/
	1661	737,646	Esteban P. Española
	1661	737,647	
	1662	737,648	
	1662	737,649	
	1663	737,650	
	1663	737,651	
	1664	737,652	
	1654	746,732	Blas Fevero Vara
	1657	746,733	
	1658–1659	746,734	
	1600	746,735/1	
	1654, 1676–1679	736,331	Juan de Artabia
	1655–1656	737,572	Miguel de Cuellar
	1657	737,625	
	1658	737,626	
	1659	737,627	
	1660	737,628	
	1661	737,629	
	1662	737,567	
	1663	737,568	
	1664	737,569	
	1665	737,570	
	1666	736,630	
	1667	736,631	
	1669	736,633	
	1670	736,634	
	1671–1675	737,573	
	1674–1686	737,574	
	1656,1660	746,735/2	José Frimiñoret
	1658–1660	717,530	Miguel de Ocampo
	1661–1662	717,531	
	1663–1665	717,533	
	1666–1676	717,534	
	1659, 1666–1668	746,245/3	Juan Antonio Sousa
	1670–1678, 1680–1689	746,246	
	1660	744,749/1	Juan Ramírez
	1661	737,618	Alonso de Contreras
	1662	737,619	
	1664	737,620/1	
	1661–1662	736,596/3	Francisco de Aguero
	1661–1662	717,532	

Location/ Document Type	Years	Roll No.	Comments
	1661–1662	746,095	Bernabé Roxel
	1663	746,096	
	1664	746,097	
	1665	746,098	
	1666	746,099	
	1667	747,203	
	1668	746,977	
	1669–1670	746,356	
	1669	746,978	
	1671	746,357	
	1672	746,358	
	1672	746,359	
	1673	746,100	
	1674	746,101	
	1675	746,102	
	1675	746,103	
	1676–1677	746,104	
	1678,1687	746,105	
	1679	746,360	
	1680	746,361	
	1681	746,721	
	1684	746,722	
	1685	746,723	
	1686	746,724	
	1688	746,106	
	1689	746,107	
	1690	746,108	
	1691	746,109	
	1692	746,243/1	
	1692	746,725	
	1661–1664	736,330/2	Esteban Española
	1662–1664	714,813	Nicolás de Maeda
	1665–1667	714,814	
	1668–1674, 1681–1684	714,815	
	1663, 1667–1668	738,020	Esteban de la Fuente
	1669–1672	738,021/1	
	1673–1674	738,021/2	
	1675–1677	737,663	
	1678–1680	737,664/1	
	1682–1684	737,664/2	
	1685–1687	737,665	
	1688–1689	736,783/2	
	1691–1693, 1699–1701	736,784/1-3	
	1663–1665	753,586/2-3	Miguel Saldivar
	1666–1669	753,587	
	1663–1677	741,712/1	Nicolás de Peralta
	1664	737,575	Pedro Díaz de Cuellar
	1668	736,632	

Location/ Document Type	Years	Roll No.	Comments
	1664	744,740/1	Pedro Ramírez Rodado
	1667	744,740/2-3	
	1668-1716	744,741	
	1665-1667	736,608	Bernito Berdugo
	1668-1669	736,609	
	1670	736,610	
	1672	736,611	
	1675-1683	737,269	
	1676-1677	737,270	
	1678-1679	737,271	
	1680-1681	737,272	
	1681-1682	737,273	
	1684-1686	737,274	
	1687-1689	737,275	
	1665-1669	756,024/1	José Ríos
	1667-1670	737,641	Antonio Delgado
	1670	737,634/1	
	1668-1669	744,736/1	Pedro Roldán Abarca
	1671	744,736/2-3	
	1672	744,737	
	1673-1674	744,738	
	1687-1689	744,739/1-2	
	1691, 1695-1696	744,739/3	
	1668-1672	717,529	Juan Manuel de Ocampo
	1673-1678	741,701	
	1681-1706	741,702	
	1707-1711	741,703	
	1668-1674	741,715	Lorenz Pérez de Rivera
	1675-1684	741,716/1-3	
	1669-1670	737,620/2-3	Pedro de Contreras
	1669-1670	746,744/2-3	Diego Valenzuela
	1670-1672	746,745	
	1669-1673	741,720	Joán Pereira
	1674-1685	741,721	
	1670	753,573/3	Antonio Zavaleta
	1671-1673	753,574	
	1674-1675	753,575	
	1676	753,576	
	1677-1680	753,577	
	1681-1684	753,578	
	1685-1687	753,579	
	1689-1693	753,580/1	
	1670-1671	744,749/2-3	José Ruiz Aguilar
	1677-1678	736,606	
	1681-1685	744,751/1-2	

Location/ Document Type	Years	Roll No.	Comments
	1671–1673	737,578	Pedro de Contreras
	1674–1675	737,621	
	1676–1678	737,622	
	1680–1684	736,627/2–3	
	1686–1687	738,099/1	
	1672–1673	753,583/2–3	Juan Jérez Serrano
	1674	738,029	
	1675–1676	753,584	
	1677–1678	753,585	
	1679–1682	753,586/1	
	1672–1674	736,594	Joseph de Aguilar
	1675–1676	736,595	
	1672–1675	716,868/2–3	Antonio de Mendoza
	1672–1675	737,544	Miguel Calderón y
	1673,	737,546/1	Rosas
	1681–1686		
	1675–1676	737,545	
	1673	753,590/2	Pedro de Contreras
	1673–1674	741,741	Nicolás Farfán
	1677–1681	738,299	
	1682–1684	736,785	
	1691–1692	736,786	
	1693–1694	736,787	
	1695	736,788	
	1696	738,023/1	
	1674	741,733	Miguel de Perres
	1675–1676	741,734	
	1677–1678	741,735	
	1679–1680	741,736	
	1681	741,737	
	1682–1683	744,446	
	1684–1685	744,447	
	1686–1687	744,448/1	
	1674–1675	737,610/3	Félix de la Campa
	1675, 1679	736,314	Ignacio de Agreda
	1676–1678	736,313	
	1680	736,326	
	1681–1683	736,312	
	1684	737,580	
	1685–1688	737,581	
	1687–1688	737,582	
	1689–1691	737,583	
	1692	737,584	
	1694	737,585	
	1695	737,586	
	1696	737,587	
	1697	737,588	
	1698	737,589	
	1699	737,590	
	1700	737,591	

Location/ Document Type	Years	Roll No.	Comments
	1675–1677	744,452	Guillermo de Pineda
	1678	744,453	Menéndez
	1679–1680	744,454	
	1681	744,455	
	1683	744,456	
	1677	737,563/2	Sebastián Coello
	1678–1681	737,564	
	1682	736,620	
	1683–1685	736,621	
	1686–1689	736,622	
	1690–1691	736,623	
	1693	736,624	
	1694–1695	736,625	
	1695	736,626	
	1696	736,627/1	
	1697–1698	737,623	
	1699–1700	737,624	
	1702	737,565	
	1702	737,566	
	1704	736,628	
	1705	736,629	
	1706	738,113	
	1707	738,114	
	1708–1709	737,571	
	1708	738,116	
	1677–1678	744,448/2	Pedro Somora de
	1679–1682	744,449	Palacios
	1683–1685	744,450	
	1686–1688	744,451	
	1680–1682	746,737/3	Nicolás Valenzuela
	1683–1684	746,738	
	1685–1686	746,739	
	1687	747,035	
	1688	747,036	
	1689	747,037	
	1690–1691	747,038	
	1692–1693	746,740	
	1694–1696	746,741	
	1698	746,742	
	1699	747,039	
	1700–1701	747,040	
	1702–1703	747,041	
	1704–1705	747,042	
	1706–1708	747,043	
	1708–1711, 1713–1714	746,743	
	1709	747,044	
	1710	747,045	
	1717	746,744/1	
	1682	753,591/3	Antonio Carballo

Location/ Document Type	Years	Roll No.	Comments
	1684–1685	744,718	Guillermo Menendes
	1686	744,719	Pineda
	1688	744,720	
	1689	744,721	
	1694–1695	744,722	
	1696	744,723	
	1697	744,724	
	1699	744,725	
	1700	744,726	
	1701	744,727/1	
	1684–1687	746,245/2	Juan Francisco Somosa
	1684–1689	714,805	Nicolás de Lorenzana
	1691–1692	714,806/3	
	1693–1694	714,806/1-2	
	1686	753,590/3	Juan Pereira
	1686–1690	741,722	Pedro Pereira
	1691–1696	741,723	
	1697–1702	741,724	
	1703–1713	741,725	
	1714–1723	741,726	
	1687–1691	741,727	Nicolás de Paniagua
	1692–1693	741,728	
	1694	741,729	
	1695	741,730	
	1696	741,731	
	1697	741,732	
	1688–1691	738,031	Anelhes Miguel de Gazetta
	1691	753,590/3	Nicolás Paniagua
	1691–1693	738,099/2-3	Diego Coronado
	1694	738,100	
	1695	738,101	
	1697	738,102	
	1698	738,103	
	1699	738,104	
	1700–1701	738,105	
	1702	738,106	
	1703	738,107	
	1704	738,108	
	1705–1706	738,109	
	1707	738,110	
	1708	738,111	
	1709	738,112	
	1710	737,554	
	1711	737,555	
	1712	737,556	
	1713	737,557	
	1715–1716	737,558	
	1717–1718	737,559	
	1719	737,560	

Location/ Document Type	Years	Roll No.	Comments
(cont)	1720	737,561	
	1721–1722	737,562	
	1723–1724	737,563/1	
	1693	738,010/1	Joseph de León
	1695, 1698–1699	738,287	
	1700–1702	738,288	
	1703–1704	738,289	
	1705	738,290	
	1706	736,773	
	1707	736,774	
	1708	736,775	
	1709–1710	736,776	
	1709–1710	736,777	
	1711–1712	736,778	
	1714–1715, 1718,1721	738,291	
	1695–1696	737,604	Francisco del Castillo
	1695–1697	736,332	Diego de Arguello
	1698–1699	736,333	
	1696	746,737/1-2	Juan Ulloa Moroscoret
	1696–1703	756,024/2	Leonardo Escobedo Quiñones
	1697	753,591/3	Fernando Escobar
	1697–1698, 1708–1711	738,294	Isidro de Espinoza
	1712	737,655	
	1713–1714	737,656	
	1715–1716	737,657	
	1698–1705	746,249	Juan de Ulloa Moscozo
	1707–1710	746,250	
	1711–1713	746,251	
	1714–1716	746,252	
	1717–1719	746,253	
	1701–1702	736,590	Ignacio de Agreda
	1703–1704	736,591	
	1705–1706	736,592	
	1707–1708	736,593	
	1702–1703	715,212	Francisco de Herrera
	1704–1706	715,213	Sambrano
	1702–1703	737,635	Phelipe Díaz
	1704–1705	737,636	
	1706–1709	737,637	

Location/ Document Type	Years	Roll No.	Comments
	1706-1708	746,363/3	Juan Ruíz de Alarcón
	1709-1710	746,364	
	1711	746,365	
	1712	746,366	
	1713	746,367	
	1714	736,368	
	1715	746,088	
	1716-1717	746,089	
	1718-1719	746,090	
	1720	746,091	
	1721	746,092	
	1723	746,369	
	1724-1725	746,370	
	1726	746,371	
	1727-1728	746,372	
	1729-1730	746,093	
	1731-1732	746,094/1	
	1706-1712, 1714	753,565/1-3	Zeledón Verraondo
	1710-1712	746,746	Diego Leonardo de Valenzuela
	1713	746,747	
	1714-1715	746,748	
	1716-1717	746,749	
	1718-1721	747,046	
	1711-1713	716,871	Manuel Antonio de Moraes Cavallero
	1714-1717	716,872/1	
	1721-1725	716,872/2-3	
	1726-1731	716,889	
	1732-1735	716,873	
	1711-1723	738,018/2-3	Lucas Fernández Pardó
	1712-1720	741,704/1	Jacinto Roque de Ocampo
	1713-1716	753,560	Juan Gregorio Vásquez
	1717-1718	753,561	
	1719-1722	753,562	
	1723-1724	753,563	
	1725-1728	753,564	
	1713-1720	714,816	Joseph de Lanuza
	1721-1722	716,862	
	1723	716,863	
	1726-1728	716,864	
	1729-1742	716,865	
	1714-1716	744,751/3	Mateo Ruíz Hurtado
	1717-1719	744,752	
	1718	744,753	
	1719-1722	744,754	
	1720	744,755	
	1721	744,756	
	1722	677,379	
	1722	744,757	
	1723-1724	746,087	

Location/ Document Type	Years	Roll No.	Comments
(cont)	1723	746,086	
	1725	746,362	
	1725–1727	746,363/1-2	
	1718–1720	714,798	Sebastián Hurtado
	1721–1723	714,799	Vetancour
	1724–1725	714,800	
	1726–1727	714,801	
	1728	714,802	
	1729	737,278	
	1730–1731	714,803	
	1718–1722	718,018	Joseph de Monterroso
	1723–1724	717,347	
	1725–1726	717,348	
	1727	717,349	
	1729–1730	717,507	
	1731–1733	717,508	
	1724–1729	736,793	Antonio Gonzales
	1730	736,794	
	1731	736,795	
	1732	736,796	
	1733	736,797	
	1734	736,798	
	1735	736,799	
	1736	738,072	
	1736–1737	738,074/1-2	
	1737	738,073	
	1738	738,032	
	1739	738,033	
	1740	738,034	
	1741	738,035	
	1742	738,036	
	1743	738,310	
	1744	738,311	
	1745	738,312	
	1746	738,313	
	1747	738,314	
	1748	737,678	
	1749	738,121	
	1751	738,122	
	1752	738,123	
	1753	738,124	
	1754	738,127	
	1755	738,128	
	1756	738,129	
	1757	738,130	
	1758	738,131	
	1759	738,132	
	1760	738,133	
	1761–1762	738,134	
	1764	738,135	
	1766	738,125	
	1766	738,126	

Location/ Document Type	Years	Roll No.	Comments
	1726	716,887/3	Manuel Andrés de
	1727	716,888	Monzón
	1728	716,890/1	
	1733-1734	716,891/2	
	1735	716,890/2	
	1736-1739	716,891/1,3-5	
	1740,	716,892	
	1742-1744		
	1745-1747	716,893	
	1748-1751	716,894	
	1752-1754	716,895	
	1757-1763	716,896	
	1726-1727	736,597	Juan Joseph Alvarez
	1727-1729	741,704/2	Domingo Antonio Ortíz
	1730-1732	741,705	
	1732-1733	741,706	
	1734-1735	741,707	
	1736-1737	741,708	
	1738-1739	741,709	
	1740-1748	741,710	
	1728-1729	736,596/4	Luis de Aguilar
	1730-1733	737,592	Manuel de Alegría
	1734-1735	737,593	
	1736	737,594	
	1731	737,285	Pedro de Carranza y
	1732-1733	737,576	Dardón
	1732-1733	737,577	
	1731-1739	741,712/2	Mathías del Poso y
			Murillo
	1732-1734	746,754/2-3	Lorenzo José de Vivas
	1735-1737	747,054	
	1733	717,522	Antonio Hipólito
	1734	717,523	Ordóñez
	1735-1736	717,524	
	1737-1738	717,518	
	1739-1740	717,525	
	1741-1744	717,526	
	1745-1746	717,527/1	
	1734-1736	746,094/2	José Rivera y Tello
	1734-1737	716,866/1	Feliciano Joseph Moreno
	1738-1739	716,866/2	
	1740-1741	716,867/1	
	1737-1738	715,140	Joseph Matthías de
	1739-1740	715,198	Guzmán
	1741-1742	715,199	
	1743	715,200	
	1745-1746	715,201	
	1747-1749	715,202	

Location/ Document Type	Years	Roll No.	Comments
(cont)	1750–1752	715,203	
	1753	715,210	
	1754–1756	715,204	
	1757–1758	715,205	
	1761	715,208	
	1762	715,209	
	1763–1764	715,211	
	1737–1739	753,588	Jacinto Zeram
	1738–1739	717,527/3	Isidro Ocaña y Armas
	1740–1742	717,528/1–3	
	1739–1742	714,120	Manuel Vicente de
	1743–1746	714,121	Guzmán
	1747–1750	714,122	
	1751–1762	714,123	
	1758–1765	714,124	
	1759	715,206	
	1760	715,207	
	1767–1769	714,125	
	1770–1775	714,126	
	1771–1774	715,137	
	1776–1778	715,138	
	1779–1789	715,139	
	1740–1741	753,580/2	José Felipe Zerrano
	1742–1743	753,581	
	1744–1745	753,582	
	1740–1746	741,717	Joseph Pérez
	1747–1752	741,718	
	1753–1756	741,719	
	1742	737,606/1	Domingo Cavallero
	1743–1744	753,569	Juan José Zavala
	1745,1747	753,570	
	1748–1749	753,571	
	1750–1751	753,572	
	1752–1754	753,573/1–2	
	1743–1746	716,874/2	Luis Antonio Muñoz
	1745–1747	717,528/4	Domingo de Oqueli
	1746	716,878/2	Diego Antonio Milán
	1747–1748	716,879	
	1749	716,880	
	1750	716,881	
	1751–1752	716,882	
	1754	716,883/1	
	1759–1761	716,883/2	
	1762	716,884	
	1763–1764	716,885	
	1765–1767	716,886	
	1768–1770	716,887/1–2	

Location/ Document Type	Years	Roll No.	Comments
	1746-1753, 1756-1762	714,117	Francisco Antonio de Guzmán
	1763-1766	714,118	
	1767-1778	714,119	
	1748-1750, 1752	739,869	Josef Díaz Gonzales
	1753-1756	739,870	
	1780-1781	739,854	
	1782	739,855	
	1783	739,856	
	1784	739,857	
	1785	714,104	
	1786	714,105	
	1787	714,106	
	1788	714,107	
	1790	714,108	
	1790	714,109	
	1791	714,110	
	1791	714,111	
	1791,1793	714,112	
	1793	721,189	
	1794	714,113	
	1794	714,114	
	1796	739,858	
	1796	739,859	
	1797	739,860	
	1797	739,861	
	1798	739,862	
	1799	739,863	
	1800	739,864	
	1801	739,865	
	1802	739,866	
	1803	739,867	
	1804	739,868	
	1749-1768	746,736	Manuel Taracena
	1752-1753	736,596/1-2	Juan Angel de Altamira
	1755-1756	717,519	Manuel Ordoñoz
	1757-1758	717,520	
	1759-1760	717,521	
	1756-1763	741,711	Francisco Joseph Palacios
	1757-1759	714,115	Joseph Miguel Godoy
	1760-1763	714,116	
	1756-1777	753,596	
	1802-1810	753,597	
	1811-1821	753,598	
	1761-1763	716,869	Lucas Martínez García
	1764-1766	716,870	

Location/ Document Type	Years	Roll No.	Comments
	1762–1765	737,596	Joseph de Asurdia
	1766–1769	737,597	
	1763–1765	736,613	Manuel Ignacio Cercano
	1769	737,283	
	1770,1773	737,284	
	1764–1765	738,050	Miguel Gonzales
	1766–1767	738,051	
	1768–1769	738,052	
	1765	738,136	Sebastián Gonzales
	1765	738,137	
	1767	738,138	
	1767	738,139	
	1768	738,140	
	1768	738,141	
	1769	738,142	
	1770	738,143	
	1771	738,074/3	
	1772	738,075	
	1773	738,076	
	1774	738,144	
	1775	738,145	
	1775	738,146	
	1776	738,147	
	1777	738,148	
	1778	738,149	
	1781	738,321	
	1782–1783	738,322	
	1783	738,323	
	1784–1785	738,324	
	1784–1785	738,325	
	1786–1787	738,326	
	1788–1789	738,327	
	1792–1793	738,328	
	1794	738,329	
	1795–1796	738,330	
	1797–1801	738,048	
	1802–1810	738,049	
	1766–1767	736,614	Miguel I. Cascamozorón
	1768	736,615/1	
	1768–1769	654,957	Miguel Joseph Gonzales
	1770–1771	714,127	
	1770–1771	714,128	
	1772–1775	714,129	
	1772–1775	714,130	
	1776–1778	714,131	
	1776–1778	714,132	
	1779–1780	714,133	
	1781–1782	714,134	
	1783–1784	714,135	
	1785–1786	714,136	
	1787–1788	714,137	
	1789–1790	714,138	
	1791–1792	714,139	

Location/ Document Type	Years	Roll No.	Comments
(cont)	1791–1792	714,140	
	1795–1797, 1801	714,141	
	1769	717,509	Francisco Marquez Rendón
	1770–1771	717,510	
	1772–1773	717,511/1	
	1769	738,292	Joseph Sánchez de León y Mendieta
	1774–1776	738,293	
	1770	746,247	José Sánchez de León
	1771–1772	746,248	
	1777–1780	746,731	
	1770–1774	753,590/1	Gerardo de Campo
	1770–1774	714,807	Joseph Manuel de Laparte
	1775–1780	714,808	
	1792–1797	714,809	
	1771–1773	746,726	Antonio Santa Cruz
	1774–1777	746,727	
	1778–1780, 1784	746,728	
	1785–1787	746,729	
	1788–1790	746,730	
	1791–1792	746,243/2	
	1771–1774	737,660	Carlos de Figueroa
	1775–1776	737,661	
	1777–1785	737,662	
	1771–1778	716,867/2-3	Pedro Domingo Moreno
	1776	737,611	Félix de la Campa
	1777–1778	736,615/2	
	1778–1781	736,616	
	1785–1788	736,617	
	1776	756,022/3	Pedro Felipe Sarruoloa
	1776–1777	736,598	Pedro Alvarado y Guzmán
	1778	737,598	
	1779–1780	737,599	
	1781	737,600	
	1776–1780, 1783–1785	736,329	Joseph Rodríguez Car- ballo, Antonio Lisana, Miguel Gerónimo de Avendaño
	1776–1813	744,885	
	1777–1778	716,874/1	Joseph Antonio Marroquín
	1777–1780	744,887/2	Pedro Alvarez
	1777–1802	753,592/3	

Location/ Document Type	Years	Roll No.	Comments
	1778–1779	736,334	Nicolás Josef Aven-
	1781–1783	736,335	daño
	1784–1787	736,336	
	1791–1795	738,096/2	
	1796–1820	736,327	
	1820–1833	736,328	
	1781–1786	753,565	Francisco María Valdez
	1784–1793	753,566	
	1794–1803	753,589	
	1781–1790	744,889	Pedro José Rendón
	1783–1791	744,888	
	1791,1794	744,539/1	Bernardino Lorenzana
	1791–1794	737,601/2-3	Manuel de la Cavada
	1795–1798	737,602	
	1797–1809	737,603	
	1791–1796	741,912	Domingo Antonio
	1797–1800	741,913	Estrada
	1804–1805	747,204	
	1805–1808	744,534	
	1791–1797	716,897	José María Martínez
	1781–1790	744,890	Cevallos
	1798–1802	716,898	
	1803–1809	716,899	
	1791–1799	741,909	Alejandro Josef Espeña
	1799–1804	741,910	
	1805–1812	741,911	
	1791–1801	753,590/3	José Palacios
	1792	738,096/1	Alexo Josef Avendaño
	1792–1793	736,780	José María Estrada
	1794–1795	736,781	
	1796–1797	736,782	
	1798–1799	736,783/1	
	1800–1801	738,019	
	1802–1803	738,298	
	1804–1807	738,297	
	1809–1810	738,296	
	1811–1813	738,295	
	1814–1816	738,015	
	1817–1819	738,016	
	1792–1803	738,030	Rafael María González
	1794–1811	737,606/2	Juan José Castro
	1797–1798	753,567	Vicente Antonio Villa-
	1799–1803	753,568	toro

Location/ Document Type	Years	Roll No.	Comments
	1797–1802	738,300	Josef Francisco
	1803–1804	738,301	Gavarrete
	1805–1806	738,302	
	1807,1836	738,306	
	1808–1809	738,305	
	1810	738,304	
	1811	738,303	
	1812–1813	736,789	
	1814	736,790	
	1815	736,791	
	1816,1834	736,792	
	1817	737,669/3	
	1818–1819	737,670	
	1820	737,671	
	1821–1822	737,672	
	1825–1826	738,025	
	1830–1831	738,026	
	1832–1833	738,027/1	
	1835	738,027/2	
	1837	738,307	
	1839–1840, 1840–1841	738,308	
	1800	756,022/1,4	Juan Toro/Pedro Miguel López
	1800–1813	756,023/1	José María Molina
	1804,1817, 1854	741,905	Joaquín de León
	1808–1816	741,904	
	1816–1820	741,906	
	1821–1828	741,907	
	1804–1807	744,535	José Gracía de Zelaya
	1808–1811	744,536	
	1812–1813 1815–1816	744,537	
	1817–1818, 1821,1823	744,538	
	1805–1811	744,541	Juan José Saravia
	1812–1817	744,542	
	1818–1828	744,543	
	1805–1813	744,540	Paulino de Salazar
	1805–1814	741,899	Antonio Arroyable y
	1805–1814	741,900	Beteta
	1805–1814	741,901	
	1806–1811	756,023/3	Jacobo Córdoba/José María Nergara
	1809–1817	741,716/4	José Ignacio Grijalba
	1813–1815	744,886	
	1815–1817	744,539/2	Antonio de Olaizola

Location/ Document Type	Years	Roll No.	Comments
	1815-1820	741,902	Francisco Berdugo
	1815-1820	741,903	
	1817-1819	741,897	Vicente Arrazola
	1820-1822	741,898	
	1818-1842	744,887/1	
	1819-1820	738,018/1	José Domingo Estrada
	1820-1823	756,023/2	José Antonio Solís
	1821-1825	741,908	Andrés Dardón
	1823,1826	756,023/4	Eugenio Mariscal
	1823,1841 1843, 1857-1858, 1861-1863	744,841	
	1897-1898	717,387	José Madriz
Huehuetenango			
	1681-1792	753,393	
	1705-1721	753,594	
	1721-1748	753,595	
Quezaltenango			
	1681-1761	744,884	
	1701-1724	753,599	
	1726-1763	753,600	
	1755-1776	753,601	
	1774-1778	753,602	
	1774-1778	756,001	
	1725-1729	717,527/2	Manuel Santiago Ordoñez
Sacatepéquez San Lucas Sacatepéquez San Lucas Sacatepéquez (c/p)			
	1878-1887	753,592/1-2	

Location/ Document Type	Years	Roll No.	Comments

Current jurisdictions are unknown or
unavailable for the following entries

Indice de Protocolos

	Years	Roll No.	Comments
	1565–1818	744,846	ODT/OL Legajo 2424
	1899	757,004	Vol 19609
	1900	757,005	Vol 19610
	1900	757,006	Vol 19611
	1900	757,007	Vol 19612
	1901	757,008	Vol 19613
	1901	757,009	Vol 19614
	1901	757,010	Vol 19615
	1902	757,011	Vol 19616
	1902	757,012	Vols 19617–19618
	1903	757,013	Vol 19619
	1903	757,014	Vol 19620
	1903	757,015	Vol 19621
	1904	757,016	Vols 19622–19623
	1904	757,017	Vols 19624–19625
	1904	757,018	Vols 19626–19627
	1905	757,019	Vols 19628–19629
	1905	757,020	Vols 19630–19631
	1905	757,021	Vols 19632–19633
	1906	757,022	Vol 19634
	1906	757,023	Vol 19635
	1906	757,024	Vol 19636
	1906–1907	757,025	Vol 19637
	1907	757,026	Vol 19638
	1907	757,027	Vols 19639–19640

Location/ Document Type	Years	Roll No.	Comments
	1907	757,028	Vols 19641-19642
	1907	757,029	Vol 19642
	1907	757,030	Vol 19643
	1908	757,031	Vol 19644
	1908	757,032	Vol 19645
	1908	757,033	Vol 19646
	1909	757,501	Vol 19647
	1909	757,502	Vol 19648
	1909	757,503	Vol 19649
	1909	757,504	Vol 19650
	1910	757,505	Vol 19651
	1910	757,506	Vol 19652
	1910	757,507	Vol 19653
	1910	757,508	Vols 19654-19655
	1911	757,509	Vols 19656-19657
	1911	757,510	Vols 19658-19659
	1911	757,511	Vols 19660-19661
	1911	757,512	Vols 19662-19663
	1912	757,513	Vol 19664
	1912	757,514	Vol 19665
	1912	757,515	Vol 19666
	1912	757,516	Vol 19667
	1912	757,517	Vol 19668
	1913	757,518	Vol 19669
	1913	757,519	Vol 19670
	1913	757,520	Vol 19671
	1913	757,521	Vol 19672
	1913	757,522	Vol 19673
	1914	757,523	Vol 19674

Location/ Document Type	Years	Roll No.	Comments
	1914	757,524	Vol 19675
	1914	757,525	Vol 19676
	1914	757,526	Vol 19677
	1914	757,527	Vols 19678-19679
	1915	756,047	Vol 19680
	1915	756,048	Vol 19681
	1915	756,049	Vol 19682
	1915	756,050	Vol 19683
	1915	756,051	Vol 19684
	1916	756,052	Vol 19685
	1916	756,053	Vol 19686
	1916	756,054	Vol 19687
	1916	756,055	Vol 19688
	1916	756,056	Vol 19689
	1916	756,057	Vol 19690
	1917	756,058	Vol 19691
	1918	754,784	Vols 19692-19693
	1918	754,785	Vols 19694-19695
	1918	754,786	Vol 19696
	1919	754,787	Vol 19697
	1919	754,788	Vols 19698-19699
	1919	754,789	Vols 19700-19701
	1919	754,790	Vol 19702
	1920	754,791	Vols 19703-19704
	1920	754,792	Vols 19705-19706

Tierras

Location/ Document Type	Years	Roll No.	Comments
Capital			
Alcabalas			
	1799	746,979/5	ODT/OL Legajo 2584
Autos de Amparo			
	1579–1713	744,588/1	Indexed ODT/OL Legajo 443
	1781	746,864/15	Legajo 6029
Autos de Avivamiento			
	1726	749,202/2	ODT/OL Legajo 5970
	1781	746,864/15	Legajo 6029
Autos de Denuncia			
	1581–1726	749,202/1	Legajo 5970
	1635–1738	749,203/3	Legajo 5980
	1726	749,202/2	ODT/OL Legajo 5970
	1740	749,203/4	Legajo 5981
	1766	747,141/2	ODT/OL Legajo 6013
Autos de Posesión			
	1757	749,207/2	ODT/OL Legajo 600

Location/ Document Type	Years	Roll No.	Comments
Autos de Residencia			
	1773	746,980/9	ODT/OL Legajo 2792
Confirmaciónes de Títulos			
	1647	746,756/29	Legajo 4581
	1701	746,351/9	ODT/OL Legajo 1572
	1707	746,351/12	ODT/OL Legajo 1576
	1708	746,351/13	ODT/OL Legajo 1577
	1720-1757	749,208/1	Legajo 6002
	1752	747,147/1	ODT/OL Legajo 6036
	1758	749,208/2	Legajo 6003
	1789	746,980/11	Legajo 2794
	1816	746,980/12	ODT/OL Legajo 2796
Diligencias de Renovación			
	1676-1768	749,202/4-5	Legajo 5970
Hipotecas			
	1650-1667	747,152/5	Legajo 667
	1817	746,980/12	ODT/OL Legajo 2796
Libros Ejidales			
	1890	744,589/17	ODT/OL Legajo 1436
Medidas			
	1569-1633	749,202/3	Legajo 5973
	1574	747,150/6	ODT/OL Legajo 6062

Location/ Document Type	Years	Roll No.	Comments
	1633	746,983/8	Legajo 5941
	1669-1682	749,203/5-6	Legajo 5982
	1722-1778	749,201/8	Legajo 5969
	1739	749,203/1	Legajo 5978
	1756	749,207/2	ODT/OL Legajo 6000
	1770	747,142/2	ODT/OL Legajo 6017
	1772-1797	747,150/4	Legajo 6056
	1779	746,864/14	Legajo 6026
	1798	747,150/5	Legajo 6059
	1816	747,150/3	Legajo 6054
Pajas de Agua			
	1816	741,893	ODT/OL Legajo 1811
Reales Concesiones			
	1712	746,352/3	ODT/OL Legajo 1579
	1817	746,980/12	ODT/OL Legajo 2796
Reclamas			
	1776-1798	747,144/1	Legajo 6022
	1798-1833	747,145/2	ODT/OL Legajo 6030
Remates			
	1784	746,980/10	ODT/OL Legajo 2793
	1793-1794	747,144/2	ODT/OL Legajo 6023

Location/ Document Type	Years	Roll No.	Comments
Títulos			
	n.d.	747,141/2	ODT/OL Legajo 6013
	1574	747,150/6	ODT/OL Legajo 6062
	1579	746,982/4	Legajo 5553
	1582,1606	746,983/5	Legajo 5937
	1582-1664	746,983/10	Legajo 5942
	1598	746,354/3	Legajo 1598
	1607	746,980/1-2	Legajo 2786
	1608	746,354/7	Legajo 2023
	1613-1614	746,353/9	Legajo 1751
	1616	746,983/6	ODT/OL Legajo 5938
	1631	746,980/3	Legajo 2786
	1637	746,983/9	Legajo 5941
	1655	746,980/4	Legajo 2787
	1671-1762	747,140/2	Legajo 6009
	1673	746,354/11	Legajo 2162
	1677,1720, 1728-1729, 1771-1773	746,979/3	Legajo 2577
	1683-1689	746,982/1-2	Legajo 4588
	1684-1759	749,209/1	Legajo 6005
	1689	746,354/6	Legajo 1962
	1691	746,985/3	Legajo 5951
	1694	746,351/6	Legajo 1569
	1694	746,983/4	Legajo 3936
	1696	746,351/7	Legajo 1570
	1700	744,588/12	Legajo 1287
	1700	746,351/8	Legajo 1571

Location/ Document Type	Years	Roll No.	Comments
	1701	746,351/9	ODT/OL Legajo 1572
	1705	746,351/10	Legajo 1574
	1706	746,351/11	Legajo 1575
	1707	746,351/12	ODT/OL Legajo 1576
	1708	746,351/13	ODT/OL Legajo 1577
	1711	746,352/1	Legajo 1578
	1711	746,352/2	ODT/OL Legajo 1578
	1712	746,352/3	ODT/OL Legajo 1579
	1714	746,353/3	ODT/OL Legajo 1581
	1718	746,354/10	Legajo 2107
	1720	746,981/3	Legajo 2865
	1721	744,588/10	Legajo 1112
	1724	746,353/5	Legajo 1584
	1725,1729, 1759,1775, 1784	746,979/4	Legajo 2583
	1725,1738	746,980/5	Legajo 2788
	1726	746,353/6	Legajo 1585
	1728	746,353/7	Legajo 1586
	1730	746,353/8	Legajo 1587
	1730,1733, 1739,1748	746,981/17	Legajo 4558
	1733	747,980/6	ODT/OL Legajo 2789
	1745-1758	749,206/1	Legajo 5995
	1749	746,981/5	Legajo 2896
	1750	744,588/4	Legajo 1065
	1753	744,588/9	Legajo 1096

Location/ Document Type	Years	Roll No.	Comments
	1755	746,355/11	ODT/OL Legajo 2576
	1755	747,980/7	Legajo 2790
	1756,1758, 1763,1766	746,981/18	ODT/OL Legajo 4559
	1758	746,982/3	Legajo 5059
	1759	749,209/2	Legajo 6006
	1760	746,354/1	ODT/OL Legajo 1598
	1760-1765	747,140/4	Legajo 6012
	1761	746,979/7	Legajo 2676
	1763-1766	747,140/3	Legajo 6011
	1765	747,141/1	Legajo 6013
	1767	746,355/3	Legajo 2314
	1770	746,354/9	Legajo 2104
	1771,1787	746,981/19	Legajo 4560
	1771-1777	744,588/2	Legajo 812
	1773	746,980/9	ODT/OL Legajo 2792
	1782	746,979/2	Legajo 2578
	1782	749,201/1	ODT/OL Legajo 5963
	1784	746,980/10	ODT/OL Legajo 2793
	1784	747,146/1	Legajo 6031
	1786	746,354/8	Legajo 2045
	1791	746,355/1	ODT/OL Legajo 2168
	1793	746,979/8	Legajo 2766
	1799	746,353/10	ODT/OL Legajo 1598
	1799	746,979/5	ODT/OL Legajo 2584
	1808	746,979/10	Legajo 2773

Location/ Document Type	Years	Roll No.	Comments
	1813–1814	747,150/1	ODT/OL Legajo 6053
	1824	746,351/5	Legajo 1484
	1833	746,355/9	Legajo 2562
	1833	746,981/9	Legajo 3633
	1834	744,588/14	Legajo 1417
	1834	746,354/4-5	Legajos 1921, 1961
	1835,1838	746,981/8	Legajo 3600
	1842	744,588/11	Legajo 1287
	1845–1847	744,588/16	Legajo 1419
	1878	746,981/12	Legajo 3987
	1885	744,589/14	ODT/OL Legajo 1433
	1892	744,589/21	Legajo 1439
	1893	746,351/1	Legajo 1443
	1894	746,351/2-3	Legajo 1445
Títulos Concedidos			
	1581,1600, 1623,1625, 1628–1629, 1722	749,201/7	Legajo 5968
	1585–1713	749,201/3	ODT/OL Legajo 5964
	1726	749,202/2	ODT/OL Legajo 5970
	1753–1775	749,201/2	Legajo 5963
	1782	749,201/1	ODT/OL Legajo 5963
	1816	747,150/2	Legajo 6053
	1885	744,589/9	Legajo 1430
	n.d.	749,201/6	Legajo 5967

Location/ Document Type	Years	Roll No.	Comments
Títulos Supletorios			
	1773	746,980/9	ODT/OL Legajo 2792
	1811	746,980/12	ODT/OL Legajo 2796
	1813-1814	747,150/1	ODT/OL Legajo 6053
	1878	717,186	
	1878	744,589/15	ODT/OL Legajo 1434
	1890	744,589/18	ODT/OL Legajo 1437
	1891	744,589/19	Legajo 1438
	1901	746,981/11	Legajo 3635
Ventas			
	1579-1713	744,588/1	Indexed ODT/OL Legajo 443
	1744	744,588/8	Legajo 1087
	1763	744,588/5	Legajo 1011
	1764	744,588/6	Legajo 1011
	1767	744,588/7	Legajo 1072

Alta Verapaz
  Santa Cruz Verapaz
    <u>Santa Cruz Verapaz</u> (c/p)

Location/ Document Type	Years	Roll No.	Comments
Títulos			
	1757	749,207/3-4	
	1760	746,354/1	ODT/OL
	1799	746,353/10	ODT/OL Legajo 1598

Location/ Document Type	Years	Roll No.	Comments

Baja Verapaz
  Salamá
    Salamá (c/cd)			

Reales Concesiones			
	1890	744,589/18	ODT/OL Legajo 1437

Chimaltenango
  Chimaltenango
    Chimaltenango (c/cd)			

Títulos			
	1681	746,984/6	Legajo 5949
	1682	747,151/1	Legajo 6063
	1691	747,151/2-3	Legajo 6064
	1775	747,151/5	Legajo 6095
	1789	747,151/4	Legajo 6071

Chiquimula
  Chiquimula
    Chiquimula (c/cd)			

Autos de Amparo			
	1743-1776	747,142/1	ODT/OL Legajo 6016
Autos de Avivamiento			
	1768	747,141/3	ODT/OL Legajo 6015
Autos de Denuncia			
	1718-1719	749,201/5	ODT/OL Legajo 5966
	1743	747,204/2	ODT/OL Legajo 5984

Location/ Document Type	Years	Roll No.	Comments
Autos de Posesión			
	1713	746,353/1-2	Legajo 1580
	1800	747,145/1	ODT/OL Legajo 6028
Confirmaciónes de Títulos			
	1704-1839	747,147/6	ODT/OL Legajo 6041
	1790-1792	747,147/3	ODT/OL Legajo 6037
	1792	747,147/5	Legajo 6039
	1798	747,149/2	Legajo 6047
	1800	747,149/4	ODT/OL Legajo 6049
Diligencias de Renovación			
	1781	747,142/2	ODT/OL Legajo 6017
Entregas de Títulos			
	1781	747,145/2	ODT/OL Legajo 6029
Medidas			
	1704	747,147/6	ODT/OL Legajo 6041
	1717-1748	747,204/3	Legajo 5985
	1732	747,144/4	ODT/OL Legajo 6024
	1742-1749	747,204/1	Legajo 5983
	1743	747,204/2	ODT/OL Legajo 5984
	1756-1796	747,148/2	ODT/OL Legajo 6044
	1770	747,142/1	ODT/OL Legajo 6016

Location/ Document Type	Years	Roll No.	Comments
	1781	744,760/3	ODT/OL Legajo 389
	1782–1783	747,145/2	ODT/OL Legajo 6030
	1795	747,148/1	ODT/OL Legajo 6044
	1800	745,145/1	ODT/OL Legajo 6028
Presentaciones de Títulos			
	1750	749,205/4	ODT/OL Legajo 1661
	1755	749,207/1	ODT/OL Legajo 5999
Reclamas			
	1794–1795	747,147/7	ODT/OL Legajo 6042
	1801	747,149/4	ODT/OL Legajo 6049
Remates			
	1800	747,149/4	ODT/OL Legajo 6049
Títulos			
	1585	746,983/1	Legajo 5930
	1597	746,983/3	ODT/OL Legajo 5934
	1613	746,983/7	Legajo 5940
	1713	746,353/1-2	Legajo 1580
	1713–1813	747,142/2	ODT/OL Legajo 6017
	1714	746,353/3	Legajo 1581
	1716	749,201/4	Legajo 5965
	1742	746,981/7	Legajo 3016

Location/ Document Type	Years	Roll No.	Comments
	1743–1776	747,142/1	ODT/OL Legajo 6016
	1768	747,141/3	ODT/OL Legajo 6015
	1773	747,143/1	ODT/OL Legajo 6019
	1776	746,981/6	Legajo 2900
	1777	746,984/1	ODT/OL Legajo 5943
	1794	747,147/7	ODT/OL Legajo 6042
	1812	747,149/6	Legajo 6052
	1834	746,355/5	Legajo 56,838
	1842	746,355/7	Legajo 2530
Títulos Concedidos			
	1718	749,201/5	ODT/OL Legajo 5966
	1756–1796	747,148/2	Disordered ODT/OL Legajo 6044
	1795	747,148/1	ODT/OL Legajo 6044
Títulos Supletorios			
	1766–1801	747,147/8	Disordered Legajo 6043
	1773	746,980/9	ODT/OL Legajo 2792
	1790–1792	747,147/3	ODT/OL Legajo 6037
Ventas			
	1650	746,984/1	ODT/OL Legajo 5943
	1782	744,588/3	Legajo 973

Location/ Document Type	Years	Roll No.	Comments
San Jacinto _San Jacinto_ (c/p)			
Reclamas			
	1921	779,726	Document damage ODT/OL
San Juan Ermita _San Juan Ermita_ (c/p)			
Diligencias de Renovación			
	1770	747,142/2	ODT/OL Legajo 6017
Títulos			
	1779-1782	747,144/5	Legajo 6026
Títulos Supletorios			
	1773	746,980/9	ODT/OL Legajo 2792
El Progreso San Agustín Acasaguastlán _San Agustín Acasaguastlán_ (c/p)			
Títulos			
	1701	746,986/4	Legajo 5957
San Antonio la Paz _Santo Domingo los Ocotes_ (a)			
Títulos			
	1748	746,355/10	Legajo 2575
Sanarate _Sanarate_ (c/p)			
Títulos			
	1862	744,589/1	Legajo 1421

Location/ Document Type	Years	Roll No.	Comments
	1878	744,589/15	ODT/OL Legajo 1434
Ventas			
	1866	744,589/3	Legajo 1424
	1883	744,589/7	Legajo 1427
	1885	744,589/14	ODT/OL Legajo 1433

El Quiché
  Santa Cruz del Quiché
    Santa Cruz del Quiché (c/cd)

Autos de Amparo			
	1775	747,143/3	ODT/OL Legajo 6021
Títulos			
	1773	747,143/1	ODT/OL Legajo 6019

    San Sebastián Lemoa (a)

Reclamas			
	1773	747,143/3	ODT/OL Legajo 6021

Escuintla
  Escuintla
    Escuintla (c/cd)

Autos de Amparo			
	1778	747,144/3	Legajo 6024
Confirmaciónes de Títulos			
	1702	746,987/2	ODT/OL Legajo 5959
	1758	749,208/3	Legajo 6004

Location/ Document Type	Years	Roll No.	Comments
	1759	746,980/8	ODT/OL Legajo 2791
Entregas de Títulos			
	1800	742,149/3	ODT/OL Legajo 6048
Medidas			
	1579,1596, 1582,1589	746,982/6-7	Legajo 5929
	1614	746,983/6	ODT/OL Legajo 5938
	1707	746,987/4	ODT/OL Legajo 5961
	1711	746,987/5	Legajo 5962
	1745	749,205/2	ODT/OL Legajo 5987
	1752	749,206/2	Legajo 5996
	1778	747,144/4	ODT/OL Legajo 6024
	1801	747,149/4	ODT/OL Legajo 6049
Títulos			
	1702	746,987/2	ODT/OL Legajo 5959
	1707	746,987/4	ODT/OL Legajo 5961
	1714	746,353/3	ODT/OL Legajo 1581
	1759	746,980/8	ODT/OL Legajo 2791
	1800	747,149/3	ODT/OL Legajo 6048
	1845	746,355/8	Legajo 2547
	1873	744,588/17	Legajo 1422

Location/ Document Type	Years	Roll No.	Comments
Vistas			
	1747	749,205/1	Legajo 5986
Palín Palín (c/p)			
Títulos			
	1837	744,588/15	ODT/OL Legajo 1418
San Vicente Pacaya San Vicente Pacaya (c/p)			
Títulos Supletorios			
	1923	779,413/1	ODT/OL

Guatemala
    Chinautla
     Chinautla (c/p)			

Reclamas			
	1585–1713	749,201/3	ODT/OL Legajo 5964
Títulos			
	1585–1713	749,201/3	ODT/OL Legajo 5964
	1692–1638	746,986/1	Legajo 5954
	1798	746,986/2	Legajo 5954
San Antonio las Flores (a)			
Títulos Supletorios			
	1893	744,589/24	ODT/OL Legajo 1440

Location/ Document Type	Years	Roll No.	Comments
Guatemala Santa Rosita (a)			
Entregas de Títulos			
	1890	744,589/17	ODT/OL Legajo 1436
Títulos Supletorios			
	1883	744,589/8	Legajo 1427
	1890	744,589/18	ODT/OL Legajo 1437
Mixco Mixco (c/p)			
Títulos			
	1778-1779	744,586/5	Legajo 359
	1885	744,589/14	ODT/OL Legajo 1433
Títulos Supletorios			
	1890	744,589/18	ODT/OL Legajo 1437
Palencia Palencia (c/p)			
Medidas			
	1881	744,589/4	ODT/OL Legajo 1425
Reclamas			
	1880-1881	744,589/4	ODT/OL Legajo 1425

Location/ Document Type	Years	Roll No.	Comments
Títulos Supletorios			
	1881	744,589/6	Legajo 1426
San José Pinula			
San José Pinula (c/p)			
Presentaciones de Títulos			
	1880	744,589/5	ODT/OL Legajo 1425
Reclamas			
	1880–1881	744,589/4	ODT/OL Legajo 1425
Títulos			
	1706–1786	749,206/3	ODT/OL Legajo 5997
San Juan Sacatepéquez			
San Juan Sacatepéquez (c/v)			
Títulos			
	1800	746,981/20	Legajo 4561
San Pedro Ayampuc			
San Pedro Ayampuc (c/p)			
Títulos			
	1884–1885	744,589/14	ODT/OL Legajo 1433
San Pedro Sacatepéquez			
San Pedro Sacatepéquez (c/p)			
Títulos			
	1878	744,589/15	ODT/OL Legajo 1434

Location/ Document Type	Years	Roll No.	Comments
Ventas			
	1878	744,589/15	ODT/OL Legajo 1434
San Raimundo			
San Raimundo (c/p)			
Títulos			
	1884	744,589/10,12	Legajos 1430–1431
Títulos Supletorios			
	1881	744,589/4	ODT/OL Legajo 1425
	1881	744,589/5	Legajo 1426
	1885	744,589/13	Legajo 1432
	1889	744,589/16	
	1891	744,589/20	Legajo 1438
Santa Catarina Pinula			
Santa Catarina Pinula (c/p)			
Títulos			
	1893	744,589/25	Legajo 1442
Títulos Supletorios			
	1892	744,589/22	Legajo 1439
	1893	744,589/24	ODT/OL Legajo 1441
Villa Nueva			
Villa Nueva (c/v)			
Títulos			
	1837	744,588/15	ODT/OL Legajo 1418

Location/ Document Type	Years	Roll No.	Comments
Huehuetenango			
Huehuetenango			
Heuhuetenango (c/cd)			
Presentaciones de Títulos			
	1799	746,979/6	Legajo 2643
Títulos			
	1767	746,979/1	Legajo 2577
	1791	747,151/7	Legajo 6099
Jalapa			
Jalapa			
Jalapa (c/cd)			
Autos de Denuncia			
	1890–1893	762,310/2	
	1890–1894	762,310/1	
	1892–1894	762,310/4	
	1893	762,310/3	
Ventas			
	1878	744,589/15	ODT/OL Legajo 1434
Jutiapa			
Jalpatagua			
Jalpatagua (c/p)			
Medidas			
	1745	749,205/2	ODT/OL Legajo 5957

Location/ Document Type	Years	Roll No.	Comments
Santa Catarina Mita Santa Catarina Mita (c/p)			
Títulos			
	1773	747,143/1	ODT/OL Legajo 6019

Quezaltenango
  Quezaltenango
    Quezaltenango (c/cd)			

Medidas			
	1684	746,984/4	Legajo 5946
	1796	747,148/3	Legajo 6045
Reclamas			
	1687	746,985/1-2	Legajo 5950
Títulos			
	1518–1719	746,986/3	Intermittent years Legajo 5955
	1684	746,985/4	Legajo 5953
	1721	746,981/16	Legajo 4557
	1881	746,981/13	Legajo 3609

Sacatepéquez
  Alotenango
    Alotenango (c/p)			

Autos de Denuncia			
	1886	716,853	ODT/OL
Títulos			
	1750	746,981/14	Legajo 4067

Location/ Document Type	Years	Roll No.	Comments
	1756,1758, 1763,1766	746,981/18	ODT/OL Legajo 4559
Títulos Supletorios			
	1877,1886, 1888–1890, 1896–1920	716,853	ODT/OL
	1900	716,854	
Antigua Guatemala Antigua Guatemala (c/cd)			
Títulos			
	1811	746,979/11	Legajo 2774
Ciudad Vieja Ciudad Vieja (c/p)			
Reclamas			
	1880–1881	744,589/4	ODT/OL Legajo 1425
Títulos Supletorios			
	1874–1887	717,594	
	1877–1920	717,595	
	1889–1892	717,596	
	1893–1917	717,597	
	1898	717,600	
	1903	717,599	Poor exposure
	1905–1916	717,598	Disordered
Magdalena Milpas Altas Magdalena Milpas Altas (c/p)			
Alcabalas			
	1881	717,662/1	ODT/OL

Location/ Document Type	Years	Roll No.	Comments
Títulos			
	1878	717,662/1	ODT/OL
	1892	717,662/1	ODT/OL
Títulos Supletorios			
	1895	717,662/2	
	1895–1899	717,661	

San Antonio Aguas Calientes
San Andrés Ceballos (a)

Títulos Supletorios			
	1881	717,500/1	

San Antonio Aguas Calientes (c/p)

Títulos			
	n.d.	747,980/6	ODT/OL Legajo 2789
Títulos Supletorios			
	1881–1889	717,388	
	1884–1889	717,389	
	1889	717,494	
	1890–1893	717,495	
	1894	717,496/1-2	
	1895	717,497/1-2	
	1896–1909	717,498/1-2	
	1910–1921	717,499	

Location/ Document Type	Years	Roll No.	Comments
San Bartolomé Milpas Altas			
San Bartolomé Milpas Altas (c/p)			
Libros Ejidales			
	1878	717,183/1	
Títulos Concedidos			
	1878	717,183/2	
	1891	717,184/1	
Títulos Supletorios			
	1891–1893	717,184/2	
	1916–1923	717,185	
San Lucas Sacatepéquez			
San Lucas Sacatepéquez (c/p)			
Alcabalas			
	1888–1919	717,741/1	ODT/OL
Autos de Denuncia			
	1888–1919	717,741/1	ODT/OL
Medidas			
	1878–1879	717,742/2	ODT/OL
Reclamas			
	1873	717,742/2	ODT/OL
Redenciónes de Tierra			
	1878	717,742/2	ODT/OL
	1888–1889	717,890/1	ODT/OL

Location/ Document Type	Years	Roll No.	Comments
Títulos			
	1760-1761	747,140/1	Legajo 6008
	1880-1887	717,742/3	
Títulos Concedidos			
	1876	717,742/2	ODT/OL
	1888-1919	717,741/1	ODT/OL
Títulos Supletorios			
	1888-1919	717,741/1	ODT/OL
	1889	717,890/1	ODT/OL

San Miguel Dueñas
  San Miguel Dueñas (c/p)

Location/ Document Type	Years	Roll No.	Comments
Autos de Denuncia			
	1894	717,352/1	ODT/OL
	1894-1899	717,353/2	
Despojos			
	1894	717,352/1	ODT/OL
	1894	717,352/2	ODT/OL
Títulos Supletorios			
	1847-1884	717,350	
	1885	717,351	
	1894	717,352/2	ODT/OL
	1894-1899	717,353/1	
	1910-1919	717,354	

Location/ Document Type	Years	Roll No.	Comments
Santa Lucia Milpas Altas <u>Santa Lucia Milpas Altas</u> (c/p)			
Títulos Supletorios			
	1910–1918	717,740/1	
Santiago Sacatepéquez <u>Santiago Sacatepéquez</u> (c/p)			
Títulos Supletorios			
	1901	717,187	
Sumpango <u>Sumpango</u> (c/p)			
Títulos Supletorios			
	1890–1893	717,674/1-2	
	1894	717,675	
	1894–1920	717,676	
San Marcos Comitancillo <u>Comitancillo</u> (c/p)			
Autos de Denuncia			
	1911–1912	717,071/1	ODT/OL
	1913	717,071/1	ODT/OL
	1916–1918	717,073	ODT/OL
	1918–1920	717,074	ODT/OL
Tejutla <u>Tejutla</u> (c/v)			
Títulos			
	1900	717,059	ODT/OL

Location/ Document Type	Years	Roll No.	Comments

Santa Rosa
  Chiquimulilla
    Chiquimulilla (c/v)			

Autos de Posesión			
	1876	744,589/2	Legajo 1423
Santa Rosa de Lima Santa Rosa de Lima (c/p)			
Títulos			
	1784	744,586/2-3	Legajo 73

Sololá
  Sololá
    Sololá (c/cd)			

Reclamas			
	1776-1787	747,143/3	ODT/OL Legajo 6021

Suchitepéquez
  Patulul
    Patulul (c/p)			

Pajas de Agua			
	1903,1911	738,335/1	ODT/OL
	1916	738,333/1	ODT/OL
Reclamas			
	1903	738,335/1	ODT/OL
Títulos Supletorios			
	1905	738,334/3	
	1915	738,331	ODT/OL
	1916	738,333/1	ODT/OL

Location/ Document Type	Years	Roll No.	Comments
Vistas			
	1905	738,334	ODT/OL

Totonicapán
  Momostenango
    Momostenango (c/v)			

Títulos			
	1684	746,981/5	Legajo 9556
	1705	746,987/3	Legajo 5960
	1900	746,981/10	Legajo 3634
Totonicapán Totonicapán (c/p)			
Confirmaciónes de Títulos			
	1783–1789	747,147/2	Disordered Legajo 6036
	1788	747,147/1	ODT/OL Legajo 6036
	1790–1792	747,147/3	ODT/OL Legajo 6037
Entregas de Títulos			
	1803	747,151/9	ODT/OL Legajo 6108
	1804	747,151/11	ODT/OL Legajo 6108
	1808	747,151/12	ODT/OL Legajo 6111
	1812	747,151/13	ODT/OL Legajo 6119
Medidas			
	1797	747,151/8	Legajo 6103
	1866	747,146/3	ODT/OL Legajo 6033

Location/ Document Type	Years	Roll No.	Comments
Títulos			
	1703	746,987/1	ODT/OL Legajo 5958
	1705	747,151/15	Legajo 6943
	1784	747,146/2	Legajo 6032
	1795	746,827/1/14	Document damage
	1804	747,151/10	Legajo 6107
	1821	747,151/14	ODT/OL Legajo 6940
	1866	747,146/3	ODT/OL Legajo 6033
Títulos Concedidos			
	n.d.	747,151/14	ODT/OL Legajo 6940
Títulos Supletorios			
	1790–1792	747,147/3	ODT/OL Legajo 6037
Ventas			
	1803	747,151/9	ODT/OL Legajo 6108
	1804	747,151/11	ODT/OL Legajo 6108
	1804	747,151/12	ODT/OL Legajo 6111
	1812	747,151/13	ODT/OL Legajo 6119

Zacapa
  Zacapa
    Zacapa (c/cd)			

Autos de Denuncia			
	1775–1779	747,143/2	ODT/OL Legajo 6020

Location/ Document Type	Years	Roll No.	Comments
Entregas de Títulos			
	1778	747,144/3	ODT/OL Legajo 6024
Medidas			
	1740	749,203/2	Legajo 5978
	1775	747,143/2	ODT/OL Legajo 6019
	1797	747,149/1	ODT/OL Legajo 6046
Presentaciones de Títulos			
	1755	749,206/4	ODT/OL Legajo 5998
	1755	749,206/5	Legajo 5998
	1755	749,207/1	ODT/OL Legajo 5999
Títulos			
	1716-1717	746,353/4	Legajo 1582
	1798	747,149/1	ODT/OL Legajo 6046
	1826-1879	746,355/4	Legajo 2511
	1837	746,355/6	Legajo 2522
Ventas			
	1753	749,206/4	ODT/OL Legajo 5998

Location/ Document Type	Years	Roll No.	Comments

EL SALVADOR
nación

El Salvador
  San Salvador
    San Salvador (cap nac)

Títulos

	1791	746,355/1	ODT/OL Legajo 2168

HONDURAS
nación

Colón
  Trujillo (cap de dpto)

Pajas de Agua

	1624	744,398/3	ODT/OL Legajo 88

Comayagua
  Comayagua

Alcabalas

	1740	744,758/3	ODT/OL Legajo 227
	1800	744,400	Legajo 352

Autos de Denuncia

	1748	744,758/3	ODT/OL Legajo 227
	1757	744,759/3	ODT/OL Legajo 388

Location/ Document Type	Years	Roll No.	Comments
Confirmaciónes de Títulos			
	1784-1787	744,760/1	ODT/OL Legajo 389
	1787	744,760/2	Legajo 389
Medidas			
	1570-1606	744,759/1	ODT/OL Legajo 387
	1692,1713	744,759/2	Legajo 387
	1755	744,759/3	ODT/OL Legajo 388
	1818	744,758/4	ODT/OL Legajo 380
Reales Concesiones			
	1816	744,758/4	ODT/OL Legajo 380
Reclamas			
	1772-1779	744,758/1	Legajo 53
Remates			
	1785	744,760/1	ODT/OL Legajo 389
	1791	744,760/3	ODT/OL Legajo 392
Títulos			
	1755	744,759/3	ODT/OL Legajo 388
	1783	744,760/4	Legajo 4560
	1784	744,760/3	ODT/OL Legajo 392

Location/ Document Type	Years	Roll No.	Comments
Tegucigalpa Teguciagalpa (cap de dpto)			
Reclamas			
	1724	744,758/2	Legajo 173

MEXICO
nación

Location/ Document Type	Years	Roll No.	Comments
Chiapas San Cristóbal las Casas San Cristóbal las Casas			
Confirmaciónes de Títulos			
	1711	746,352/2	ODT/OL Legajo 1578
Títulos			
	1755-1758	746,355/11	ODT/OL Legajo 2576

NICARAGUA
nación

Location/ Document Type	Years	Roll No.	Comments
León León León (c/cd)			
Alcabalas			
	1792	745,816	ODT/OL Legajo 152

Location/ Document Type	Years	Roll No.	Comments

Current jurisdictions are unknown or
unavailable for the following entries

Agua Caliente

Medidas

	1779	746,864/14	Documents place in Quezaltenango Legajo 6026

Canales

Pajas de Agua

	1792-1793	744,586/4	ODT/OL Legajo 73

Títulos

	1792-1793	744,586/4	ODT/OL Legajo 73

Cristóbal Aceitum

Títulos

	1583	744,586/6	

Pinula

Títulos

	1837	744,588/15	ODT/OL Legajo 1418

Portillo

Títulos Supletorios

	1893	744,589/23	Legajo 1440

Location/ Document Type	Years	Roll No.	Comments
Sacatepéquez			Documents fail to specify whether San Juan, San Lucas, San Pedro, or Santiago Sacatepéquez in Sacatepéquez departamento
Entregas de Títulos			
	1781	747,145/2	ODT/OL Legajo 6029
	1792	747,147/4	Legajo 6038
Medidas			
	1773	747,143/1	ODT/OL Legajo 6019
	1777	747,144/4	ODT/OL Legajo 6024
Presentaciones de Títulos			
	1750	749,205/4	ODT/OL Legajo 5986
	1755	749,206/4	ODT/OL Legajo 5998
Reclamas			
	1752-1781	747,146/4	Legajo 6034
Títulos			
	1556-1557, 1563,1565, 1567-1568, 1587,1591	746,981/1-2	
	1565	746,982/5	Legajo 5928
	1579	749,205/5	Legajo 5994
	1586-1589	746,983/2	Legajo 5931
	1597	746,983/3	ODT/OL Legajo 5934

Location/ Document Type	Years	Roll No.	Comments
	1598	746,354/2	Legajo 1598
	1613	746,983/6	ODT/OL Legajo 5938
	1658	746,984/2	Legajo 5944
	1662	746,984/3	Legajo 5945
	1752	749,206/3	ODT/OL Legajo 5997
	1786	749,205/3	Legajo 5991
	1799	746,979/9	Legajo 2768
Títulos Concedidos			
	1804	747,149/5	Legajo 6050
Títulos Supletorios			
	1758	747,143/1	ODT/OL Legajo 6019
	1760	749,210/1-2	Legajo 6007
Ventas			
	1671	746,984/5	Legajo 5947
San Pedro Milpa			Documents place near León, Nicaragua
Títulos Supletorios			
	1803	745,419/10	ODT/OL Legajo 1334
Santa Cruz			Placement on film suggests Chiquimula
Reclamas			
	1783	746,981/4	Legajo 2866

DOCUMENTOS MISCELANEOS

Location/ Document Type	Years	Roll No.	Comments

GUATEMALA
nación

Capital

Bautismos

	Years	Roll No.	Comments
	1636	746,805/5	Written in Indian language Legajo 5895
	1694	746,803/2	Legajo 169
	1704	746,803/17	Legajo 203
	1708-1809	746,804/47	Disordered Legajo 8406
	1733	746,804/13	Legajo 1975
	1734	746,803/23	Legajo 204
	1736	746,803/4	Legajo 180
	1738	746,805/8	Legajo 5895
	1743	746,804/36	Legajo 4614
	1743-1748	746,804/37	Legajo 4633
	1754	746,804/38	Legajo 4683
	1757	746,803/16	Legajo 203
	1759	746,804/26	Legajo 2654
	1761	746,803/51	Legajo 708
	1762	746,803/1	Legajo 80
	1764	746,803/20,21, 27	Legajos 204,2654
	1765	746,803/13	Legajo 202
	1765	746,804/28	Legajo 2755
	1766	746,803/19	Legajo 204

Location/ Document Type	Years	Roll No.	Comments
	1767	746,805/9	Legajo 5895
	1767-1791	746,804/44	Legajo 4800
	1768	746,803/22,48	Legajos 204,378
	1768	746,804/39	Legajo 4791
	1769	746,803/27	Legajo 204
	1769	746,804/3	Legajo 1073
	1772	746,803/7	Legajo 194
	1772	746,805/11	Legajo 5900
	1774	746,803/44	Legajo 211
	1776	746,803/11	Legajo 201
	1776	746,804/40	Legajo 4798
	1777	746,803/9,39	Legajos 199,211
	1778	746,803/10,15, 49	Legajos 200,203,582
	1779	746,803/40	Legajo 211
	1780	746,803/43	Legajo 211
	1783	746,803/26,30	Legajos 204-205
	1784	746,804/41,43	Legajos 4796,4799
	1784-1808	746,804/46	Legajo 4805
	1785	746,803/14	Legajo 202
	1785	746,804/12	Legajo 1963
	1786	746,803/24	Legajo 204
	1786	746,804/42	Legajo 4797
	1787	746,803/12	Legajo 201
	1788	745,109/1	ODT/OL Legajo 2758
	1791-1807	746,804/45	Legajo 4804
	1793	746,804/24	Legajo 2653
	1794	746,803/25,28	Legajo 204
	1794	746,805/3	Incomplete Legajo 5895

Location/ Document Type	Years	Roll No.	Comments
	1795	746,803/32,46, 50	Legajos 206,211,601
	1799	746,803/45	Legajo 211
	1800	746,804/22	Legajo 2653
	1801	746,804/5-6	Legajo 1077
	1802	746,804/4	Legajo 1077
	1803	746,803/29, 34-35	Legajos 205,207-208
	1807	746,805/15	Legajo 6940
	1808	746,803/31	Legajo 206
	1809	746,803/36,38	Legajo 208
	1814	746,803/42	Legajo 211
	1814	746,804/23	Legajo 2653
	1817	746,803/41	Legajo 211
	1817	746,804/21	Legajo 2653
	1818	746,803/37	Legajo 208
	1818	746,804/20	Legajo 2653
	1819	746,803/47	Legajo 211
	1819	746,804/18-19	Legajo 2577
	1820	746,804/25	Legajo 2653
	1826	746,804/16	Legajo 2556
	1831	746,804/17	Legajo 2556
	1832	746,804/14	Legajo 2404
	1835	746,804/11,32	Legajos 1962,3600
	1840	746,804/30-31	Legajo 3600
	1841	746,804/33-34	Legajo 3600
	1844	746,804/29	Legajo 3590
	1852	746,804/35	Legajo 3601
	1857	746,804/2	Legajo 859
	1866	746,804/1	Legajo 743

Location/ Document Type	Years	Roll No.	Comments
	1869-1891	746,804/15	Legajo 2405
	1875	746,804/7	Legajo 1087
	1880	746,804/9	Legajo 1758
	1888	746,804/10	Legajo 1758
Cuentas Desudotes			
	1635	745,113/7	Legajo 6056
	1651-1807	745,113/6	ODT/OL Legajo 5927
	1658-1794	745,112/1	
	1795-1811	745,112/2	
Exhumaciones			
	1887-1888	744,856/1	Legajo 23359
	1895-1899	744,857	Legajo 23361
	1900	744,858/1	ODT/OL Legajo 23362
	1903	744,582/1	Legajo 23363
	1904	744,582/2	Legajo 23363
	1905	744,582/3	Legajo 23363
	1906	744,583/1	Legajo 23364
	1908	744,583/2	Legajo 23364
	1909	744,583/3	Legajo 23364
	1910	744,584/1	Legajo 23366
	1911-1913	744,584/2	Legajo 23366
	1914	744,584/3	Legajo 23367
	1915	744,585	Legajo 23368
	1917-1920	744,859	Legajos 23372-23374
Guías			
	1761	744,398/5	ODT/OL Legajo 193

Location/ Document Type	Years	Roll No.	Comments
	n.d.	746,828/2/5	
Listas de Defunciones			
	1703	744,878/1	ODT/OL Legajo 2660
Mausoleos			
	1902	744,858/1	ODT/OL Legajo 23362
	1908	744,583/2	ODT/OL Legajo 23364
Nacimientos			
	1895–1897	736,310/1	ODT/OL
	1897–1901	736,311	Legajo 8
	1911	736,308	Legajo 53
	1911–1912	736,309	Document damage Legajo 53
Revistas de Comisario			
	1771	746,829/2/11	
Testamentos			
	1776	744,765/4	ODT/OL Legajo 9
Tutelas			
	1636	744,860/1	Legajo 1125
	1638	744,860/2	Legajo 1126
	1832	744,860/3,5	ODT/OL Legajos 2561,3599
	1861	744,860/6	Legajo 3601
	1863	744,860/7	Legajo 3601
	1864	744,860/8	Legajo 3601
	1880	744,860/10	Legajo 3601

Location/ Document Type	Years	Roll No.	Comments
	1882	744,860/11	Legajo 3601
	1888	744,860/12-13	Legajo 3602
	1888	744,860/14-16	Legajo 3602
	1894	744,860/17-18	Legajo 3602

Chimaltenango
  El Tejar
    El Tejar (c/p)

Bautismos

	1742	746,805/7	Legajo 5895

Chiquimula
  Jocotán
    Jocotán (c/v)

Bautismos

	1762	746,805/6	Legajo 5895
	1784-1786	746,805/1	Legajo 5895
	1786-1787	746,805/2	Legajo 5895

Escuintla
  Escuintla
    Escuintla (c/cd)

Nacimientos

	1886	759,998/1-2	Legajos 4-5

Tutelas

	1879	744,860/9	Legajo 3601

La Gomera
  La Gomera (c/v)

Avisos

	1906	752,158/1	
	1907	752,158/2	

Location/ Document Type	Years	Roll No.	Comments
Guatemala 　Guatemala 　　Las Vacas (cas de Santa Rosita)			
Nacimientos			
	1878–1883	736,310/4	
	1897–1898	736,310/2	Legajo 17
	1899–1893	736,310/3	Disordered
Villa Canales 　　Villa Canales (c/v)			
Guías			
	1780–1781	746,827/1/10	
Huehuetenango 　Huehuetenango 　　Huehuetenango (c/cd)			
Testamentos			
	1810	747,296/20/7	
Izabal 　Morales 　　Morales (c/p)			
Nacimientos			
	1896–1922	714,144	ODT/OL
Jutiapa 　Jutiapa 　　Jutiapa (c/cd)			
Revista de Comisario			
	1900	737,250/1	ODT/OL
	1901	737,250/3–4	
	1902	737,250/5	

Location/ Document Type	Years	Roll No.	Comments

Quiche
  Sacapulas
    Sacapulas (c/p)			

Bautismos			
	1756	746,805/14	Legajo 6115
Testamentos			
	1810	747,296/20/16	
Uspantán Chicamán (a)			
Testamentos			
	1810	747,296/20/15	

Sacatepéquez
  San Lucas Sacatepéquez
    San Lucas Sacatepéquez (c/p)			

Mausoleos			
	1909,1928, 1930-1931, 1935, 1937-1941	717,742/4	ODT/OL
	1941	717,743/1	ODT/OL
Testamentos			
	1914-1916, 1918-1919, 1922-1923, 1926-1927	717,743/2	
Santa Lucía Milpas Altas Santa Lucía Milpas Altas (c/p)			
Testamentos			
	1904,1911, 1923,1926	717,740/2	

Location/ Document Type	Years	Roll No.	Comments
Sumpango <u>Sumpango</u> (c/p)			
Listas de Defunciones			
	1914,1919	717,673/3	
Nacimientos			
	1879-1922	717,673/1	
	1890-1895, 1897, 1899-1905, 1915	717,673/2	
Testamentos			
	1907,1912	717,673/4	
Santa Rosa Chiquimulilla <u>Chiquimulilla</u> (c/v)			
Guías			
	1780-1781	746,827/1/10	
Suchitepéquez Patulul <u>Patulul</u> (c/p)			
Avisos			
	1902-1904	738,335	ODT/OL
	1903	738,335	ODT/OL
Exhumaciones			
	1903	738,335	ODT/OL
Inventarios de Agricultura			
	1915	738,331	ODT/OL
	1915	738,332	ODT/OL

Location/ Document Type	Years	Roll No.	Comments
Listas de Defunciones			
	1905	738,334	ODT/OL
	1914	738,331	ODT/OL
	1914-1915	738,331	ODT/OL
Matrícula de Armas			
	1905	738,334	ODT/OL
Nacimientos			
	1905	738,334	ODT/OL
	1914	738,331	ODT/OL
Revistas de Comisario			
	1905	738,334/1	ODT/OL
Tutelas			
	1915	738,331	ODT/OL

Zacapa
   Estanzuela
     Estanzuela (c/p)

Nacimientos			
	1896-1922	714,144	ODT/OL

Zacapa
   San Pablo (a)

Guías			
	1780-1781	746,827/1/10	

Location/ Document Type	Years	Roll No.	Comments

EL SALVADOR
nación

La Paz
  Zacatecoluca
    Zacatecoluca (c/cd)

Guías

| | 1780-1781 | 746,827/1/10 | |

San Salvador
  San Salvador
    San Salvador (cap nl)

Bautismos

| | 1720 | 746,805/4 | Legajo 5895 |

Guías

| | n.d. | 773,996/1/10 | |

HONDURAS
nación

Colón
  Trujillo (cap dl)

Revista de Comisario

| | 1795 | 744,401 | ODT/OL
Legajo 382 |

Comayagua
  Comayagua (cap dl)

Testamentos

| | 1570 | 744,759/1 | ODT/OL
Legajo 387 |
| | 1807 | 744,760/3 | ODT/OL
Legajo 392 |

Location/ Document Type	Years	Roll No.	Comments
Municipio unknown Sagrario			
Bautismos			
	1865	746,803/52	Legajo 743

MEXICO
nación

Chiapas Heredia			
Bautismos			
	1811	746,805/13	Legajo 6067
San Cristóbal las Casas San Cristóbal las Casas			
Listas de Defunciones			
	1634	744,764/1	ODT/OL Legajo 1
Testamentos			
	1601	744,569	Legajo 221
	1636-1637	741,580/3	Incomplete Legajo 35
	1687,1733	741,580/2	Legajo 35
Tutelas			
	1786	744,546/2	ODT/OL Legajo 271
	1810	744,558/1	ODT/OL Legajo 286

Location/ Document Type	Years	Roll No.	Comments
NICARAGUA nación			

León
  León
    León (cap dl)			

Avisos			
	1708	773,995/1/8	
Bautismos			
	1717	746,803/5	Legajo 186

Current jurisdictions are unknown or
unavailable for the following entries

Location/ Document Type	Years	Roll No.	Comments
Ermita			Gaz/various
Listas de Defunciones			
	1915	738,331	ODT/OL
La Laguna			
Bautismos			
	1715	746,803/3	Legajo 178
San Juan			Gaz/various
Bautismos			
	1774	746,805/10	Legajo 5895
San Martín			Gaz/various
Bautismos			
	1776	746,805/12	Legajo 6056

Location/ Document Type	Years	Roll No.	Comments
San Nicolás de Bilbao			
Bautismos			
	1711	746,804/8	Legajo 1481
Zubuyaqui			
Bautismos			
	1745	746,803/8	Legajo 198

Locations are unknown for
the following entries

Bautismos			
	1724-1739	673,092	
	1742	746,803/6	Legajo 193
	1769	746,803/33	Legajo 206

The following represent entries for which
document type classification
was not possible

Capital			
Unknown document type			
	1603	746,355/2	Illegible
Chimaltenango Chimaltenango <u>Chimaltenango</u> (c/cd)			
Unknown document type			
	1775	747,051/6	One page in Indian language

Location/ Document Type	Years	Roll No.	Comments
Sacatepéquez San Antonio Aguas Calientes <u>San Andrés Ceballos</u> (a)			
Unknown document type			
	1890-1917	717,500	Poor focus